# Two Pilgrims Meet

## in Search of Reconciliation between China and Japan

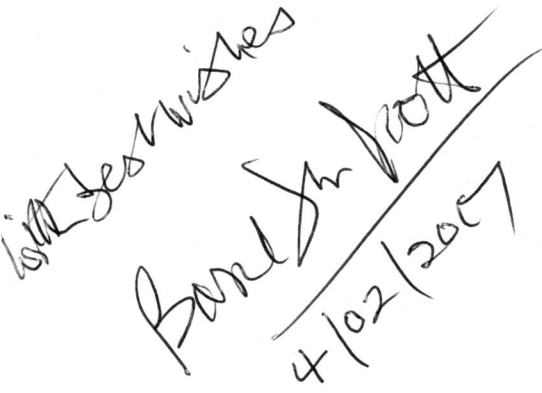

## Minoru Kasai & Basil Scott

Published by New Generation Publishing in 2016

Copyright © Minoru Kasai & Basil Scott 2016

First Edition

The authors assert the moral right under the Copyright, Designs and Patents Act 1988 to be identified as the author of this work.

All Rights reserved. No part of this publication may be reproduced, stored in a retrieval system or transmitted, in any form or by any means without the prior consent of the author, nor be otherwise circulated in any form of binding or cover other than that which it is published and without a similar condition being imposed on the subsequent purchaser.

ISBN: 978-1-78719-043-6

**www.newgeneration-publishing.com**

*We dedicate this book
to
Yoshiko and Shirley*

# Acknowledgments

It is impossible for us to thank all the many people who have made this publication possible. But we cannot fail to mention some who have played a major part in bringing this book to birth.

In particular, we must thank Prof. Toshi Yamamoto and his wife Midori for their crucial part in our story. Without them we would never have been reunited in 2005. That was but the beginning of their crucial contribution to the formation of our joint enterprise. Without the use of their apartment for Minoru and Yoshiko's visits in 2011 and 2015 this book could not have been written.

We must also thank Minoru's former student, Uno Ayako, who has come to our rescue in the latter stages of the typing of the manuscript. Her patient work not only in typing our dictations and revisions, but also in printing and sending them by email has been invaluable. She has also contributed in many other ways, such as by providing photos and making connections with some who are mentioned in this book. We also thank Hannah Smith who performed wonders to reduce our recorded reflections to order by her audio-typing skills.

We are grateful to all our many friends, especially those in China and Japan, who have helped us on our pilgrimage.

Most important of all we thank our families who have supported us over the past ten years in fulfilling our joint project. They have done more than they realise to make this publication possible. Without them none of these pages would have been recorded.

# Contents

Foreword ............................................................................ 1

Preface .............................................................................. 3

Basil's Shanghai Roots ........................................................ 7

Minoru's Pilgrimage .......................................................... 26

Basil's Meeting with Minoru in India .............................. 49

Minoru's Pilgrimage Continued ....................................... 67

Reunion ! ........................................................................... 90

Japan and Prisoners of War ............................................ 115

Signs of Hope in Japan and China .................................. 137

Vision for Reconciliation ................................................. 173

Preparing for Partnership .............................................. 189

Reflections on Key Issues ............................................... 219

   Awakening to the blessed reality ............................. 220

   Why is Takamori Soan important as a witness
   in Japan? .................................................................... 234

   No More War .............................................................. 246

   Nuclear Weapons ...................................................... 258

   Ma Licheng's View of Reconciliation between China
   and Japan ................................................................... 265

   Responsibility for the Past ........................................ 274

   Student and Youth Exchange Programmes .............. 288

   United as Brothers and Sisters in the Human Family 297

Looking Forward Together to a United Future .......... 306

Postscript .......................................................................... 318

# Foreword

The authors of this book invite us to share dialogue, meditation and intimacy. Themes include the healing of traumas and an ever present openness to creativity. They also offer many specific proposals to soften the tense relationship between China and Japan, ideas that are well grounded in the context of post-war political and civil society initiatives.

Their text is being published in 2016, when the lives of so many human beings, along with the natural world which is their home, are being destroyed in an apparently endless succession of wars. So far, thankfully, East Asia has not been directly affected, having avoided armed conflict for the past 60 years. Readers might even wonder, what is the point in revisiting the faraway tragedies of the 1940s, when we have countless contemporary ones closer to home?

One important consideration is that China will very likely play a dominating role in the international economy, and in technology and politics, through this century. As long as the Chinese maintain a healthy reciprocal relationship with their close neighbours, the whole region of East Asia should be a global source of stability, education and environmental improvements. The peoples of East Asia constitute about one sixth of world population.

Reconciliation also has global significance. Even if today's violent conflicts are somehow contained or resolved, their sequels will persist for generations. The healing of traumas will be an aspiration for a long time to come. An idea in this book that bridges the social and the spiritual is creative coexistence: with former enemies and with the Nature that is also destroyed by war and by other human activities.

Several spiritual traditions pervade the text. Both authors present themselves as Christian, the presence of Christ shining through their deliberations. In addition, the transformative power of study and pilgrimage in India inspires and deepens their vision.

Last but not least we may feel the subtle spirit of East Asia, whose citizens might prefer to hint at peace through a couple of humble brush strokes revealing a dragonfly or morning glory. Here is a gentle reminder that the massive scale of human arrogance and destructiveness is not to be found elsewhere in the natural world. Conversely lightness and grace, wisdom and maturity, are seldom found in politics, where they are most needed. But we may perhaps glimpse them, reading between the lines of this book.

Alan Hunter
Professor of Asian Studies
Centre for Trust, Peace and Social Relations, Coventry University

# Preface

How is it that a Japanese and an Englishman come to be writing a book together about reconciliation between China and Japan? Here we tell how we met and why this quest is so important to us. We record our pilgrimage from wartime Shanghai in the 1940s to our present quest for reconciliation between China and Japan. The story of the way our lives have crossed and re-crossed is the sub-plot that holds the book together. Underlying all of this is a search for the reality which gives meaning to our human existence and opens our eyes to what is unseen and eternal.

This book is about the reconciliation of enemies and opposites, not as an exercise in academic abstractions and theories, but as a search for reality. It is undergirded by the story of two very different people whose lives began in the same place; though they grew up unknown to each other, they were destined to meet.

Minoru grew up in Shanghai. By the time he was shipped back to Japan in 1946 he had lived nearly all his 13 years in China, as a son of the imperial power. Basil grew up in China, in Sichuan, Shandong and Shanghai, but found himself on the wrong side in the war, interned in a Japanese prison camp. When we met as students in Banaras Hindu University we made the surprising discovery that during the war we had both been children in Shanghai. At that time we had been on opposite sides in every way. We lived on opposite sides of the river – Minoru lived on the north bank in Shanghai proper, Basil was on the squalid south side of dumps and derelict factories. We were on opposite sides of the war – Minoru was Japanese, Basil was British. We belonged to different religions – Minoru prayed in the Shinto temple for America's defeat, Basil's parents were Christian missionaries. We were poles apart in our living conditions – Minoru part of the ruling power, Basil in a Japanese POW camp.

Minoru traces the path his life has taken from Shanghai in 1945 back to his family roots in Japan. He had already begun his journey to reconciliation when he enrolled as a student in International Christian University, Tokyo, to find out whether Christ could be a light in the darkness. He then went to America to study at Princeton. He was attracted by Martin Luther King's renunciation of force in the fight against racism. In 1960 he went to study for a Ph.D. in Banaras Hindu University and found Gandhi to be a convincing guru of ahimsa in the cause of peace. On returning to Japan he was able to pursue the quest for reconciliation between people and nations through a spiritual community and the Zen-Christian association he helped to found.

1945 saw Basil regain his freedom and return to the England he had never known. Nearly twenty years later he left for India. He marvels at the way he met Minoru for the first time in a Hindu university on the banks of the Ganges, whilst studying Indian philosophy from 1963 to 1965. This was his first encounter with a Japanese person after the war; it turned into a profound experience for him of reconciliation. But in relation to this book it was only a seed which might never have taken root, because we lost all contact with each other.

Forty years later, however, our paths crossed again. A chance meeting with Prof. Yamamoto, a retired Japanese professor in Cambridge, put us back in touch. As a result Basil and Shirley travelled to Japan to meet Minoru and Yoshiko. The journey to Japan showed Basil that the road to reconciliation was longer than he had thought. It had taken sixty years for him to reach Japan after the war. On this first visit Minoru and Basil went together to Shanghai

*Preface*

and together they visited the places where they had lived, first on one side of the river and then on the other. Reconciliation is not only meeting in the middle of a bridge, but going together to both sides to see the other's point of view.

It was only after Basil visited Japan several times and Minoru came to Cambridge in 2011 that the idea of writing a book together became a shared commitment. The seed sown in India began to grow. Our common project developed through encounter and dialogue. Reconciliation between China and Japan emerged as the focus for our discussions. In this renewal of friendship we found a task, which was inspired by and through prayer.

Since then there have been more visits to Japan. We have seen Keiko Holmes' heroic efforts to bring peace by welcoming British POWs to Japan. We have gone together to Hiroshima, where Yoshiko was living as a child outside the city when the atom bomb was dropped. We also planned to go together to the Nanjing Massacre Museum, which records the horrors of the Japanese assault in 1937.

We are both concerned for heart to heart reconciliation between China and Japan. We approach this subject from different angles. Clearly Minoru looks at future relations with China from a Japanese perspective, yet with love for China in his heart, for he lived there all his childhood and China is part of him and in his bones. Basil is not Chinese, but he grew up in China and experienced China as his first motherland. His love for China is deep-rooted and has been refreshed by many visits to the mainland over the last fifteen years and through many Chinese friends. We find ourselves united in prayer for there to be no more war between Japan and China.

Reconciliation between nations is an ongoing process which is never complete and has to be renewed in every generation. So there are no quick solutions, but at the same time differences cannot be ignored. This year marks the seventieth anniversary of the end of the Sino-Japanese war. Those who lived through it, as we did, have not forgotten the devastation caused by world war and have a duty to pass on to subsequent generations our passionate hatred of war and our longing for the harmony between nations, which should be the rightful inheritance of all the world's citizens.

Minoru is most concerned to work for reconciliation between Japan and China. His mountain retreat near Mt. Fuji witnesses to his commitment to bring nations and religions together in the search for peace. India remains in his heart and Gandhi earns his admiration for overcoming war with non-violence. Japan's peace constitution is precious to him and he goes on regular pilgrimages for peace.

In the concluding part of the book we discuss together some of the issues that continue to be of importance in the quest for reconciliation between China and Japan.

We do not attempt to present arguments that will convince the powerful - such as national leaders, politicians, economists, industrialists, academics, theologians or the media. You will find here no academic treatise, though Minoru has studied and taught in universities most of his life. Our book is a witness to what God has done for us and what we see God doing now and in the future.

Reconciliation requires a new vision for the future, not an agreement, but something better which enables Japan and China to work together with trust and in harmony. As the world steps forward into the unknown we pray that both countries will be surprised to discover they are brothers and they are free. With this gift from above both can move forward in thankfulness and hope.

# Basil's Shanghai Roots

## An Internment Camp

It had been a long journey from Shandong in the north to Shanghai. The slow moving train had taken a day and a half to transport us children from our previous internment camp at Weihsien (now Weifang). I had been both scared and excited to taste the freedom of life outside internment, even if it was only a train. Still, it had been fun to move from one compartment to another on our way to the dining-car. What we had to eat has long been forgotten, but it was certainly better than we had been used to in camp. The guards were surprisingly pleasant. Some even smiled at us. Perhaps we reminded them of their own children back in Japan. Who knows? There were only twelve to fifteen of us children, so we posed no threat. Besides it was an ordinary civilian train, not a military transport.

As I look back I find it strange to account for the Japanese authorities taking the trouble to move a handful of children a few hundred miles, so they could be with their parents in Shanghai. By November 1943, when I was taken to Shanghai, all movement of foreigners had ceased. Our school teachers in Weihsien had requested the military authorities to send us children to our parents in Shanghai. They had also wanted two teachers to accompany us on the journey, so we could be properly cared for – and controlled! The Japanese did not agree to this, but they did agree to reunite us with our parents – an amazingly considerate action in wartime. So it happened that my sister and I were together as we arrived in Shanghai and were sent across the river in the small group bound for Pudong.

Night had fallen before we crossed the Huangpu river. A tall figure loomed up out of the darkness. I could not see his face. Only a familiar hand reached out towards me and took hold of me. The stranger was my father. The last time I had seen him was nearly three years before, when he had waved me off from the Shanghai docks to boarding school. Then I was six. Now I was nine.

When we stepped ashore we could hardly see the narrow road that led between brick walls to our new home. Twenty minutes later we were once again behind barbed wire and locked gates, but this time we were on the top floor of a three storey factory building. Apart from a narrow gang way between rows of bamboo matting, every foot of floor space was occupied. My father guided us through the matting to our space and my mother's arms.

Our new 'home' measured 6 ft. wide by 14 ft. long. The space allotted for each person was 7ft. by 3ft., or 21 sq. ft., and that times 4 came to 84 sq. ft. or the size of our area. The width was just enough to put a double bed across and leave room on either side for 2 camp beds for my sister and myself. Despite being compressed into so tight a space, the very closeness to my family was a psychological blessing that outweighed the loss of freedom. My sister and I had been separated from our parents for years in a boarding school in Chefoo (modern Yantai). This had been much worse for my sister, five years older than me, as she went to this school in 1936 and only saw her mother and father for holidays in 1939 and 1940. The separation left us both with deep emotional scars. For me the years apart from 1940-1943, partly due to the outbreak of war following the Japanese attack on Pearl Harbour in December 1941 and a year in a Japanese camp, were devastating. So to sleep with my mother and father, to get up with them, to eat with them, and not to be cut off from each other even for a day was very comforting. At the end of internment, as we looked forward to going home my mother would remark with sadness that we would probably never live together again for so long.

On one side of us we had English friends, Ken & Vera Price. At night the curtain went up between us, but during the day it was removed, so we could move past our double bed. On the other side we had a White Russian couple. The matting wall between us never came down. We never got to know them, and I have no recollection of their names. All I remember was that they smelt of garlic, and that put me off the smell of garlic for life.

At the end of our space we had a window and that window looked across the fields and the river to the Shanghai Bund. For two years the Bund skyline was the backdrop for my dreams. It imprinted itself not just on my memory but on my feelings. At the same time it was a symbol of the future, of the day when we would once again be able to cross the river to freedom.

The Pudong camp – an artist's impression of the camp and Bund beyond from *The Moon Looks Down* by Ken & Frances McAll

*Two Pilgrims Meet*

Pudong camp was not my introduction to Shanghai. The summer of 1939 saw me arrive in Shanghai for the first time. My father had been called from Sichuan to be the secretary of the China Inland Mission. I had travelled with my parents on a fascinating journey from Chongqing via Kunming, Hanoi, Haiphong and Hong Kong. The reason for this vast, circuitous route was the Japanese occupation of the eastern half of China from 1937 onwards. The mission headquarters were in Xinza Road. The 2 six story blocks, then new and modern constructions, still exist and are now used as a children's hospital. Here I lived for at least a year, plus the winter holiday of 1940. It was a comfortable environment compared with up-country Sichuan. There were also British families and children to play with.

From our secure home in Xinza Road I had the chance to explore Shanghai whenever I was taken out. Those were the days when Shanghai's International Settlement still sparkled with glitz and glamour, despite the Japanese occupation of the city in 1937. The Japanese left the International Settlement and the French Concession untouched. All that was to change, but not until after Pearl Harbour was bombed. For me it was great fun to ride on a clanking tram or a swaying trolley bus. If that was not possible I could perch on the high seat of a rickshaw being pulled through the crowds, whilst avoiding the tram tracks. Nanking Road was the place to be with excited crowds and fashionable shops. The famous department stores, Wing On and Sincere, were in full swing. Best of all for a small boy were the ice-cream parlours and the taste of 'Knickerbocker Glory', a 1930's speciality, served in a tall glass and topped with nuts, cream and a cherry.

Nanking Road led to the Huangpu river and the famous buildings that made up the Bund on the river front. Here were the Customs House with its tall clock tower, the Hong Kong Shanghai bank and the Cathay Pacific Hotel, the stars of Shanghai's 'billion dollar skyline'. When I go back to Shanghai nowadays, the first thing I want to see is the Bund, even if it is completely dwarfed by countless stupendous skyscrapers on both sides of the river.

## Life in Camp

If we had been locked in our rooms and never allowed out, our 6' x 14' home would have been intolerable. But I soon found out there was a big new world to discover in Pudong camp. I could get down to floor level by inner or outer stairs. Once outside our block there was space between two more blocks and a communal meeting room. Beyond these was a sports field with a small area for allotments inside the barbed wire fence. This limited space was crippling for adults used to complete freedom, but for a child like me used to a boarding school it was not so bad.

Apart from loss of freedom the main problem was food or the lack of it. The rice was poor and contaminated by grit and rat droppings. Sometimes we had cracked wheat with a generous supply of weevils. Rice came with watery soup. Occasionally there were bits of leathery meat and gristle, most notoriously when the Shanghai greyhound circuit dogs were slaughtered and some were added to our diet. The one ingredient I disliked the most was the daikon added to our soup. The daikon now served in Japanese restaurants is delicious and bears no resemblance to the smell and taste of what we were given in Pudong. In the last year of the war the food got even worse. The fact that 14 stone men shrank to 6 stone tells its own story.

## Two Pilgrims Meet

Our physical condition would have been a lot worse but for the parcels we received from time to time. Parcels came from two sources. Surprisingly, our German friends in Shanghai, who were not interned, because Germany and Japan were allies, were able to send us food parcels, sometimes once a month. What I remember with great affection was the salami hanging in a protected corner of our 'home'. How delicious even the thinnest slice of that salami tasted. We also got a jar of jam, which like the 'widow's cruse of oil' was never exhausted.

The other source of parcels was altogether more exciting. During the war there were two occasions when we received American Red Cross parcels. Their arrival generated enormous excitement throughout the camp. I had never seen such goodies in my life as popped out of those parcels. Large tins of powdered milk, solid bars of concentrated chocolate, spam, cheese, coffee and cigarettes. The cigarettes became the currency for buying and selling. A tin of milk powder sold for ten or fifteen packets of Camel cigarettes.

I had my own third source of extra nutrition. In one corner of the camp, in front of the men's block, was a large, rectangular mill pond, which had been used before the war by the tobacco factories where we were now housed. This pond was walled in on three sides and had a narrow ledge running round the water beneath the wall. I was frightened of falling in, as the water was deep, and I did not dare go to the far corner where the water often covered the slippery ledge. The great attraction was fishing. I got a rod and a float, and cast my line into the murky waters. When I was successful in landing fish, I took these small six to eight inch carp to the camp grill. This iron sheet, eight feet by five, was heated underneath by a coal fire and even had a small oven at one end. My grilled fish were so crisp that they vanished in a few mouthfuls.

Beyond the blocks and the mill pond was a playing field. The favourite sport was baseball. The black American crew of a scuttled US merchant ship were the stars. They still had the energy to blast home-runs. Shouts of 'Strike One', 'Strike Two', ring in my ears when I think of those days. Football was another team game that attracted players. My father used to enjoy a game, but I was too small to get on the pitch. The playing of hockey had to be stopped, because too many players suffered broken bones due to malnutrition. There was a lack of calcium in our diet, so mother crushed egg shells into powder and sprinkled that on our food, when we were lucky enough to have eggs from our friends outside camp. I also got used to eating burnt toast as that was supposed to be good for us – and I still love burnt toast!

Around the games field were the "Happy Gardens", the fruit of months of labour by the men of the camp, who had levelled a vast area of rubble. The debris was all that had been left of a once flourishing Chinese village, bombed by the Japanese attack on Shanghai in 1937. The gardens, like mini-allotments, were intersected by paths named "Regent Street" and "Anzac Avenue". For me these gardens are indeed a happy memory. Here I grew my first tomatoes in a tiny plot and experimented on radishes. Here too I fell in love with portulaca. I am delighted whenever I see their bright colours shining in the summer sun.

Among the 1200 people in the camp there were representatives from every profession. Some were teachers, so there was school for children and there were classes for adults. My sister, being sixteen, had serious exams to pass. In the summer of 1945 she and ten other teenagers took the Cambridge School Certificate exam.

The papers were set by university staff in the various camps dotted around Shanghai. After the war the exam papers were submitted to the Cambridge Board and all the candidates were passed. In the meanwhile I must have attended my classes, but I cannot remember a single one or any of the teachers either. This strikes me now as very odd, since I recall with perfect clarity school in my previous two camps, including Weihsien, where I only stayed for two months.

What I enjoyed was learning in my own way from books and people in the camp. My favourite adopted uncle, Alex McLeod, from Canada, looked after me like his own son. Later I discovered that his own son was my age, but separated from Alex for years and by thousands of miles in distant Toronto. Alex gave me his precious pocket atlas. This was my most prized possession and gave me a love for maps. With the aid of this atlas I tracked advancing armies and fought the war with paper and pencil.

Fortunately there were other boys of my age. Bruce lived very close to me on the third floor of our building. He and his parents had the distinction of living in the factory lift. The lift was located in the corner, outside the main room, where they had a little more space and privacy than the rest of us. Nevertheless, I was glad I did not sleep there. It gave me nightmares just to think of the lift suddenly plunging all the way to the ground floor. Bruce's father had been a missionary in Gansu, in China's north-west. A powerfully built man, he was down to earth and practical, always good fun, the sort who are the salt of the earth. When we were not fighting each other, Bruce and I would go in search of Ben, whom we teased remorselessly as his mother's darling.

## Relations with Japanese

For the purposes of this book I must reflect on my attitude to our Japanese captors. When the war with Japan began I was only seven; by the time it ended I was eleven. A child sees things very differently from adults, but also absorbs the views of adults, whether parents or friends. I was probably very fortunate not to have been a teenager in the war, as a younger child is resilient and adjusts to circumstances without introspection.

The Japanese were to be feared. I kept out of their way. The ones I knew were all guards or soldiers. Fortunately for me the Japanese guards left us alone most of the time. The daily running of the camp was handed over to the internees to organise. Our own people ran the kitchen, distributed the food, manned the showers, taught the children and set up the games. My parents looked after me. There was however at least one point in the day when we came face to face with our guards, and that was at roll-call. At 9 a.m. we lined up on the games field, where 1200 prisoners could be counted. Here I learnt to number off in Japanese: *Ichi, ni, san, shi, go, roku, shichi, hachi, ku, ju* ...and so on up to 30. I think the guards wisely reckoned foreigners could not learn to count in Japanese beyond 30, so after 30 we just began again at one.

Roll-call could be frightening. The guards marched up and down shouting at us. We were expected to stand to attention and not move a muscle. Woe betide anyone who talked, or smiled, or misbehaved. Sometimes roll-call could be held at night. This happened whenever there was an emergency; most often this would be when the guards had found that someone had escaped or got through the barbed wire fence. Such nights scared me out of my wits.

On one of these midnight roll-calls I was ill and left behind in my parents' double-bed. To make matters worse, I was lying on top of a hidden electric hotplate, which we were not supposed to possess. The guards came round, peered at me with their torches, marched round the bed, but fortunately did not force me to get out. I look back on this event as a joke, but it was anything but a joke at the time.

We were not allowed to have or to use electric hotplates, for the simple reason that they used up valuable electricity. On our floor ingenious camp electricians had hidden cables behind wooden boards and beading, so that they could be pulled out and connected to a hotplate. We used ours regularly, so did our neighbours. One of our guards made it his business to catch hotplate users. We called him, "Hotplate Harry", because we could hear him coming as he marched up the stairs in his boots with his five foot sword clanking on the steps. One day however he crept up in gym shoes without a sword and rushed into our line of matting. One of our neighbours was caught red-handed as he threw a sheet of cardboard over his stove, just as 'Harry' marched in to see the sheet go up in flames. That gave us something to laugh about for weeks, and to congratulate ourselves on for not being caught!

Another point of friction was black out for the lights. Our electric light bulbs gave out very feeble rays, but even these had to be boxed in with black cardboard, so that American planes could not see any glimmer of light from our camp. As the war dragged on and American bombing increased, black out was strictly enforced. On more than one occasion the Japanese naval base close by fired bullets at our building, when they saw light appearing during an air raid.

Not all our contact with Japanese was negative. I have already mentioned the kindness of the guards, who accompanied us by train from Weihsien to Shanghai. It also surprises me that Japanese helped us with medical supplies and allowed us to receive food parcels from Shanghai. Nevertheless Japanese were the enemy.

I fought the war on paper. I made maps of the Russian front and later of the bitter fighting on the Normandy front round Caen and Cherbourg. I also followed the Pacific war intently. Our news came from the Japanese in the form of propaganda announcing ever greater battles and annihilating victories over American forces, which moved westwards towards Japan. We learnt to read the information backward, to understand that heavy American losses actually meant heavy Japanese naval and military defeats. We also got news that could not be posted on camp notice-boards from secret radios that were put together from parts smuggled into the camp.

When American planes started to appear over Shanghai I used to stand on the fire escape and watch the B29s glistening serenely in the azure sky at an altitude beyond the reach of Japanese planes and anti-aircraft guns. Bruce and I cheered wildly if we saw a Japanese plane being shot down. On one such occasion when a Japanese fighter plane was spiralling down to earth, we were given a severe reprimand by Miss Ginger, a missionary spinster. "How dare you boys cheer when a man is dying", she shouted. Her words have stuck in my memory simply because they were completely contrary to my jingoistic frame of mind and the general patriotic fervour of the camp. Out of the blue came a totally different voice that condemned delight in the defeat of an enemy. She was right, and for a moment I felt conscience stricken.

Where we and our Japanese guards were most sharply divided was over the treatment of Chinese. Looking out of our camp across the barbed wire to the road outside I could sometimes see the brutal attacks on Chinese coolies and rickshaw pullers. The Japanese did not attack us though we were prisoners, but Chinese were treated as a subjugated race.

I loved China, despite the poverty of the masses and the filth in the streets, of which I had seen plenty in villages and cities alike. I had a high regard for the best in Chinese civilisation and loved Chinese food. In Sichuan I had been used to playing with Chinese children and talked a child's level of their language. If you ask how I acquired this respect for the best in China, it must have come from my parents, who loved China and had given the best years of their lives to serve its people. This high regard for China also came from growing up in the historic city of Langzhong with its elegant courtyards and Confucian examination centre. My love for China is more easily explained. I grew up in China and this was my home land for the first nine years of which I have any memory. Sichuan was good to me. Boarding school in Chefoo cut me off from my parents, but the bays and beaches were mesmerizingly beautiful. Shanghai was sophisticated and an exciting place to live in.

## The Indelible Scar

Disaster struck me in June 1944. I woke up with a vicious headache pounding my temples. Never before or since have I experienced anything like it. My temperature soared and I was taken down to our camp hospital on the ground floor. For the next five days I drifted in and out of consciousness. One moment I do recall was the jabbing of a needle into my spinal column without an anaesthetic to extract fluid for a test. The next day, the test had to be repeated, and this time I knew only too well what to expect. The fluid tests were sent across the river to the Japanese hospital, which confirmed that I had contracted pneumococcal meningitis.

A few days before I was taken ill, our camp received its one and only consignment of drugs and medical equipment from the American Red Cross. Among the drugs was one lot of tablets which were new to the camp doctors. Their name indicated that they belonged to a new group of anti-infective sulpha drugs. There was nothing on the packet of drugs to say how they were to be used or what they were for. However, by God's grace, Frances McAll had recently qualified as a doctor from Edinburgh University, and she recognised what the drugs were and knew that they could be used for pneumonia. Frances had to guess what dose to give me and hope the drugs might have an effect on meningitis. Within two days I began to show signs of improvement and after a few more days I was off the danger list. Frances used to say my survival was one of the two real miracles she saw during the war.

When I was carried upstairs to the third floor, a new battle began. I found that meningitis had partially paralysed my left side. My left leg was pathetically weak, and I kept on falling over. A new group of friends then came into my life, who nursed me back to mobility. There was a Danish American, who created all sorts of contraptions for me to exercise my leg. He carried me around on his back and coaxed my limbs back to life. Others were physio-therapists, who massaged my muscles to get them functioning again. Gradually I regained the ability to walk without a limp, for which I am profoundly thankful to them and to God. However, my left side has been thinner ever since and my left leg is very much weaker than the right.

The indelible scar I have carried with me since internment in Shanghai was not a bitter memory, but a painfully weak physique. I was able to play all the games at school and survive the rigours of military training during National Service in the army. But I felt as if I had to work twice as hard as anyone else, just to keep up. Psychologically I had something to hide, a skeleton in my cupboard, and that skeleton was my left side.

## Liberation

What every prisoner longs for is freedom. I was no different, but there was no deadline in sight. The Japanese military forces were clearly being pushed back by the Americans. They were losing the ferocious and long drawn out battle for Okinawa. The front line was moving closer and closer to Japan and China, but that did not mean the war was nearly over. No one thought the Japanese were about to surrender. In fact the American sailors, my baseball heroes, pinned their hopes on 'Golden Gate in Forty-Eight'. In other words they did not expect to get home to San Francisco till 1948.

The world changed with the dropping of the atom bombs on Hiroshima and Nagasaki. The first we knew about this was a rumour. A terrifying new bomb had been dropped on Japan. We had no idea what this mystery terror might be. The front page report in the Shanghai Times was said to have been blacked out. Our secret camp radio was not able to explain what had happened.

For a few days uncertainty and excitement grew in our camp. Then on Wednesday 15 August the Japanese Commandant called the British Camp representative to accompany him to the Swiss Consulate across the river. There he learnt officially of the Japanese surrender and that all guards would be withdrawn from our camp. Back in Pudong we were almost sorry for our dejected guards, who had just listened to the Emperor's broadcast from Tokyo telling them to surrender. They melted away, and there was no desire in the camp to seek revenge, only a longing for freedom and home.

The most exciting sign of the war being over was the sight of parachutes descending from the skies full of amazing tins of food of all kinds – peaches, apricots, tomatoes, spam, chocolate and all sorts! The parachutes were dropped by American planes that knew exactly where we were located. After 15 August they came every day until we had collected enough. We had fun racing out not only for the tins but also to rescue the parachutes with their valuable material. Sometimes these food drops became quite scary. I remember being out on the playing field and looking up at a plane above me only to see dozens of tins dropping out of the bomb bay, as I ran for my life!

After the war was over the American military command in Shanghai revealed that 2 weeks after August 15th a major invasion would have taken place north and south of Shanghai. Our camp would not have been spared, as the Americans would have had to attack the Japanese naval base a few hundred yards away between us and the Huangpu. We would also have had to contend with our guards, who would not have surrendered but would have fought to the bitter end. What plans they had for dealing with their civilian prisoners we do not know, but feared the worst.

The record of the battle for Okinawa shows that Japan would have fought to the death if Honshu had been invaded. Similarly, the Japanese armies in China would not have surrendered. If the war had continued hundreds of thousands of Chinese, Japanese and allied nationals both military and civilian would have perished. The carnage does not bear thinking about. My attitude therefore to the dropping of the atom bomb is ambiguous, as I believe my family and up to a million or more individuals would have died if the Emperor had not been forced to order his Japanese subjects to lay down their arms. At the same time I cannot condone the unspeakable horrors inflicted on Hiroshima and Nagasaki. Those who went through the Second World War know that in such a war all are losers. This book is written to warn generations that follow us of the misery of war and that nuclear warfare should never be justified.

From this distance in time, 70 years after the end of the war, it might be assumed that soldiers and prisoners alike would soon have gone back to their countries. That was not the case. Hundreds of thousands had to be transported home by ship. We did not leave Shanghai till November, and it was to be much longer before our guards returned to Japan. On December 4th I got my first view of England, actually Wales, as Anglesey loomed out of the cold grey mist with its hedged fields looking like a patchwork quilt. We docked at Liverpool and were soon transported to our Lancashire family roots in Preston.

England was not a bed of roses. The street we lived in had not been bombed, but rationing reigned. We needed coupons to buy anything essential, both food and clothing. It was a shock to go to school. I was years behind kids in their first year at grammar school, and to begin with I was physically hopeless at sport. It took me the next five years to catch up with my peers. My sister soon left home to go for nursing training. I was sent to a boarding school. My parents moved to inner London. My mother's fears proved well-founded – we never lived together again apart from holidays.

## On Reflection

It may seem strange, but as I look back now on those years of detention by the Japanese military, I am glad that I had that experience. On reflection, I only realise now how much I learnt in those three years.

At the top of my list is the supreme importance of hope. When hope dies, people die, and in the harsh conditions we lived through that literally meant death. Fortunately I never lost hope and my parents' strong relationship with God meant they never lost hope either. As I have already mentioned the US sailors' slogan, "Golden Gate in '48", was a symbol of their realistic hope. They did not pin their expectations on a quick release, just round the corner. They were willing to wait for the freedom they were sure would come, even if that would take another three or four years.

Camp life taught me to make the most of the little we had and never to waste anything. Even now my natural instinct is to save and conserve, and keep the best to last. No luxury can be taken for granted. I never forget the taste of powdered milk when those American Red Cross parcels arrived, never mind the joy of concentrated chocolate.

Some of the people I lived with and met in camp were amazing. My adopted uncle, Alex McLeod, was so generous. I realise now that he lavished his love for his distant son on me. Others also were generous with their affection. We lived close to each other. Nothing separated us apart from a curtain at night.

In the midst of war, when we are either enemies or allies, it is like a flash of lightning when someone speaks up for the enemy. That is why I remember Miss Ginger's startling rebuke, when she condemned me for cheering as a Japanese plane crashed to the ground. Thank God for such people who remember that even an enemy is a human being.

In the past twenty years I have worked with refugees in Britain. They have often been in despair waiting to be released from a detention centre. Occasionally I have said, "I know how you feel. I was a prisoner for 3 years, when I was a child." I have something in common with them, even though it was a long time ago. I know they need never give way to despair, for God still cares for them.

There's no doubt that what affected me most in the Pudong camp was the attack of meningitis that left me half paralysed. I know I should not have survived the camp and I definitely should not still be alive seventy years later. This was God's miracle gift for me. You can read more about it in Frances & Kenneth McAll's book, *The Moon Looks Down* (p.73-74). Everyone who overcomes a handicap develops determination. I certainly had to fight hard when I came back to school in England to cope with boys of my age and to catch up with those who were far ahead of me at school. Since then it has always seemed to me that because of my weak left side I have had to work twice as hard as others just to keep up. Paul expressed it well when he wrote in the New Testament: "We know that suffering produces perseverance, perseverance character and character hope."

If hope keeps people alive, it is freedom that we hope for. Nobody knows how precious freedom is unless he or she has been deprived of it. The day we regained our freedom was a day of celebration like no other. Suddenly the skies were opened and gifts came, literally, flying down. Today Chinese and Japanese deserve freedom not only from the past but from any enmity that keeps them apart.

There is much more I could mention, including some of the things I have referred to in my story of the Pudong camp, but this is enough to indicate why I do not regret those three years in detention.

# Minoru's Pilgrimage

## From China to Japan

I was born in 1932 in Ichinoseki city in Iwate prefecture. My father's home was near the city where a famous poet lived, Miyazawa Kenji. He was a teacher and a strong witness to spiritual reality. His heart and soul were focused on the suffering of the people. He maintained belief in the creative coexistence not only of the cosmos and humanity, but of all nature, including animals, trees, flowers, rivers, earth and sky, sun and moon, and the stars. The people were very much affected by his life and activities. He is still remembered among the people, both locally and all over Japan. There is a museum about him, founded and maintained by his native town. He was a Buddhist of the Nichiren sect. This heritage unconsciously affected me through my family's love of nature.

Three months after my birth my mother took me to Shanghai and after that I stayed in Shanghai until 1946, one year after the end of the war. In Shanghai my father had worked in a printing company, but he was not successful in this job, so he moved to a Japanese business where he was employed to the end of the war. My mother worked in the international concession in Shanghai in a beautician's shop. So she knew westerners. I remember later when the fighting against America was fierce that I was shocked to hear my mother say: "White people are kind and some especially Christians are good people." However, she stopped her work because my young brother was drowned in a pond, playing with his friends. She did not blame anyone else but herself. I do still feel his life in my own life.

In August 1945 I was told that a massive bomb, an atomic bomb, had been dropped on Japan. There had been intense bombing of Japanese cities, but the atom bomb dropped on Hiroshima and Nagasaki caused Japan to surrender. The news of Japan's defeat was an unbelievable shock. The myth of Japan as God's kingdom, which had never been defeated was broken. The meaning of my life as consisting in complete loyalty to the nation and to the Emperor was lost. For me, as for many others, the Emperor and the nation were identical. The Emperor was the nation and the nation was the Emperor.

In April 1945 I had just entered Middle School at the age of 13, dreaming of entering naval college for the sake of the Emperor and the nation. But my dream was gone and the meaning of life was gone as well. My school was closed from August 1945 until March 1946. Instead we studied in an informal school called Juku in Japanese and I was separated from most of my classmates.

Life in Shanghai during the war had been comfortable and secure with no bombing and no battles after 1938. Even after the end of the war life in Shanghai was secure and relatively safe compared to other areas. At the end of March 1946 we had to leave Shanghai with very few possessions, though compared to Japanese being repatriated from other places we were better off.

With the experience of loss becoming real and hard to endure, we returned to Japan, first to my father's eldest brother's house in the north in Iwate prefecture. On the way the suffering in Japan became obvious to us as we travelled from south to north. We observed all the big cities which had been burnt down by bombing and saw the devastation in Hiroshima. The destruction in Hiroshima, clearly visible to me, was beyond words to describe. In Tokyo the huge number of orphans was overwhelming. I could see that for ordinary people life was just a struggle to survive. My impression at that time was that Japan had been totally destroyed and multitudes had been uprooted. Coming back from China at the age of fourteen, I was overcome by the feeling of uncertainty which was prevalent everywhere.

I could see on my way to my uncle's home many, many mothers just searching desperately for food for their children. My uncle was amazed to see us, as they had received no warning that we had returned to Japan and were on our way to his house. We were exhausted and hungry. My uncle's family must have been shocked to see us in this condition and to receive our large family of six, father and mother, my elder sister and my two brothers, one older and the other younger than me. It was completely dark at night without any electricity. The only form of communication was by post. However we were so fortunate to have such a family. They wholeheartedly welcomed us, though they had little money and they looked after us for a whole year. So whenever I think of them now I am overwhelmed with thankfulness for their kindness in those days when life was just a struggle to survive.

As there were no jobs and no employment in that part of northern Japan, my parents decided to move to my mother's home in Shimabara Island in Nagasaki prefecture. In this difficult situation my elder sister and my elder brother decided not to continue with their studies at school, but to look for a job, so they could support us. I had been encouraged to continue to study, so I went to the middle school in Ichinoseki. Fortunately I was accepted by the school from April 1946.

However, I was surprised to find that I was so different from my classmates. They treated me as being different from them and I found that I was indeed different. I wondered whether this was due to my upbringing in

China, since I had lived for thirteen years in Shanghai from my birth to my return to Japan in 1946. My classmates and I found it difficult to get on together.

We lived very close to the island, where Christians, in the early part of the 17th-century had fought to defend themselves against the powerful *samurai* army who had come to attack them, because they refused to give up their new found faith in Christ. They endured for three months before they were overwhelmed and killed. My mother's parents were much older than my uncle and aunt with whom we had been staying in the north. They were also poorer and had little income, yet they were so generous. I used to ask myself, why they should give us so much when they had so little.

In my mother's home town there were no jobs available for her, and my father's health was poor and he was often sick. However, it was fortunate that my father got a job in one of the smallest coal mines, so that we could survive without depending on others. Later I also worked part-time in a small coal mine to earn money, so I could continue to go to school. Here I met the poor and the forsaken, who had been uprooted by war. I found myself with those who were crushed and broken, and heard the cries of the suffering. This has made me sensitive to the voice of the least and lowest in society.

In this way I was able to continue to study in high school, but my mind was not at peace. I kept asking, 'Why am I here? What is the meaning of life?' In Shanghai I had been motivated to study and work hard for the sake of the Emperor and the nation. For me the Emperor and the nation were identical and absolute. But that cause was dead and that cause had gone. Now what was there to live for?

Then one day I saw a pamphlet on my table at home about a school that was called *Seisho Gakuen* - 'A learning community inspired by the Bible'. This school consisted of junior school, high school and junior college. Its aim was to assist the birth of the new man for a new Japan. I did not have any knowledge of Christianity at that time, nor had I any contact with any Christian institution. All I knew was my mother's statement in Shanghai in the midst of the war: "American and English people are not such devilish people. Christians are fine people." Those words had struck my heart so forcibly that I was freed from the language of hatred. My sense of identity in those days had come from the feeling of duty. The aim of the school – the new man for a new Japan – touched my heart and I decided to go to that school. It was the right decision. I am thankful for this, because it marked the beginning of my pilgrimage as a Christian. First I was struck by the environment - here I could enjoy communion with the sunrise and the sunset, as they lit up the hills on the horizon. Most of the teaching took place in the morning, so I was able to work outside the campus as a tutor for junior and senior high school students. I had to be financially independent from my parents, because they were responsible for my younger brother. They fulfilled their task so well that my younger brother was eventually able to graduate from university and then took responsibility with his wife for caring for my mother. My mother was a saintly person, surrounded by people who needed her help wherever she was. She always reminded me of Christ's presence, full of love in action.

In this new school, from the beginning to the end, I was deeply moved by the old retired couple, who cared for the dormitory students of the Junior and Senior high school as their advisers. The relationship between the old couple and the dormitory students was amazing. It was a relationship of trust and affection. The parents of those children had to work day and night to survive, so they could not look after their children at home and had to entrust them to this school. Their appreciation of the old couple was so evident, that I observed it with wonder. This couple were the key people to open my eyes to the reality of Christ living in the darkness. They were members of the church of the Holy Spirit. During the war they had suffered so much, because of their loyalty to Christ and because they were pacifists, in protest against Japanese militarism. They firmly believed that peace is the only way to break through the arrogant and violent ways of the world. I talked with them regularly three times a week after my work. They used to wait for me with tea and dialogue. I learnt so much from them, that I was awakened to the reality of Christ as the light in the darkness and I was baptised in the church which was attached to the school. My pilgrimage began as a Christian in this way. I still feel their witness to Christ is alive in my heart, as a torch light. My thankfulness for their lives goes beyond words.

## International Christian University, Tokyo (ICU)

After two years in the Seisho Gakuen school, I was recommended to study at the International Christian University (ICU). Unknown to me this new university had been founded after the war in 1953 in Tokyo. I decided to apply and was accepted as an undergraduate.

When I arrived at ICU, I was astonished to see the campus of the university, bordered by a forest and with a traditional tea garden (*Taizanso*). From the roof of the university hall I could clearly see Mt Fuji in the distance, though it is miles away. I was so moved by this environment that I anticipated deep communion with nature, which would lead to prayer. When I was admitted as a student this became part of the blessed reality given to me by God. In this process I often met the university gardener, who worked silently from early morning to evening. In my communion with the environment of the campus and in my prayers I was often reminded of the gardener's presence. He was deeply appreciated by the university President, Prof. Hachiro Yuasa, as a most vital person for the progress of the university. In my encounter with the ICU professors important as they are in my heart, the central message is the importance of the cosmos and humanity as a healing family.

I can never forget the president of ICU, Hachiro Yuasa. He always reminded us that ICU had been founded in response to the prayers of the victims of the atomic bombs dropped on Hiroshima and Nagasaki. Therefore it was essential that ICU should continually remember the prayers of the victims and respond to God's calling for the university to be a blessing to mankind. For this we must die to ourselves and be reborn by God's Spirit, so that we forgive others and are reconciled to each other, living creatively together. This is the gift of God's blessed reality and also the destiny of mankind. He used to tell students that the purpose of the university was to be a venture with God, which was given by God and guided by God, and this purpose is to work for the destiny of humanity.

Prof. Yuasa had migrated to the USA at the age of seventeen. He established himself as an entomologist through his experience in working on farms. He was then invited by Kyoto Imperial University to be a university professor for about ten years. He looked back on those years as the happiest and most peaceful of his career. But then he was obliged to take up the position of President of Doshisha Christian University in Kyoto. He and his family suffered under the fanatical, military regime in Japan. He was forced to resign from his position as president, because his loyalty to the Emperor and to the nation was regarded as being suspect. At that time he was invited to attend a Christian conference in Madras, India, as a representative of Japanese Christian laymen. He was then invited to go to America and, as the Second World War started soon afterwards, he was compelled to stay in USA during the war period. After 1945 he was reappointed as President of Doshisha University in Kyoto. But when ICU was founded after the war in 1953, he was needed so much there that he resigned from his position in Doshisha and became President of ICU.

When Prof. Yuasa was no longer the ICU president but head of the trustees of ICU, his spiritual convictions were profoundly influenced by a visit to Nepal at the age of 86. His son was working there as a doctor at a leprosarium. The intense spiritual experience he underwent, he described as a dialogue with the Himalayas. In his vision of God's reality he saw humanity and the whole cosmos as a healing family. God's family includes not only humanity but also the entire universe. Nevertheless, I confess that seeing the cosmos and humanity as a healing family and as a blessing given by God was not intelligible to the members of the university, except for Prof. Yuasa. However the encounters with the professors in this university were such a blessing to me that I remember them with thanks.

One of the professors, who made a lasting impression on me was Prof. Tateo Kanda. He was the professor of Classics and the New Testament. His expositions of the Greek New Testament impressed many students and inspired me to become a specialist in the study of the New Testament. The way he revealed the gospel of Christ as an astounding event still remains in my heart. Prof. Kanda was the first person I met who was a leader of the *Mukyokai* movement, a Japanese independent church

(*Mukyokai* or 'No Church Movement' was founded by Uchimura Kanzo).

Another person who I always remember with affection was Prof. Yoshito Shinoto, a botanist and a world renowned scientist. His concern for students went beyond boundaries. He embodied in himself the atmosphere of ICU at that time, when the university was seen as a close community embracing all, both students and staff. Hope for the future shone in him as a burning light. Many years later when I was on my own and feeling isolated in Banaras Hindu University, he and his wife deliberately broke their return journey to Japan to stop in India and visit me. I will never forget his concern for me. He also was a member of *Mukyokai.*

A professor from Switzerland, Dr Emil Brunner, made a deep impression upon me through his dedication and openness to discuss with students the painful issues arising from the war. In my first year there was a lot of suffering as students struggled with conditions in the aftermath of the war. Most were very poor and found it difficult to get the money to pay their fees and to buy enough food to stay alive. The whole country was suffering from depression after the war.

I went to see Emil Brunner in his own house, as he held open home for students to come and see him. I asked him: "What is suffering? What is pain?"

Prof. Brunner replied: "Why do you ask such a question?"

I said: "We are all suffering, and students are no exception. Our parents have lost their inheritance, their savings, their property, so we have to work to continue our studies and face all sorts of difficulties. We ask ourselves, 'Why is this so?'"

We could not see any future for Japan. The country had been completely destroyed. In this vacuum we could not but reflect and wonder why we were in that situation. Naturally we were very critical of the past institutions which had failed our country and led to this hopeless state. We could not see any hope in that situation. Daily we were experiencing this pain. So I asked Prof. Brunner: 'What is pain and suffering?' He listened very patiently, because my English language was so poor. So he tried to clarify the meaning of my question and then responded beautifully. I think he also referred to the European war and its disasters. But because I did not understand his language I did not feel he was really responding to my question. So I said: "Unless we experience the same pain together, it may be impossible for you to understand our situation. I hear what you say, but it does not touch me and does not answer my situation."

The next Sunday I went to church. As he began his sermon Emil Brunner said he was going to respond to a question put to him by a student, who had asked him, 'What is the answer to the suffering we are going through at this present time?' The student was not satisfied with my response and said: "Only if you have suffered as we have done would you be able to answer my question."

Emil Brunner then went on to say: "A year before I came to Japan I was celebrating with my son and his fiancée the prospect of them getting married and having a family. It was a moment of great joy. When they left us they were very happy. An hour later there was a telephone call from the station saying, 'There has been an accident at the station and your son has been killed.' We went to the station. There we saw the body of our son lying cold and bloody." They were stunned. Emil's thoughts froze; he had no words to say. Then in the silence suddenly out of his mouth came these words:

"The Lord gave and the Lord has taken away. Blessed be the Name of the Lord."

On that morning in the ICU church Emil Brunner's wife was sitting in the same pew where I was sitting, just a little further along. She was sobbing, and Emil Brunner was also overcome. There was a long silence. At the end of the silence he said 'Amen' and that was the end of the sermon. But that was the answer I was looking for.

I was surprised on that Sunday morning that Prof. Brunner was actually responding to my question with reality, not with an intellectual answer. We could not see the situation as it really is, so we could not enter into this reality, despite knowing many things intellectually from books. But when we entered into reality and became reality, then we could say that Christ is born in our hearts continuously, and the good news is here.

The memory of that story and that morning is still burning in my heart. Later I saw Emil Brunner's wife, who was suffering from depression, walking slowly with a young woman. This girl was the fiancée of their son who had come to be with them and help them in Japan. Dr Brunner also suffered from ill health and was forced to return to his own country. I last saw him in a wheelchair on his way to board a ship from Yokohama for Europe.

Prof. Brunner was convinced that every Christian should be an evangelist. He was invited to establish a cell group movement in ICU. Each cell was to consist of five or six students, who were to meet once a week for Bible study and share their problems. Through this mutual learning from each other they would be convinced that God is at work among them. Once a month they had a general meeting of all the cell groups. In this way Dr Brunner believed they would become transparent and be transformed by God's working amongst them. The Brunners offered their home as a place where all the cell groups could meet. The cell group inspired me to be open to the unknown. I was ridiculed and nicknamed "Saint Kasai"!

In Japan, whether at school or university, I was different from my classmates. I realised that fourteen years in China had left their mark on my life. The blessing of China on my life is beyond my comprehension. I am still discovering the real riches of this blessing.

## From ICU to USA

Immediately after graduating from ICU, I was given a scholarship to study in USA at Princeton Theological Seminary. My hero at that time was the Japanese Christian leader, Uchimura Kanzo. Following his example I wanted to share the good news of the New Testament in Japan, free from institutional churches. I came to America by God's grace, to prepare for my witness in Japan. I firmly believed this was the only way I could help Japan, so I had to learn in the States. I worked day and night, because this was the first time in my life that I could concentrate on learning after returning from China. But learning was very hard for me there, because I had to read at least two books a week in English. But by the second year, though there were some difficulties, I found learning languages, including Greek and Hebrew, was rewarding.

But as I stayed there, I became very disturbed by racial incidents, particularly between black and white Americans. At that time Martin Luther King came to the university chapel to preach; that was in 1959. The chapel was packed with students. I was surprised, because usually you would always see seats available there, but on this occasion it was packed with students. Many students were standing, and I was one of them. Fortunately, I was just in front of the pulpit, so I could see Martin Luther King. His preaching still resounds in my heart, as he spoke of the blessed reality of being members of God's family.

What Martin Luther King was saying was radically different from my understanding of Christianity at that time. Although my faith was firm and the fire was burning in my heart, I was striving for a kind of futuristic perfection. But in listening to Martin Luther King's preaching I felt this message was for now, not for the future, but for here and now. 'Please be awakened', he seemed to say, 'to the blessed reality. We are brothers and sisters in God's family, so let us be awakened to receive this gift from God, and let us live and walk as brothers and sisters in God's family! Let us be liberated, emancipated from the mark of segregation in history, and from anything man-made. So be free, let us be free now!' I felt that this was not for the future, but to experience the blessed reality right now. To be liberated, here and now. This really moved me and touched me. This was a revolutionary moment for me. It was a message of liberation and reconciliation. I felt Christ was speaking through Martin Luther King not only in the context of America, but also in the context of the whole world.

Hearing Martin Luther King speak, shook me and moved me so much that I could not restrain myself from expressing my pain, so I wrote to a newspaper with a brief article on this matter, which was printed in one of the papers. My roommate who was so kind and helpful and had arranged to share a room with me, thought after reading my article in the newspaper that I would not be allowed to remain much longer in America. I really appreciated his care and his kindness, so then I restrained myself and concentrated on my studies. The library was my home again.

But at the same time there was another friend, Stan Mumford, who was really tormented as a Christian by this racial segregation of black and white. He supported Martin Luther King's movement. He found my position to be very much akin to his position. Talking with Stan, I found Martin Luther King had been greatly influenced by Gandhi and was sustained and inspired by him. To me Martin Luther King was a genuine Christian, and I was struck by the love and justice in him, which really inspired me from Japan. Also, he was completely free from bitterness and hatred. But Gandhi was a Hindu man. Stan - who was impressed by the Hinduism of Gandhi – suggested there must be something strong enough to go beyond racial boundaries and deep enough to be shared even beyond religion. There must be a reality which has not been fully recognised, because our historical experience is still provisional.

Sometimes Stan would share his desire to go to India, to learn through experience in India, rather than just reading books. He also asked me to go to India with him, so that we could share our learning. But I told him bluntly that I would not go, only for him to keep repeating his request.

But Stan Mumford kept asking me to go to India with him. My friend had studied more about the relationship between Martin Luther King and Gandhi, and said that Martin Luther King had been sustained by Gandhi's witness. I began to wonder, what is Hinduism in general, and what is the Hinduism of Gandhi? This man must be a very special person. In this way, and in particular because of our deepening relationship and our sharing of the same common problems, I finally decided to go with Stan to India.

## From USA to India

Stan Mumford belonged to an international studies programme, a voluntary association of university Christian students concerned with the destiny of America in the world situation. Most of the members of this fellowship had an Inter-Varsity Christian fellowship background. But they felt a calling from God to live in the midst of non-Christian civilisations. For this they felt the need to understand their calling and the conditions in other countries. For this purpose they were strongly convinced that they needed to live in the same situation as other university students, identifying and sharing with the students who came from a non-Christian background. The first group were sent to Egypt and India in 1958. The letters and reports from those who went convincingly affirmed the vision of the programme, though trials were unavoidable because they were living in a totally different situation, even occasionally at the risk of their lives. No official foundation was willing to sponsor this programme, so financially individual donors were needed who understood the circumstances of the students and wished to support them.

Stan and I found the cheapest boat available for the passage from New York to Bombay, a Greek cargo ship, *Hellenic Torch*, which took passengers. It was scheduled to take forty days to Bombay. On the way it would stop at different ports for a few days or even a week to offload cargo. To our surprise most of the passengers were foreigners being expelled from America, so the journey was a learning experience. Every day we met for Bible study and prayer and to share what we were discovering. In Egypt we were much surprised to find that Japan was highly respected. But the existence of the new state of Israel was a source of intense pain.

We left the boat in Karachi, because we wanted to learn about the situation in Pakistan. As we left we requested an Indian Christian pastor on the ship to send our luggage to Banaras Hindu University in India. Travelling by train in Pakistan we were struck by the hatred of Muslims for Hindus and the hostility against India. When we got to Varanasi we discovered that our luggage had not arrived (in fact it never arrived), so we had to start life in India only with what was in our rucksacks. On reaching Banaras Hindu University we first settled in the International House for foreign students.

Whilst staying in the International House in the campus of Banaras Hindu University (BHU), we registered as students in the department of Indian Religions and Philosophy in the Indology College. We then searched for accommodation in a hostel for Indian students. Within a few months we were allowed to stay in a hostel for graduate students. Unfortunately we were given two separate single rooms, so we could not stay together, but the rooms were next to each other.

Every morning we started with silent prayer and reading the Bible together. After that we would have breakfast together. We used to have lunch and supper in the hostel canteen of Birla Hostel. The simple menu was the same every day. Not surprisingly this was a strain on our digestion and we suffered from stomach trouble, so it was just as well that the toilet was not far away!

Fortunately we found a group of students studying the Bible. They were Christian students, mostly from Kerala in south India. They came from traditional churches that were founded long ago, according to legend in the first century AD. It was a fascinating opportunity to learn about their background and through getting to know them personally as friends to be invited by them to visit their homes in Kerala in the vacation. Together with them we regularly attended the church in the cantonment, where we could participate in a service in English. After the service the pastor from England used to invite us to his home where we shared lunch with his family. The pastor's wife was a medical doctor. In this initial phase of our life in India when we were ignorant of so many things, these Christian brothers and sisters were very helpful. This initiation to India continued from my first year up to June 1967.

In the first year I was surprised to meet a classmate from Tamilnadu, who was a devotee of Tamil Saivism, Nirenkanta Hiremata. He came from a respected family, which was responsible for maintaining that tradition. He was responsible for the Sanskrit learning of his sect of Saivism in Varanasi. He was spontaneously helpful and kind, so that through him I began to ponder the deep sources of living Hinduism. I felt he was a *jivan mukta* (a man of enlightenment). He was like a brother.

Another person whom I cannot forget was Man Singh. He was a hostel-mate in Birla Hostel. He was sincere and always helpful and his subject was classical Sanskrit literature. When I was tormented by both malaria and sunstroke simultaneously on my visit to India in 1971, he and his whole family took care of me for a whole month at their home. When a medical doctor first examined me at my friend's home, he said my case was very serious. At that time, I felt my life was about to end. Man Singh could not trust the Indian hospital at that time, so he asked me to stay at his home. That whole month was an unforgettable and blessed time.

## Dr RS Misra

Dr RS Misra was the advisor for my Ph.D. studies. He was another unforgettable person. When he first met me he thought I was a Buddhist, as I came from Japan. So he wholeheartedly welcomed me and inquired about the state of Buddhism in Japan. But when he found out that I was a Christian, he was very puzzled.

Dr Misra felt rather uneasy about my becoming a Christian. Our conversations stopped rather abruptly and he did not talk to me for a year. Nevertheless, I attended his lectures together with Stan Mumford. Stan left India in March 1963. I moved to Birla Hostel in June 1963. Dr Misra was living with his family in the residence on the roof of the hostel, as hostel warden. I asked Dr. Misra to be my Ph.D. supervisor for my thesis, comparing Hinduism, Buddhism and Christianity, with special reference to three texts, the Bhagavada Gita, the Bodhicaryāvatāra and the Gospel of John. To my surprise, he accepted my request. As soon as I had settled in Birla Hostel, Dr Misra came one day to my room with a Bible. Surprisingly he had never read the Bible before, but because of my thesis he read the Gospel of John. On reading the first chapter of the Gospel, he said that he was so impressed that he read right through to the end of the Gospel. He then kindly arranged a schedule of meetings so that we could discuss the text. For this he invited me to come to his residence. His wife always provided tea and sweets when we had these discussions. To my amazement, these occasions became a time of encounter and dialogue. More and more the focus was not only on the literal meaning of the text but on a sharing of our existential experience of faith. Through this process I was led to understand Dr Misra as a man of the

Hindu faith. I could see he was brought up in a very pious Hindu joint family. His father died when he was in primary school, but his uncle took care of Dr Misra's family. Dr Misra enjoyed learning and wanted to go to university. But his uncle had a son of his own, who also wanted to go to university. Due to his financial situation the uncle could not afford to send both of them to university. So Dr. Misra had to give up his longing for further education. Then, to his amazement, his uncle decided to send Dr Misra to university instead of his own son. So Dr Misra was so thankful for the Hindu tradition through actually experiencing the reality of the Hindu *Dharma*. Philosophically he holds the Advaitic position, but religiously and spiritually he and his family belong to the Vaishnavite *bhakti* tradition.

Thus my learning process with Dr Misra became more and more a sharing of our spiritual pilgrimage in the Hindu and Christian faith. So in this way we were able share our existential position. One day Dr Misra shared about the suffering of his family. On one occasion when we were discussing the suffering in the world he told me about the tragedy of his second son. In his childhood he had a very high fever, which caused brain damage. After that his mental growth was disrupted and became dysfunctional. Since then he has been severely handicapped. Mrs Misra suffered so much because of her son's condition that often she could not sleep at night. Dr Misra asked me, what would Christ's attitude be to such suffering. I did not expect such a question, because it was so personal. However, strangely I responded to him: "Christ is suffering with your son and with Mrs Misra and with you." I was struck myself with my own response. Sensing Christ's presence, Dr Misra kept strangely silent. We shared a deep silence. Then Mrs Misra bought us tea.

## Murray Rogers' Ashram

In search of the truth I went with Stan Mumford to a Christian ashram (spiritual community). Our meeting with Murray Rogers at his Ashram near Bareilly was most unforgettable. In my case the silence in the morning worship before sunrise in the Ashram touched my heart, because there, as I recalled the experience of loss in my own pilgrimage, I was given a glimpse of the reality of God. Stan Mumford had also been in torment through some bitter experiences he had been through in America. He too was led to silence. Like me he also glimpsed God's presence. Before sunrise sitting in the chapel, keeping silence in worship, touched our hearts. Before silence in the early morning worship this invitation was given (which I still keep with me):

"Be silent and still, aware, for there in your own heart, the Spirit is at prayer. Listen, Learn, Find and Open. Heart wisdom. Christ."

After this early morning worship and breakfast we saw a line of children with small buckets. Female members of the ashram had prepared powdered milk with which they filled the buckets. After finishing this distribution of powdered milk, we saw a small line of adults, who were suffering from illness or physical handicaps. They were taken care of by the female members. Meanwhile the male members and visitors went to work in the fields. Before lunch and before supper and before going to bed there were brief meetings for prayer.

This description of life in the Ashram sounds so simple, but Stan and I were deeply touched and moved, because it somehow related to our previous experiences in Japan and America.

## Two Pilgrims Meet

After Stan's departure from India, I regularly visited this Ashram, particularly in the Christmas season. Here I met a very distinguished and unforgettable Christian, Swami Abhishiktananda. Originally he came from France to India and obtained Indian citizenship. When I met him, I found his smile strangely welcoming. The Ashram people also loved his smile. Meeting together at meals and other times, he often burst out laughing. I also discovered that he was a kind of Christian *sanyasi* (one who has renounced worldly life), deeply rooted in the Catholic tradition, but going beyond the boundaries of the Catholic tradition through his life in India. Therefore he visited this Ashram, and the Ashram members looked forward to his visits. There was a deep and thankful relationship between them, which went beyond Catholic and Protestant traditions. But in addition to this going beyond the boundaries, I found he had been deeply united with a few Hindu *sanyasis*.

I found out more about this when I went on pilgrimage with him and with a young French man who came from France to learn more from Abhishiktananda. On this pilgrimage I was fortunate to meet with a few of his dear Hindu friends. One had been an officer in the British Indian army. He had endured a bitter wartime experience in Europe. After the war ended he returned to India. Instead of returning to his home, he went to the Ashram of Shri Ramana Maharishi to learn from him. I met him in Lucknow. There I was given a small room. In the early morning he came to my small room, filling it with his huge frame. He talked with me. Finally before leaving he said: "You must die, as I was driven to death by Ramana Maharishi."

Then I met another person who was closely united with Abhishiktananda in Haridwar. Satchitananda was a *sanyasi* from Rishikesh. They were deeply united, despite being rooted in their own traditions. It was a touching scene to see them together. Their meeting was a sign of the Spirit at work. After finishing the pilgrimage Abhishiktananda came with me to Dehra Dun to see me off on the train. He took a firm hold of my hand, gazing up at my eyes, and as the train gradually started to move he ran with the train until he finally let my hand go and raised his arms as the train left. In this way I was greatly touched by him and particularly when we bathed together in the Ganges at Rishikesh. It was in October and bitterly cold. The Ganges was split into seven currents and in the early morning before sunrise, bathing in the river was risky, because the river was in spate after the monsoon. It was running fast with a huge roaring sound. We were holding hands tightly in the freezing cold water. After bathing in the river the three of us, including Mark, a French young person, partook of Holy Communion together. God's presence here and now was most real.

In Murray Rogers' Ashram I also met Raimon Panikkar, an extraordinary, dynamic Christian. Talking with him I learnt that from his childhood he had been faced with a question. He was born in Spain and brought up by his parents. His father was Indian and a devout Hindu. His mother was Spanish and a very pious Catholic. With this background he grew up wondering how his father and mother could be so closely committed to each other, though both were deeply rooted in different traditions. He grew up wondering how this combination of religions was possible. He had to go through a religious crisis in Spain, in Europe and in India. He could see very clearly the threat of self-destruction hanging over him. Therefore naturally he was absorbed in a search for the way out.

In my talks with Panikkar I began to understand the conclusion he had reached in his search for truth and a way out of his personal crisis. Here again I found that suffering led to a discovery of the divine reality. Put briefly he termed his solution as 'radical relativity'. Though this is abstract and complex terminology, the context was the awakening of a person to reality, which can be likened to being reborn. This awareness can be shared with people of many different backgrounds, whether the differences are religious, racial or something else.

Panikkar defines three positions. The first tends to atheism. It arises from a painful rejection of traditions which are closely cherished. Although drawn to the source of reality, the conclusion is to negate God as Being.

The second position responds to painful religious divisions by negating God as non-Being. Overwhelmed by the divine presence seen as distinct from traditional religious understandings, this experience leads to silence and to a kind of apophatic position, or negative theology, speaking of God only in terms of what He is not.

The third position, termed 'radical relativity', affirms the experience of being related to God, as well as being related to oneself and to other persons. Here the response to God's grace and generosity is amazement at the all-embracing nature of God's love, which goes beyond all differences. The gift of knowing reality leads to thankfulness, and in relation to others we pray that we may be one family, loving each other.

Recalling Panikkar's witness to this truth, I was so surprised later to read Desmond Tutu's description of the rainbow people of God. Although they probably never met each other their experience had much in common. In the midst of the suffering of black people in South Africa there came a discovery of the divine reality – a gift from God – which provided a way out from an impossible situation, which led to reconciliation instead of bloodshed.

# Basil's Meeting with Minoru in India

## The Journey to India

Growing up in Shanghai, I would never have thought that one day I would reside in India and study at a Hindu university. Even when I had returned to England the possibility of travelling to India seemed remote. In the 1960s the British ties with India, which had been so strong, had been severed by Independence in 1947. So what did happen to bring me to study in India and to Banaras Hindu University in particular?

After the war my parents had to settle in Britain. Their health had been severely affected not only by the prison camp but also by nine years in China. They were never able to return to the land they loved, and within a few years the communist take-over in 1949 led to the expulsion of all missionaries. My parents moved to London and I went to a boarding school near Bath.

It was a shock to find myself so far behind other boys whose educational progress had not been halted in wartime Britain. Although we had kept going with classes in camp, I knew nothing about Latin or French or the sciences. It took me many years to catch up with my peers, in fact I only really caught up with the bright ones at university.

Another severe challenge was presented by the physical demands of sport. Although I had survived meningitis without a limp, my legs were more like thin pencils than healthy limbs. Like anyone who responds to disadvantage, I developed the determination to compete whatever the odds, which has stood me in good stead since then. I put the past behind me and adapted to the present. Conditions in post-war Britain were amazingly tough in comparison with the luxuries that are now at our command. It is difficult to remember that rationing of essentials continued well into the 1950s.

My life changed dramatically in 1955. That was my 'annus mirabilis' or year of miracles. In February I came out of the army after two years of national service, including 10 months in Malaysia. In April I experienced God for myself in a way that I had never felt before. I had often longed to know God personally as my parents clearly did. But despite many prayers, I had not encountered God as others said they had. Suddenly God became a reality and my prayers were being answered. As I look back on that year I am amazed how God shaped the direction of my life and gave me not just career directions but a calling that still controls what I do fifty years later. On two separation occasions God called me to ministry in the church and to service in his mission to the world.

From October 1955 I was fortunate to be an undergraduate at Cambridge. Those three years were foundational for my life in every way. I owe the Christian Union a huge debt for grounding me and training me in the basics of Christian life and understanding. The fellowship of dedicated Christian students meeting daily for prayer converted me from a loner to a team player. The friends we made then were friends for life. Even if many of us have rarely met since then, the memory of those days has been an inspiration to look back to.

It was in the first term of my first year reading history that God gave me my marching orders. After listening to a moving exposition of Christ's sacrifice on the cross for us all, students at the Christian Union meeting were left to pray in silence. I asked God whether there was anything he wanted me to sacrifice for him. There was one thing I had vowed not to be and that was to be a missionary, unless God gave me an unmistakable calling which I could not avoid. I had other plans, but on that day God spoke to me with deafening clarity. Was there something I should sacrifice? Yes, was the resounding response; he wanted me to be a missionary. God has never spoken to me so clearly before or since.

For a hundred years from the 1870s to the 1970s Christian students in Cambridge held a daily Prayer Meeting during term. On weekdays this took place in the Henry Martyn Hall. Apart from praying fervently for the needs around us, we prayed for the world. All around us in the hall were boards listing the countless number of Cambridge graduates who had gone out to all parts of the world in the service of Christ. The names of those people are long forgotten, but they were for me a cloud of witnesses inspiring us to go wherever Christ wanted us to be, to be his presence in his world.

Discovering where God wanted me to go in the world took seven years. I realised I had to be open to going anywhere God wanted to send me. I could not choose what I preferred, or even what I thought was best; instead I had to find out the direction God wanted me to move in. So I gathered information about the progress of the church throughout the world, listened to reports from Latin America, Africa, the Middle East and Asia, met missionaries and exposed myself to the needs of many countries. Fortunately I had time to wait and pray, and God was certainly not in a hurry. Gradually, as I prayed about all these different possibilities, the focus fell on India.

People ask me, 'why did you go to India?' Humanly speaking, the seed for this idea may have come from students I met at Cambridge. The connection had to be confirmed by God. But I have often looked back to the good time I enjoyed with a group of Sri Lankan Tamil students. They taught me to eat their curry and watch with wonder as the beads of perspiration rolled down their foreheads as they ate the hottest chillies they could find. They also opened my eyes to the bitter struggle that was even then being waged between Tamils and the Singhala majority in Sri Lanka.

Sri Lanka is not India, so this may have nothing to with my journey to Banaras. In any case it was many years later that God began directing my thoughts towards India. I cannot say how this happened, I only know that during 1961 and early 1962 the conviction took root in my mind that India was where God wanted me to go.

As I thought about India I wondered how I would get there. Who would support me? What organization could I join? I began to search for a society that worked in India which I could apply to. Whilst at Cambridge I had met Jack Dain, who was the Secretary of the BMMF (Bible & Medical Missionary Fellowship). Jack had been an officer in the navy and had worked in India. Students, who had volunteered for service in other parts of the world had received help from him in preparing for this vocation. Impressed by his vision and open-minded spirit, I began to inquire if I could join this society. At the same time I found out about other societies and churches with experience of working in the Indian sub-continent.

If India was to be the country, then what was to be my work? By 1962 I had been ordained and was working as a curate in a church south of London. Even at that time I believed Indian churches needed to be led by Indian ministers, not by foreigners. There must be a more suitable role for a foreigner and a better way for me to assist the church in India. So I was not looking for a post in a church.

As my thoughts were turning to India, I heard that Shirley had come back from south India. Shirley had been a year ahead of me at Cambridge. Both of us were historians and knew each other through the student Christian Union. I wrote asking for her advice on where to go and what to do. She had gone from Cambridge to be a lecturer in a women's college in the temple city of Madurai in Tamilnadu, and was in close touch with the leaders of a new student movement, the Union of Evangelical Students of India (UESI). Her love for India and contact with students confirmed the direction I was moving in. The idea of working with university students appealed to me and seemed a God-given direction to move in. Shirley and I also were drawn to each other and after a rapid, if not whirlwind courtship, we were engaged two months before I left for Bombay in January 1963.

BMMF and its predecessors had established schools and hospitals and other institutions in the northern part of the Indian sub-continent. So I did not look to go south as Shirley had done, but to go somewhere in the north. The first challenge would be to learn Hindi, the national language. For this I could go to a Language School in Allahabad at the confluence of the Ganges and Jumna rivers in Uttar Pradesh, India's most populous state.

The idea of going to Banaras Hindu University (BHU) came from Bob Brow, a lecturer in Allahabad. He was in touch with the UESI and was one of their supporters in founding new groups for Christian students. When he heard that I had applied to join the mission he belonged to, he suggested that I should study at BHU. He rightly thought that becoming a student at a Hindu university would be an ideal way of introducing me to India and to student life in the sub-continent.

Travelling to India in those days was not so easy or quick as it is today. You could go by plane, but that was expensive and comparable to a first class ticket now. Most people, even business men, went by sea. That was the time honoured method. There were still plenty of passenger ships, though not many tourists. I was booked on an Anchor Line boat, the Circassia, which sailed out of Liverpool. The trip to Bombay via the Suez Canal took 20 days.

So it came about that when I arrived in Bombay at the beginning of February 1963, I went straight to Allahabad. Within a few days I had learnt my first words of Hindi and visited Varanasi (Banaras) for the first time. A week later I met Bob Brow and went with him to Varanasi. No doubt he was the one who suggested that I must meet a Japanese Christian research student in BHU, as soon as possible. This student turned out to be Minoru Kasai. So it was that on Friday 15 February I met Minoru for the first time.

## Meeting Point

I kept striking my head on the low canopy of the rickshaw, as I peered out. For the first time I was getting a glimpse of Varanasi traffic. The cyclists, the cows, the tongas, the bullock carts, the rickshaws and pedestrians – all tumbling together and weaving in and out. Only the occasional bus or motor scooter challenged for a place on the highway.

The road twisted and turned past street vendors, wayside shrines, temples, sacred bathing pools, broken walls and mysterious houses. At Lanka the road suddenly broadened out with low shops on either side. Books and stationery and students showed that the university must be close at hand. Sure enough the road narrowed and the rickshaw slowed to pass under the gateway to Banaras Hindu University (BHU).

'Where is Birla Hostel?' I asked the guard at the gate in my faltering Hindi.

With a wave of his arm the guard pointed ahead and to the right. Soon a large sign showed we were passing the Medical College Hospital. More sandstone buildings appeared on the right, and then a board saying 'BIRLA HOSTEL'. The long two-storey block was lined with student rooms. I paid off the rickshaw and went in search of a hostel warden, who said I could go to Minoru's room. But when I got there the room was locked. In fact most of the student rooms were locked and empty. The February evening was rapidly turning dark. Someone would need to help me if I was to find the way.

'Where is everyone?' I asked the first person I could find.

'The students are all out at a special function. Who are you looking for?'

'I am looking for Minoru, a Japanese student. Where do you think he might be?'

'He will not be at the function. But you can try the university library. He often goes there.'

I thanked the helpful stranger and went out to look for another rickshaw. The evening air was turning cool. Though the day had been warm, summer was still a month away and the temperature dropped at night. A rickshaw soon came trundling into view and I got in.

The quiet roads of the campus bore no resemblance to the city streets outside. The hostels were well spread out and most stood well back from the road. At a crossroad the rickshaw turned away from the hostel road, past a sports field and tree-lined avenues. There were only a few cyclists and pedestrians to be seen. Here all seemed calm and peaceful. It is true that only a few years before striking students had closed the university for nine months. But that evening there were not many of the 10,000 students to be seen.

Lights were twinkling after sunset and I could not make out the names of the buildings we were passing. At last the rickshaw stopped at a pair of imposing wrought iron gates. I got out. It was the library.

I had been in India only two weeks, but it already seemed an age, separating me from all that had gone before. And Minoru? What would he be like? Why would a Japanese be studying in BHU? And how would I get on with him? The last time I had been with Japanese was in a prisoner of war camp nearly 20 years before, when I was a child. I was not thinking of that now, just eager to meet the person who I had heard so much about.

But where was Minoru? I asked the clerk at the library reception desk: 'I want to see Minoru Kasai, a Japanese student. Is he here?' The receptionist called a peon to take me to where Minoru was sitting. Minoru stood up to greet me.

'This is amazing! How did you get in?'

Whatever was going through Minoru's mind, he did not show it, except for surprise that a non-student had been allowed into the library. He had been carrying out research for a Ph.D. in BHU for three years, exploring the relationship between Hinduism, Buddhism and Christianity. During that time he had seen many foreigners come and go. How would this Cambridge graduate be any different?

Polite as always, he took his guest out of the library to a tea stall outside. There we found a bench and sat down under the welcoming trees. Where better to talk than sipping chai in Indian style in the cool of the evening?

Minoru may have wondered why an English student should come in search of him so soon after his arrival in

Varanasi. But he knew from letters he had received that I wanted his advice on how to enrol as a student in BHU.

'You can study as I do,' he said, 'at the Indology College. If you are interested in learning about India, that's a good place to begin. There are courses in Sanskrit and Pali, Indian Art and Archaeology, History, and Indian Philosophy and Religion.'

'But let me warn you,' he went on, 'that the Indology College will not want to admit another Christian who has studied theology, like you. They have recently had Americans from Princeton and a Jesuit priest from Belgium.'

BHU had been founded in 1916 to promote all that was good and great in Hinduism and the ancient civilization of India. One of its special features was the provision of Hindu religious instruction for Hindu students. The university was fiercely proud of its role and its situation near Mother Ganges and the most holy pilgrimage centre of Varanasi. At the same time, Pt. Madan Mohan Malaviya, its guiding genius, had insisted that the university would be for all students, whatever their religion. So BHU is an All India university, drawing students from all parts of the country. From the beginning it has also aimed to provide scientific and technical education of the highest quality.

Despite his warning Minoru went on to say: 'Nevertheless I suggest that you apply for the MA course in Indian Philosophy and Religion. I am 90% sure that you will get in, as no one has actually been refused so far.'

Reassured by this positive advice, I went on to ask about the hostels, as I wanted to know which would be a good one to apply for. Like Minoru I had no desire to live in the International Guest House with foreign students. This was a little world of its own with a fascinating mixture of Buddhist monks from Burma and Thailand, communists from Poland, westerners from Europe, America and elsewhere. But I had not come to India to view the country from the outside, but to get close to Indian students and empathise with their hopes and fears.

Minoru described his experience of living in Birla hostel. 'Birla is an Arts faculty hostel and as the Arts students are not so well qualified and come mainly from the villages, the standards are pretty low. The science faculties, particularly engineering, have a good reputation, whereas the Arts faculty is generally poor, providing a low standard. There is only one wash place and one wash basin for a hundred students. The food is provided by several different canteens, according to how much you can pay. Most students have only two meals a day and have a very poor diet with watery dal and chapattis.'

'Do you keep well?' I asked.

'Yes, yes. Now I am alright, perhaps only ill once a month.'

'What's the worst thing?'

'The noise from other students' rooms nearly drives me mad. But, Fr. Van Troy and I are both agreed that we really experience the atmosphere of rural Indian mentality in a way that would be impossible elsewhere.'

It would be a challenge, but Minoru's comments only made me more determined than ever to live in an Indian hostel. Immersion in the culture would demand much more than academic study, it would mean sharing the life style. I wanted to be here in Varanasi, to enter the soul of India, to discover what shaped the mindset of millions of Indians, even if they were ignorant of Hindu philosophy.

As we parted we wished each other well. I left wondering whether I could cope with the rigours of Birla hostel, when I joined the university in July. Unknown to me, Minoru was contemplating a move from Birla to a hostel for research students. Both of us wondered whether our meeting on that

February evening would be the beginning of a friendship that would grow deeper in the days to come. Would we be able to overcome the obvious barriers of race and nationality, and what would we discover about each other, which might unite or separate us?

## The Experience of Reconciliation

In July 1963 I returned to Varanasi. The monsoon had broken and four days of torrential rain had lowered the temperature from the furnace heat of mid-summer. Minoru took me on July 19 to the Indology College office in BHU, and with his help and persistence I got all the forms I needed to apply for a room in one of the hostels. The next day Minoru introduced me to the College Principal and to Prof. Devaraja, the head of my department. After more form filling and paying my university fees, I was finally given a room the next week, not in Birla Hostel as we had originally planned, but in Gurtu Hostel.

Gurtu Hostel, BHU, Varanasi

## Two Pilgrims Meet

When Minoru and I met in Varanasi, we were drawn together by common interests, as students studying in the same University and the same College. Two things were particularly important: we were both foreigners in the same Indian university, and both of us were disciples of Christ. I needed someone who understood a foreigner's problems and had learnt how the university operated, as Minoru had done through three years at BHU. I also appreciated Minoru, because he understood my beliefs as a fellow pilgrim on the way with Christ.

There was also something else that we had in common, something unusual. I do not remember how we discovered that we had lived close to each other in China as children without ever meeting. On some occasion we must have been talking about our past. Probably I said: "I used to see Japanese during the war when I was in Shanghai." Minoru must have been very surprised. "How could you be in Shanghai? I was there too." That would have amazed me. How could Minoru have been in China during the war? The reason for both of us being in Shanghai was the same – our parents were there. His father was not a soldier but in private business, and my father's office was in Shanghai. Now twenty years later we were meeting for the first time not in China but in India. It sounded like a good opening for a novel, but this was reality. We both had roots in Shanghai.

The fact that we were different in many ways was not a barrier. As Miroslav Volf says in his book *Exclusion and Embrace*, differences are not the problem. All human beings have been created uniquely different. Difference constitutes the basis of our individuality. What separates us is the barrier of enmity.

At the personal level, Minoru and I were not enemies. We had never been enemies to each other. Nevertheless underneath the surface there were barriers that needed to be overcome. Our upbringing and identity as Japanese and British citizens threatened to keep us apart. By nationality we had been divided by war. At one time we had both been on opposite sides, on opposite sides in the Second World War, living on opposite sides of the river in Shanghai. We had experienced the pain that war inflicts. How was this inherited barrier of national identity to be overcome?

The experience of reconciliation took place for us at two levels. The basic level of practical friendship was important for me. When I went to Banaras Hindu University in July 1963 I found myself in a vast campus of three square miles, with thousands of students and dozens of hostels. It was a bewildering encounter with a new culture. The only friend I had was Minoru. He helped me to get admission to the Indology College and he was there to welcome me when I arrived at the beginning of the academic year. I am still indebted to Minoru for looking after me in those first few weeks when I was so ignorant of a strange environment. He introduced me to the professor of Indian philosophy under whom I was to study. He helped me to get a good room in a student hostel. He guided me through the initiation of form filling and fee paying. I would have been lost without him.

Some may wonder, 'How did you feel about being befriended by a Japanese?' This thought was not uppermost in my mind, because Christ had united us in love for him. On the other hand I have many times pondered how extraordinary it was that I had to depend entirely on a Japanese student, when I first went to India. As far as I remember Minoru was the first Japanese I got to know after being in a prisoner of war camp. He was certainly my first Japanese friend. Not that I was particularly hostile to Japanese, as none of my family had been tortured or subjected to forced labour in our civilian camp. Nevertheless there was something that had alienated us in the past, which had to be overcome by Christ. The way Christ did that for us has always been a powerful example of what the gospel of Jesus is all about – reconciling enemies not only to God but also to each other. This is particularly impressive when you experience deep friendship with someone of a totally different culture, whom your country regards as an enemy.

Our friendship led to a deeper level, where we were united in prayer. Even before I came to BHU Minoru had written to me in March saying that he was looking forward so much to fellowship with me. What thrilled me was his suggestion that we should pray together daily. He longed for 'a new living and burning fellowship which would melt the hearts of non-Christians too.' So it happened that when I took up residence in BHU, we began to meet daily for prayer.

In the months of July – September 1963, when I had moved to BHU for the new academic year, we prayed together as far as possible every day. Whatever else we may forget we will never forget those times, when we entered into the mystery of oneness in Christ. In my diary I wrote, 'it was as if I saw straight into Minoru's soul.' There were no barriers, nothing was hidden. We were one in Christ. This was much more than meeting 'face to face'. As Minoru recalls, it was meeting 'heart to heart' and 'beyond nationality'.

This was an unforgettable experience. As a human being I could never hope to know what a Japanese man was thinking. But as we prayed together, nothing was hidden, our innermost being was laid bare. There we knew a oneness in the presence of God where all thought of enmity was banished. There was nothing hidden, nothing in between, as we met beyond barriers.

A quote from Miroslav Volf, a Croatian author who has experienced the bitterness of ethnic conflict, illuminates why this came about:

" ... *Christians can never be first of all Asians or Americans ...and then Christians. At the very core of Christian identity lies an all-encompassing change of loyalty, from a given culture with its gods to the God of all cultures*" (M.Volf, *Exclusion and Embrace,* Nashville, 1996, p.40).

However we explain what happened to us, we were reconciled by Christ. All our national differences and wartime memories simply melted away in his presence. We wanted to be friends and we became friends by his grace. It was a sheer gift from Christ, which we had never sought or imagined. What God has given us is entirely due to Christ who embraced us and gave us the love to embrace each other. The embrace of Christ goes very deep, because he has identified with the suffering of humanity on the cross. He did not shrink from it. So he has understood our pain and forgiven our hostility to himself and to others.

As I reflect on what meeting with Minoru has meant to me and as I ponder the liberating effect of reconciliation across national barriers, I am profoundly moved by what God has done for me.

I look back now without any bitterness on those POW camps. There is no bitterness for our guards. It does not mean that I have lost my critical faculties. I know many things done by both sides were wrong and some were emphatically evil. I have not lost my senses, but I have lost all sense of resentment. I owe this to Christ and I owe it to Minoru.

As I think of friends I know who could never forgive the Japanese people for what they suffered in the war and never got over the bitterness they felt, I am grateful that

Christ has delivered me from that dead end. I have been enlarged by friendship with Japan through Minoru, instead of being limited by national sentiment. Forgiveness enlarges the heart, resentment narrows the arteries of compassion. Because we had both experienced the liberating power of being forgiven by Christ, we were able to embrace each other. This in turn meant we could live beyond the limits of national loyalties. We could relate to each other as brothers in the family of God. We accepted each other as members of the one human race. What we have in common is more important than what we have that is different. Our differences – even national, racial and cultural differences – no longer divide us, instead we are enriched by them.

One of God's most valuable gifts is healing of the memories. The memory of suffering lives on long after the event and can return to trouble us at any time. To survive in peace we repress the memories of painful experiences, especially the ones we cannot cope with. These painful times may resurface in our dreams, they may also come back to haunt us when we are least expecting them. By filling our days with work and a busy schedule we can keep the horrors we have experienced out of mind, but when we have time on our hands the real nightmares of the past come flooding back. For this reason those who experienced the horrors of the Second World War and are now retired may once again be overwhelmed by flashbacks to the gruesome scenes of war. If we cannot cleanse our minds of these memories they will continue to torment us.

Is there a solution? It is not surprising that one of the doctors in our concentration camp, Kenneth McAll, sought for an answer. He turned from general medical practice to specialise in a search for memory healing (see his book *Healing The Family Tree*, London, 1982). As I look back now I recall perfectly clearly the worst things that happened to me in the camp, but I no longer feel them as pain. I have not forgotten the evil or the suffering. The solution was not to forgive and forget. Far from forgetting, I remember the worst with joy. If that sounds unbelievable, the easiest analogy I can suggest by way of explanation is that of a student. The student preparing for a final exam is petrified with the fear of failing and exhausted by endless hours and nights of study, but when the exams are over and the result is success, he or she can glory in all that they suffered to achieve the goal. The difference in my case is that I achieved nothing; the healing of my memories was a pure gift from God. God removed the pain by uniting me with Christ and through Christ with Minoru.

A more profound analogy is seen in the way we recall the crucifixion of Christ. The extraordinary thing is that Christians look back on the cross and the appalling execution of the Son of God with joy. We actually celebrate the crucifixion as the glory of Christ's love for the world. We do so because he overcame the abyss of suffering by rising to the heights of heaven. Every day Christ's death is celebrated throughout the world as a thanksgiving, the Eucharist. Miroslav Volf argues in his masterly book, *The End of Memory*, that the memory of pain remains a serious threat to peace of mind. He argues that in eternity the memory of the death of Jesus will be unnecessary and undesirable. This is not the view of John's Gospel, where the cross is seen as the glory of God, nor is it the view of the book of Revelation where Christ in heaven is still viewed as a sacrificial Lamb, whose sacrifice for every human being has won the eternal victory of cosmic salvation through suffering. The glory of Christ is not to be forgotten because it was painfully achieved, or because it was revealed on earth in time and not in heaven for eternity.

Reconciliation brings hope. This was another gift I received from friendship with Minoru. The world is full of suffering caused by enmity between nations, religions, races, classes, families and individuals. Some of these divisions run so deep that they appear to be unbridgeable. To reunite old enemies seems impossible. But the impossible is possible with God. Our experience showed me that Christ specialises in reconciling enemies. This is the heart of the gospel and the beauty of the cross of Christ. Christ died for his enemies and for all humanity at enmity with God. Consequently Christ has the power to unite all who come to God through him. This power is a living reality. Our experience of meeting with God in prayer in the depths of the soul was a convincing demonstration of God's presence. The hope born of this encounter was therefore not wishful thinking but an expectation that what God had done for us he could do for others. Whether people are Indian, Chinese, Japanese or British, whether they are Hindu, Buddhist, Muslim or Christian, Christ can unite them. No division is insuperable for him.

# Minoru's Pilgrimage Continued

## Year at Harvard

After I had finished my Ph.D. studies at Varanasi, I returned to America as a teaching Fellow at Harvard University. As a teaching Fellow I had plenty of time for discussion with students and other Fellows. I was greatly blessed through these intensive discussions. In particular I met three professors who impressed me. One was Prof. Wilfred Cantwell Smith, a historian of Islam and comparative religion. The second person was Prof. Robert N. Bellah, whose speciality was the sociology of religion. I found him to be an unusual person, because he insisted that in order to understand society one must begin with one's own pilgrimage in search of the truth. This was most striking in the situation of a prestigious university. The third person was Prof. A.K. Saran, from the Indian university of Lucknow, who specialised in the sociology of religion

I found my discussions with Cantwell Smith very moving. As a young scholar, he had been in Pakistan, attending Forman Christian College in Lahore. While he was there he lived through the traumatic events of the Partition of India when hundreds of thousands were slaughtered on both sides of the border. Hatred and bitterness spread everywhere. In his college the Muslim, Hindu, Sikh and Christian staff met to discuss the crisis. They felt it was their responsibility to maintain sanity in the face of the turmoil going on all around them. In that serious situation the teachers were deeply united as they strove to maintain sanity in the midst of insanity. They felt helpless, but were led to devote themselves to prayer.

Each of the staff had to pray according to their religious tradition. For the Muslim this meant returning to the source of Islam. For the Hindu it meant returning to the source of Hindu belief. Similarly the Sikhs had to go back to their founding Gurus. For Cantwell Smith it meant returning to the source of Christianity in Christ and the gospel. The only way out for each one was to go back to the source of inspiration in their religion. In this way their faith was deepened. They also found in relation to each other a new bond, as they sought together in one community to find one solution to the problem of division. To find reality in the face of the unknown became a process which transformed the teachers. Sharing the same problem together produced a kind of brotherhood in their college community.

Cantwell Smith wrote his Ph.D. thesis out of this experience with the title: "Modern Islam in India". His thesis was submitted to Oxford University, but was rejected. However the thesis was appreciated by Islamic specialists in India. Academically Cantwell Smith suffered a severe disappointment in the rejection of his thesis, but actually the writing was an inspiration to him and later he wrote another book, *Islam in Modern History* (1957), which was published by Princeton University. Out of this experience he developed a study of religion based on three levels. The first is in the third person, or the level of 'they'. The second level is the level of 'you' – 'to you', 'about you' and 'with you'. The third level concerns returning to the Source, as a pilgrimage. At this level there are new apprehensions of reality, which are difficult to describe. It involves seeing our community as a brotherhood with all other religious communities, facing contemporary issues together. The above is just a rough description of my appreciation of Cantwell Smith. Later I translated one of his books into Japanese as a token of my appreciation of his kindness. I also agreed with his emphasis on returning to the Source as the only way to break through the present impasse, which is self-destructive.

R. N. Bellah was a professor of the sociology of religion. I was impressed by his emphasis on the need of a search for meaning and truth, as a necessity for the scholar's own self-understanding. In the academic world this quest for self-understanding is unusual. Bellah saw the search for the Source as the spring for action. He developed a framework for the study of history, dividing history into primitive, ancient, historic, early modern, modern and post-modern. In the contemporary situation he saw two phases: the loss of faith and the faith of (or out of) loss. The turning point between these two phases was a personal pilgrimage for him. In his childhood his father died. His passing felt like a loss of faith. He was brought up by his mother in the pious tradition of Christianity in the deep south of USA. They then moved to San Francisco, where he was thrown into a typical city situation with segregation and separation based on race and wealth. He lost faith in the piety with which he had been brought up and became a communist. Marxism seemed to provide a way out of differentiation based on race or economic status. In this situation he was fortunate to receive a scholarship to study at Harvard University. In Harvard he found others who believed in Marxism as the way out of the American contradiction. They met regularly and learnt from each other. But in Harvard he was also exposed to other religions, and was attracted by Zen Buddhism with its sense of beauty and awareness of nature and the environment. He could also see that though Marxism was an ideal, the actual condition in communist countries was different under Soviet control and the rule of force. This produced a conflict in his heart.

Then McCarthyism swept over America and made him critical of McCarthyism and Marxism. It was difficult for him to find an alternative. At that time he was introduced to the writings of Paul Tillich with his different view of Christian doctrine. However, having been a member of the Communist group, he could no longer stay in Harvard and had to move to Canada. At McGill University he met Cantwell Smith and stayed at his institute of Islamic Studies. Cantwell Smith stressed the importance of dialogue. In the institute half the members were Muslims and half were Christians, so as to encourage dialogue and foster encounter. He stayed there for two years.

The problems of America were Bellah's main concern. Fortunately the McCarthy witch hunt abated and he was able to return to Harvard, where he stayed for ten years. He found that there was still hope for America in its tradition of liberalism and self-criticism. During this period the Vietnam War started. This provoked student protests all over America. But Harvard remained relatively peaceful. Prof. Bellah, however felt a calling to move to California and to the University of California, Berkeley, because he felt there was such confusion among the students who were agitating against the Vietnam war. He believed the Vietnam war was not justifiable by any means. So he came to be regarded as a leader of the liberal protest movement. He felt that the danger was that whatever America decided to do in Vietnam would be seen as a Christian response and therefore that it would be regarded as right. On the other side the anti-Vietnam war movement would become intolerant of anyone holding other views. So Bellah tried to express his position non-violently. He sought through encounter to find a breakthrough between these conflicting positions.

At this time he had two daughters who were very dear to him. The elder daughter supported the anti-Vietnam war movement but was really tormented by the campus student violence. It also pained her that her father was attacked for advocating non-violence by the anti-Vietnam protesters. In the end she committed suicide. That was a terrible blow for Bellah. For six months he could not speak in public. However after six months he preached in a Congregational Church in Berkeley. The title of his sermon was "Reflection on Reality in America". His speech had such a powerful impact on his audience that when he finished there was total silence. He said that America was going through a period of profound darkness and no one could say when the night would be over and the sun would rise again. But in this darkness there are people who are witnessing a breakthrough that brings hope in the midst of the gloom. This is the real spirit of America, deeply rooted in God's blessing, in God's guidance and in God's prayer. We do not know when the morning will come but we wait for it in hope. He confessed that his position now was one of faith arising out of loss. Everything made by man is not reliable. However man is proud of his achievements. Pride leads to self-justification, and this has led to the Vietnam war. But there is still hope and there are individuals who witness to a way out through returning to the source of being. He described his position as faith born out of loss, which instead of bringing despair brings hope and results in thankfulness. I was struck by Bellah's insistence on life as a ceaseless pilgrimage, repeatedly going beyond the past and the point that one has reached, and finding new realities and God's blessing, which leads to thanks and prayer.

A.K. Saran was a representative of the influential Lucknow school of sociology, which emphasised the need for a scholarly traditional framework to understand India. The sociology of religion has been cultivated in India, in order to understand religion and society. The Lucknow school of sociology developed after the war and was unusual in that it treated the sociology of religion as a modern science, which is inadequate to understand traditional Indian society. When I first attended his seminar, I was struck by his statement: "Hinduism is no longer alive, it is dead." He considered that though there are many leading scholars in the study of Hinduism, overall it would be true to say that it is a case of the blind leading the blind. The only exception was M.K. Gandhi. As far as the spiritual tradition in Hinduism is concerned he only accepted three representatives: Ramakrishna, Ramana Maharishi and Aurobindo. His views gave me a new understanding of the situation in India.

A. K. Saran surprised me by his statement that Hinduism is dead, but I found that despite holding such a radical position in India, he was a very warm hearted and affectionate person. My friendship with him continued throughout his life until he passed away. The core of his position is the one expressed by M. K. Gandhi in his book, "Hind Swaraj", written in 1909, in a chapter where he deals with the question, 'What is the condition of India?'. Gandhi's verdict was one word, 'misery'. That misery really pained Gandhi. What was the reason for this misery? Gandhi put it briefly: "India is walking against God." Religions aid the people of India in walking (or working) against God. By religions Gandhi meant Hinduism, Islam and other religions. Religions are responsible for the misery of India and they are encouraging the people to walk against God. By accepting modernisation as progress India is working against the source and the foundation of religions. Modernisation is arrogant and self-sufficient and claims to stand for progress and civilisation. This movement against God is still curable, because there are people who have been awakened to reality. A. K. Saran took Gandhi's position to be fundamental, though he was ignored and rejected and expelled from the academic community in India. Even his own Lucknow school of sociology totally ignored him. Cantwell Smith was very impressed with A. K. Saran's paper, "On Hinduism and Economic Development". So he invited A. K. Saran to come to Harvard. So I was privileged to meet A. K. Saran, because his argument challenged me. After six years in India I had been impressed by Hindu spirituality. But I thought modernisation was absolutely necessary for India to be free from the misery of poverty. But A. K. Saran challenged my understanding of Indian spirituality, and also confronted my perception that modernisation is essential for progress in India.

My discussions with these three professors made my year in Harvard extremely beneficial. In particular the vision shared by Cantwell Smith and R. N. Bellah of humanity as a healing family was a blessing to me. It is necessary to be awakened to this reality. A. K. Saran added to this by insisting that nature and the cosmos are also an inseparable part of the healing family. According to him this was the vision of M. K. Gandhi.

I was greatly blessed by my time in Harvard. Originally it was to be only for one year, but then I was offered an extension for a second year. However I also received an invitation to return to my own university, ICU, in Tokyo and I accepted the ICU offer and returned to Japan after ten years abroad.

## Return to ICU

Returning to my university in Tokyo in 1968, I was confronted with a most unexpected and painful situation. There was a nationwide student protest against government interference to the university's right of self rule.

*Two Pilgrims Meet*

ICU was not an exception to the national trend. On my return, I was sad that the university was in such turmoil with students occupying university buildings. As a result there were no lectures going on. The university was dysfunctional. I was appointed, as the residential adviser of the first men's dormitory, very close to the centre of the student movement. I had to live in the dormitory residence with my family in the midst of this painful process. The general atmosphere at that time was marked by hostility against the university administration and the faculty.

But unexpectedly, the dormitory students asked me to open a class in the common room of the dormitory at night. I was surprised by their request, because as a faculty member, a dormitory adviser and later an assistant to the acting President of the University, I would be considered as a part of the existing system and a political enemy. I suggested the theme for the class: the search for the meaning, "Who am I?" and social transformation. They accepted my suggestion. This was similar to the task of R.N. Bellah in Harvard University. The meaning of self-identity, "Who am I?" is crucial in social transformation and in the history of the post-modern period, for we have the instruments to destroy the whole of humanity (nuclear weapons). They knew the prayers of the victims of the atomic bombs in Hiroshima and Nagasaki are for the peace of the whole world, a world free from the hatred-revenge mentality, though their pains are beyond words.

I had a collection of Prof. Bellah's papers from his earliest days as a scholar in Harvard University and knowing my position, he kindly and continuously sent me his papers. As a class method, the students began to read his papers chronologically and discussed them among themselves. I always joined their discussions. They really appreciated this way of learning. The class was held once a week from 9 o'clock in the evening. It went on beyond midnight and even to dawn on rare occasions. It continued for about three years. Even after the university started to function normally, this night class continued. As a result, it became a book and was published. The title of the book is *Between Religion and Social Sciences* (published in Japanese in 1974). The students understood why Prof. Bellah was persistently against the Vietnam War. Now, his position of faith from Zero remains as a question. From my point of view, it indicates the blessing of reality given by God.

Then some students in the protest movement, who were not residents in the dormitory, came with sticks and helmets to my residence in the dormitory and asked me to begin an open class to study Gandhiji's views of non-violence and social change. They were very much disturbed by the role of violence as a means to pursue their political goals in the protest movements. This open class continued for one year till my new appointment in the Philippines. It was not easy to understand Gandhiji's position: non-violence is the only way to the truth. In order to understand the position, it is necessary at least to have a glimpse of the blessed reality given by God as the Truth, in which we are brothers and sisters as members of God's family. In this reality the following prayer may be born in our hearts:

*Let all earth's nations honour you and all people shout out praise to God as the Truth:*
*Christian, Muslim, and Jew, atheist, agnostic,*
*Buddhist, Taoist, Hindu, black, brown and white....*
*Let all of them feel your presence and sing out in the fullness of joy.*

*Two Pilgrims Meet*

It is difficult to have a glimpse of the blessing of reality given by God, but the witness of both Mahatma Gandhiji and Martin Luther King is powerful enough, so that the joy and thanks of awakening may be shared by many, as has happened in India, America, the Philippines and South Africa.

Studies on Gandhiji's witness still continue to take place once a month at the ICU campus. I participate in these after deep communion with nature and God in the ICU garden of Taizanso and enjoy radical relativity (in Raimon Panikkar's phrase) in the studies with thanks. Now we are using the text written by Narayan Desai. He has just passed away, but wrote a four-volume biography of Gandhiji, which we are studying now. This study continues to be held at ICU, and so when I go for this discussion on Gandhiji's legacy, I am able to go for silent prayer to the same quiet garden that I used to frequent as a staff member.

Taizanso – traditional tea garden

Minoru meditating in silence at Taizanso

What surprised me most was the invitation of God to meet him in that garden. This invitation became like a call to pilgrimage – a pilgrimage to meet with God, to be renewed and awakened to that reality with prayer. Sadly this experience is not known and there has not been much response when it has been shared. But this has become more real to me than anything else. This helps me in defining the meaning of society. Normally in our articulation at the simple level, society means the relationship between people, person to person. Then it becomes a movement and is institutionalised. But for me society must be constituted of three pillars: one is the relationship between God and man, that is the foundation of society, and if this relationship is deepened, it becomes the relationship between one person and another person, which is not confined to the present, but exists also in the past. I recognise how greatly I have been enlightened by people who have passed away. At the same time I find that society also consists of a relationship between man and nature. Through nature we will naturally become thankful, because through nature God speaks to the heart, very deeply. The given-ness of the blessed reality is a present reality. So my prayer is that people will be aware of this blessing. Then it will be increasingly painful if people remain blind to the tremendous gift of being able to walk with God.

God's invitation to spend time with him in the garden was shared with visitors from outside who came to ICU. One of these was Fr. Oshida. When he came to this garden he immediately felt the reality of prayer. He was impressed and moved, and commented that it was such a blessing to have such a place in the campus. He was not a traditional Catholic, but more like a non-conformist catholic. He was well known to Catholics as an unusual priest and unorthodox in the catholic tradition. So I appreciated it greatly when he visited ICU, though it is not a Catholic institution, and spoke to the community. They responded with extraordinary appreciation to his preaching. Then he visited the garden with me. He shared with me the wonder of the blessed reality which he found there.

Another visitor who came with me to the garden was Rajmohan Gandhi. His visit was an extraordinary event for me, because when he came to the campus he planned to leave at 2.30 pm, immediately after he had given his lecture. But the students persuaded him to stay, so he cancelled his programme for the rest of that day and stayed on the campus responding to the students.

Before the final session Rajmohan was exhausted and wanted to have a quiet time to restore himself before another session. So I took him to the garden. As soon as he entered the garden he felt something quite different in the atmosphere in the garden and he asked me: "What is this place?" I responded by saying to him: "Every morning I begin the day here with prayer and silence." He immediately asked me if he could share in that, so I opened the quiet house in the garden and we sat together. He felt the invitation to pray so clearly that he responded and joined me in silent prayer.

Rajmohan Gandhi at Minoru's home, ICU

In time I felt more and more aware of the importance of the threefold relationship between Man and God, Man and Man, and Man and Nature. Nature reveals the value of this relationship as a pure gift and points to the real source of life itself. When we become aware of this gift we are drawn together in thankfulness to God.

For university education the relationship between God and man is fundamental. We make all sorts of tools to raise our living standards, consequently we have many instruments of violence, which can easily destroy us and torment many people. The contrast here and now between the darkness and the blessing is drastic. But unfortunately through education the most fundamental gift is missed. Knowledge has increased, but this progress blinds our eyes to the blessing of the given reality. My prayer is a yearning for an awakening to and sharing of this blessed reality.

## In the Philippines

In 1960, when I had to fly back to Japan from India because of my father's death, I had to stay in Manila for one night. I was not allowed to go outside the hotel, because of security reasons. I was told: "A hate-revenge mentality among the Filipinos still remains due to the Japanese occupation."

In 1972, I was appointed as the director of the Japan Studies Program of Ateneo de Manila University. I went to the University with my family. At first, I felt uncertain because of my previous experience. But the situation was different this time. I and my family were fully accepted as part of the University community. Soon after our arrival I heard Fr. Kruz, the president of the University, giving a public address to all the University community. He said: "We are blessed here and now because of God's love. We are surrounded by many challenges within and without. We are so much blessed to be in all these challenges, as God's love goes beyond the hatred-revenge mentality." I was deeply moved by his address. He was much loved and respected by the students. His vision was like that of M.L.King and M. Gandhi.

I worked hard, especially for exchange initiatives on many levels of life. Everything was so unexpected. With the help of Fr. Nebreda, originally from Spain, I invited Fr. Oshida. Fr. Oshida's speech spoke to people at a heart to heart level. Prof. E. Weibright, professor of psychology, was particularly grateful to meet Fr. Oshida. He and his Filipino wife, and Fr. Nebreda understood my task and my prayer and helped me so much, because my prayer was for a universal task. There is no future without reconciliation and creative co-existence. The way to reconciliation and creative co-existence is open from person to person and from nature to the individual. But it is extremely difficult at the level of the nation-state.

One day, Prof. Fr. Horacio de la Costa, former president of Ateneo de Manila University gave me a paper that he had written. The subject was "The Eastern Face of Christ" is Gandhi. If freedom and justice, as expressions of our God-given dignity are rejected by political rule, then we must stand against the violence with love and non-violence. This spirit continued down to the 1986 EDSA Revolution in the Philippines. The paper was given as an address at the Commencement Exercise of the University of the Philippines.

My two year stay was too short, just like a passing moment. But it was an extraordinarily condensed and blessed time. I say, my identity is "Japan, the beautiful and myself", but I feel - naturally and spontaneously - "The Philippines, the beautiful and myself." This is not intelligible, but the feeling is actual and real.

Just before my departure from Manila, I was told, "Do you know that Fr. Kruz's father, elder brother and two male members of his family were killed by Japanese soldiers?" I was shocked and the pain struck deep into my heart.

## Takamori Soan

I was invited to speak at the Zen Christian Dialogue Fellowship in 1968, soon after my return from Harvard University. I was so moved to find such an audience of well known people, listening intensely to an unknown person like me. After the meeting Fr. Oshida, a Catholic priest belonging to the Dominican order, asked me to visit his ashram in the remote village of Shinano Sakai in Nagano prefecture. I visited his ashram community in November 1968. When I arrived he was not there. Unexpectedly he had been hospitalised. That night there was a telephone call from the hospital to say that his condition was critical as he was spitting blood into the wash basin. I went to the hospital with some members of the ashram. We were told by the doctor not to speak to Fr. Oshida, but just to give him a silent greeting. I greeted him in Japanese style, bowing to him with folded hands. He responded with a smile, greeting me with folded hands and a prayer. I stayed for a few more days in the ashram without Fr. Oshida being present. Then gradually I became aware of God's call to me, an invitation from God through silent prayer in the House of Prayer and at the place where a stream pours out of the spring at the foot of the mountain. This place is surrounded by mountains including Mt. Fuji.

I responded to God's call by regularly visiting this ashram. Later I discovered rice fields belonging to the ashram, which were cultivated by the community without the use of chemical fertilisers and relying only on simple tools. At that time I used to work in the fields with Fr. Oshida and ashram members. Several times I saw Fr. Oshida talking to and listening to the rice plants when he was alone.

Minoru working in the rice field during the 1981 Conference

Then, the memorial garden in the woods struck me very deeply. Starting with a memorial for the victims of the atomic bombs that fell on Hiroshima and Nagasaki, there are a series of memorials on wooden pillars. These commemorate the victims of Japanese invasions of Korea, China, the Philippines and South-East Asia, as well as the sufferings of aborigines at the hands of the civilised. On a final memorial plaque Fr. Oshida has expressed in poetic form his purpose in establishing this memorial garden to the memory of the victims of Japanese aggression. This can be translated into English in the following way:

*In the sea of infinite, ceaseless tears, I stand for ever.*

This memorial touched the hearts of the Bahuguna couple from India, who are well known in India as followers of Gandhi, leading the Chipko movement to protect the Himalayan forests. When they were visiting the memorial garden in the woods, I asked Shri Bahuguna, whether this concern for the victims of suffering would have been Gandhi's position in the closing years of his life. He strongly affirmed that this would have been the case. He also said that this has been his position in the struggle for justice for the past fifty years. His response was unexpected and I was deeply moved.

My granddaughter's girl friend wanted to come to Japan to see her friend's home. Her father is a leading lawyer in the Philippines. In 1986 he and his wife stood facing the tanks of the Marcos army. He and his wife visited the ashram, and as they stood in front of the memorial for victims in the Philippines, they asked me why this memorial had been placed there. When I explained our sorrow for the many victims, our spiritual brothers and sisters, tears came into his eyes, because male members of his family had been killed by Japanese soldiers during the war. He was astonished to find a memorial for them here in Japan. He was grateful for this. This was his moment of reconciliation with Japanese brothers and sisters.

Similarly I remember a couple of Chinese girls coming to Takamori Soan from Hong Kong. They too were moved to tears to see this memorial for Chinese victims of Japan's invasion of China. Talking with them, it seemed to me that their tears were for the Chinese victims as a part of the whole of humanity, the whole of humanity bearing the suffering from war and violence, which continues to this day.

I found in Takamori Soan the same longing for the experience of reality, which had become so important to me in my own pilgrimage. In the practice of silent prayer and the dedication to no more war I found my own convictions confirmed.

**The Pilgrimage for Peace** arose after Fr. Oshida died. When he died we spent time in reflection, wondering what we should do to continue the work he had begun. As a result of our reflection the consensus among members was that the pilgrimage for peace would be a fitting continuation of the heritage given through Fr. Oshida by God. So ashram members began to go on regular monthly pilgrimages in the Nagano prefecture. Recently, in the past two years, it has been decided that we should not confine this pilgrimage to the remote mountain areas, but go to Tokyo and meet with more people there. In the present critical period when the government has proposed to change our peace constitution this pilgrimage for peace is extremely relevant. It is very easy for us to give way to arrogance and self-interest. We desperately need to be awakened to the gift of the blessed reality. In this way we will be united with all people who long for peace, including the many in China who have the same yearning for a new era of peace as we do.

The aim of the Pilgrimage for Peace is to deepen and widen prayer for peace, together. This prayer is bound to be born when we are awakened. In the midst of the darkness we have been so greatly blessed. We simply need to be awakened to this reality. Then there will be a natural and spontaneous response. No one can stop this response, when people are awakened. This will enable us to go beyond the limits of the past. The world is waiting, joyfully and thankfully, for the coming generation. Everywhere there are people who will respond. But at the same time the political situation is very critical. That is why our task is so urgent. Why are we so stubborn and find it hard to be awakened to reality, and to receive this blessing?

## Postscript 2016

### I. I was given something precious from China.

I shared this feeling with Basil, expressing the feeling, "China is in my bones and flesh." But, I was not sure what it was.

However, it became clear to me after seeing the film, "Riding Alone for Thousands of Miles", directed by Chan I-Mou, and the leading actor being Takakura Ken, together with a documentary programme depicting how the film "Riding Alone for Thousands of Miles" was created by NHK (Japan Broadcasting Corp.). The theme of the film is love. The story is simple. Takakura's son went to Lijiang, a small town in Yunnan and saw a local dance. He was so impressed by it that he promised to come and see it again the following year. But he became seriously ill, so he could not keep his promise. Thus instead of him, his father, Takakura Ken, came to fulfill his son's promise. But the dancer was in prison, so it was arranged for him to see the dance in the prison. But just before the dance, the dancer was crying, saying without seeing his son, he cannot dance. So Takakura went to his village and returned with the dancer's son. Thus, seeing his son, the dancer performed his dance. Takakura filmed it, so that his son might be able to see the dancing.

The core of creating this film, "Riding Alone for Thousands of Miles" was the relationship between Chan I-Mou and Takakura Ken, characterized by mutual affection, respect and trust. In the process of creating the film, their relationship became deeper and deeper. This affected and permeated the whole group of people involved in creating this film, so that, in spite of hopeless diversities - local people as non-professional actors and actresses, and the only professional actor being Japanese (Takakura Ken), not knowing the local language - the whole group became a living community. Surprisingly, in the process of creating the film - beautiful mountains, land and village became part of a living community in which each one is so precious to each other. It became indeed, China, the beautiful. I felt I was invited into this living community. Thus I found my other identity: "China, the beautiful and myself." Now, I see the meaning of "something precious from China" is my other identity, which deepens my Japanese identity, "Japan, the beautiful and myself."

Chan I-Mou is one of the most well known directors in the world, who was working in a factory after the Cultural Revolution. His eyes for the reality of films were opened by Takakura Ken's film, "Hot Pursuit". He wanted to make films with Takakura Ken for many years. He fulfilled his dream. Now, I have found "China, the beautiful and myself" in the film, "Riding Alone for Thousands of Miles." My joy and thanks are infinite.

## II. Niitsu Haruko

I appreciate Sun Gu's (*Sun Ge* in Chinese) view on the value system still alive among ordinary people, who may not be formally educated in the modern sense in China, but are willing to stand against the general trend and even against the power of the nation state. She cites the case of Chinese parents who adopted Japanese orphans (as quoted in Sun Gu's recent interview with a reporter of Asahi Newspaper on beyond the framework of the nation state).

I have been much impressed by the witness of Niitsu Haruko, the daughter of a Japanese orphan adopted by Chinese parents as their son. Her father was brought up as a Chinese and naturally identified himself as Chinese. When his Chinese parents died, he was thirteen years old. Before their death, they told him for the first time that he is Japanese and showed him the evidence of his father's photo and writings. They urged him strongly not to reveal his identity as a Japanese until the right time comes. He had to survive. Fortunately he was employed as a boy resident in a small repair factory, and as he worked hard, he studied hard. He became a key person in the small repair factory. He married Haruko's mother. They were poor, but happy. But after 1972, the door for Japan was opened for Japanese orphans. Haruko's father decided to return to Japan. When it became known in her school that Haruko's father was Japanese stones began to be thrown at Niitsu by her friends. She returned home crying. Her mother's youngest brother stood up against the throwing of stones at the children and their families, and the throwing of stones stopped. At that time, she had to see anti-Japan films at school almost every day.

On returning back to Japan, she had to overcome all kinds of difficulties. But now, she is the key person in maintaining Haneda Airport in Tokyo as one of the cleanest airports in the world. In 2013 and 2014, Haneda Airport was chosen as the cleanest airport in the world by Skytrax in England.

She has a vision of Haneda Airport, as an open house serving visitors from all over the world and becoming a bridge between China and Japan. We have many things to learn from her.

I am so grateful for Niitsu's Chinese grandparents who adopted her father as their son. Her position is unique in the process of reconciliation between China and Japan.

## III. Onagawa – Tsunami Story

- a new witness in the process of reconciliation between China and Japan.

It is a beautiful, and unforgettable story.

There were 162 young Chinese female trainees working in a small town, Onagawa, facing the Pacific Ocean. There, 162 young trainees were divided into 19 small sea food companies, each company being responsible for the welfare of the young trainees. They seemed to enjoy working together in this beautiful town.

Then, suddenly they had to face the disaster of the Tsunami rising 17.5 metres high on March 11, 2011. How did these small companies fulfil their responsibilities for the trainees? We are thankful that all these 162 trainees were saved and returned safely to their homes in China.

In order to see the situation, let me take one example. Manager Sato guided all 20 trainees working for his company to a high, safe place where a Shinto Shrine was located. Then he returned to take his family to this safe place. But the Tsunami was so powerful and fast that he was overtaken by the Tsunami and disappeared. All these trainees saw this happen. It must have been a traumatic experience. 831 people of Onagawa town died. Among them, there may have been other courageous persons like Manager Sato.

However, I was astonished to see that the trainees, despite their traumatic experiences, are returning back to Onagawa town, in spite of family opposition. The townspeople are so grateful to them. They need them to restore the new Onagawa. Among them there is mutual affection, respect and trust. If this relation is deepened, the community will be reborn despite diversities, with one task: to restore together the beautiful Onagawa.

The position of the trainees who returned to Onagawa is expressed in one of the letters written by them. "Now, there are no national boundaries. Let us cooperate to restore this beautiful Onagawa. Onagawa is our second home."

This is the powerful witness for reconciliation on the level of person to person between China and Japan.

"No more wars between China and Japan" will continue to be my prayer.

# Reunion !

**After 40 years apart Basil describes how he met up with Minoru again and the consequences of this surprising reunion.**

I used to think as I looked back on my chance meeting with Minoru in BHU, Varanasi, that here were all the ingredients for a dramatic post-war novel tracing the lives of two boys, the one Japanese and the other English, who grew up on separate sides in Shanghai, then criss-crossed the world, only to meet in the heart of India. Not being a novelist I never committed that idea to paper, and this book would never have been written but for a strange event nearly forty years later.

It was a Sunday morning. I left to visit refugees at the Oakington Immigration Centre, outside Cambridge. Shirley went as usual to Holy Trinity in the centre of Cambridge. At the end of the service she turned round to greet the couple behind her. In the course of conversation she found out that they were from Japan and lived in Tokyo. Remembering friends we had not seen or heard of for 40 years, she asked:

"Do you happen to know Prof. Minoru Kasai?"

"Yes," said Toshi, "he was my classmate at International Christian University, Tokyo. We knew each other very well as students. Midori, my wife, was also a good friend of Yoshiko, Minoru's wife."

Prof. Toshi Yamamoto often comes to Cambridge and he has an apartment near the city centre. On this Sunday morning he and his wife had decided to visit Holy Trinity rather than the churches they usually went to. Toshi is a professor of English, who specialises in the writings of

John Bunyan. But this does not explain how he reconnected us with Minoru & Yoshiko.

When Minoru hears this strange story, he is amazed. "No one knows Minoru Kasai in Japan. If you were to turn round in a bus or in a church in Japan and ask: 'Do you know Minoru Kasai?' they would not know who I am. So how is it possible that Shirley could turn round in a church in England and, seeing two Japanese, ask them, 'Do you know Minoru Kasai?' and they say, 'Yes'?"

A casual meeting and a simple question put us back in touch with Minoru and Yoshiko after 40 years. Shirley's meeting with Toshi and Midori took place in the early summer of 2005. Toshi was able to communicate with Minoru in Tokyo and tell us how to contact him. Once we had an address we were able to write, and later to speak to Minoru and Yoshiko on the phone.

The next question was how to meet and where could a reunion take place. If we had simply exchanged letters and a phone call and no more this book would never have been written. Two more strange coincidences combined to turn Shirley's chance encounter with Toshi & Midori into a reunion.

Minoru surprised us by revealing that he was planning to come to England in the autumn of that year, 2005. He and Yoshiko wanted to see their old friends, Murray Rogers and his wife in Oxford. One of his former students was also at Oxford completing a Ph.D. in the field of comparative religion, which Minoru had supervised. We hoped they might be able to come to Cambridge. Here again Toshi was most helpful. He suggested that Minoru & Yoshiko could stay with them in his apartment, as he would be in Cambridge in October.

The second coincidence was even more extraordinary. Our daughter Carol and her husband, Patrick, had been working in Yekaterinburg across the Urals on the Siberian

## Two Pilgrims Meet

side of Russia. They had come home in August and after a holiday with us were planning to transfer their base to Japan and live in Osaka. Quite why they decided to move to Japan, where they had no connections, is still something of a mystery to us. They were booked to fly to Osaka on October 10$^{th}$, just two days before Minoru & Yoshiko were expected in Cambridge.

Carol & Patrick's flight was delayed for two days. This enabled them to meet Minoru & Yoshiko on October 11$^{th}$, because Minoru had decided to come to Cambridge a day earlier than he had planned. I remember taking Carol & Patrick over to Toshi's apartment. It was the first time I had seen Minoru for 40 years. He looked amazingly well and not at all old. It was a brief encounter, to enable Minoru to meet our daughter and her husband on their way to a new chapter in their lives in Japan.

Three days later on October 14$^{th}$ Shirley and I met Minoru & Yoshiko for a proper reunion in our own house. What a day that was, after forty years of silence! Words flowed as we caught up with each other's stories. Amongst other things we told Minoru about our five week trip round China in 2003 and the reawakening of memories of my Chinese childhood. I noted in my diary that Minoru was "keen to go to China with me, as they had only had a week in China with a tour guide." But before we could go together to China, we had to get to Japan.

Visiting Japan had not been on our agenda at all. But now with a daughter and family in Osaka we had to think new thoughts. Minoru & Yoshiko's visit and Carol & Patrick's departure for Japan were the two events which lifted us off on a new journey.

*Reunion!*

Yoshiko & Minoru

Basil & Shirley

## Japan – a new challenge

On 17 September 2006 we arrived in Japan for the first time. A typhoon off Kyushu delayed our plane on its flight from Shanghai to Osaka. In the old days a typhoon off Taiwan would have delayed a ship much longer and might have kept it in port till the storm had blown itself out, or the ship would have avoided the typhoon season altogether. As it was we arrived in Osaka when the

## Two Pilgrims Meet

weather was still warm, and a slow moving fan kept us cool at night.

Our twenty years in India did not prepare us for Japan. In many ways Japan is the exact opposite of India. Japan impressed us immediately with its neat, clean and efficient trains, crowded yes, but running precisely on time to the nearest minute. Osaka was incredibly quiet for a big city. People were smartly dressed, and very polite. Every day our grandchildren, Lawrence & Deborah, took us to the nearby park with its spacious walks and colourful botanical gardens.

On our second Sunday we went with our family to a local church on the corner of a busy crossroads. After the service a dentist, Shinichi Yamamoto, surprised me with his question:

"Do you love Japanese?"

Did he mean: "Do you like Japan?" I suspect that was what he meant to say, because his English was not fluent. However the question he asked put me on the spot. What could I say? I had only just come to Japan and knew very few Japanese. But I did know Minoru and Yoshiko, as well as Toshi and Midori; so thinking of them, I quickly said "Yes." He was satisfied, but I was not.

The question stuck in my mind: "Do you love Japanese?" Nobody had ever asked me that question before. If I had been asked, "Do you love Chinese?" I would have immediately said, "Of course". Why the difference? The question Yamamoto put to me pushed my thinking beyond the comfortable bounds of, "Do you like Japan?"

I wrote in my diary, "May be this whole experience is extending my boundaries of 'love' and 'affection' to include Japanese. Why not? Should I not love all humanity? Why should I not go out of my way in

Cambridge to meet Japanese as well as Chinese and Koreans?"

Volf in his book, *Exclusion and Embrace,* draws attention to the need to go beyond forgiveness, if there is to be complete reconciliation. This going beyond must include making space in oneself for the other. To embrace the other requires more than forgiveness. "Forgiveness is the boundary between exclusion and embrace....Yet it leaves a distance between people, an empty space of neutrality...." (Volf p.125). Although I had embraced Minoru and been embraced by him, and I had thought that I now harboured no ill feeling for Japan, I had never thought of going to Japan, or of getting to know more Japanese people. Was it not true that I was stuck in that empty space called neutrality?

Within two weeks of arriving in Japan I began to sense that I had more to learn about reconciliation for myself, in addition to understanding the process of reconciliation between nations. I was on a spiritual journey not just a physical one from one place in Japan to another. God was trying to enlarge my thinking, more than that he was enlarging my heart to love people I had not thought of embracing. The love God requires is not emotion but action, and the action I needed to take was to make space for the other, to listen to a people I did not know and to take an interest in their concerns.

After two weeks we left Osaka to meet Minoru and Yoshiko in their mountain retreat near Fujimi. On the way we linked up with Toshi and Midori who had kindly agreed to come from Tokyo to see us. They guided us by train to the little station near Mt. Yatsugatake (eight peak mountain) where Minoru and Yoshiko were waiting for us.

The next morning at 6 am Minoru walked with me to his 'ashram' (to use an Indian name for his spiritual community). Taking our shoes off at the door, we joined three others who were already there. The room was plain with wooden walls and one window. For half an hour we sat on the rush matting in silent prayer, and only after that did we read from the Psalms and Job, saying the Lord's Prayer together to finish with. The silence was striking. Minoru explained that silent prayer is so important for him. It is a time to focus on the reality of God's presence. I often think of that quiet time we had together.

Minoru had not forgotten the suggestion he had made in Cambridge the year before about going together to Shanghai. After leaving their mountain retreat Yoshiko drove us to their home in Tokyo on the top floor of an apartment block where they had a view of Mt Fuji. In the evening Minoru went to see whether his travel agent had been able to book a ticket for him to fly to Shanghai. He came back beaming saying, "All the bookings have been made for me to fly to Shanghai next weekend."

I left the next day for Shanghai to see friends and get everything ready for Minoru. Sixty years before we had been on opposite sides in a war, now we were coming together as friends to retrace our childhood and show each other where we had lived; more than that we were going together first to one side of the city, then to the other. Minoru arrived on Friday evening. On the Saturday morning we set out on our day of pilgrimage.

The day began on my side of the Huangpu river in Pudong. In the old days no one wanted to live in Pudong. It was deserted apart from old factories and the remains of villages that had been destroyed by the invading Japanese army in 1937. Now Pudong rivals New York for skyscrapers. The iconic Oriental Pearl Tower rises by the waterfront and the Jin Mao Tower housing the Hyatt hotel towers above other competitors. We went first to the Lujiazui Park beneath the Hyatt. I reckoned that this was approximately where our concentration camp was located about 800 metres from the river. I took Minoru to the Pearl Tower museum of Old Shanghai for a nostalgic glimpse of Nanjing Road as it used to be and life size models of old streets and shops. From there we went to the river.

Overlooking the river we found a perfect spot in a corner along a small promenade where bushes gave us shade. Here we sat together and looked across the river at the Bund, which I had gazed at for two years from my prison camp windows. The clock tower of the Custom's House stood erect reminding me of Big Ben. Beside it rose the dome of the impressive bulk of the Hong Kong Shanghai bank, and further along we could see another landmark, the old Cathay hotel. After all these years here we were, two boys from opposite sides, sitting together on my side and seeing my view. To cross over the water and get to the Bund had been the symbol of freedom to me. On this morning it was a moment to give thanks that God had preserved my life in 1944, and that I was still alive long after I thought I would be dead or crippled. Sensing God's presence we prayed and opened our hearts to each other.

Then it was time to go with Minoru to his side of the river, to do what I had never done before, to see things from his territory. As the Bund Tourist Tunnel was too congested we went under the Huangpu by metro and took a taxi across the Suchow Creek up the Wusong Road to what used to be the Japanese quarter of Hongkiew. Minoru wanted me to see his junior school. We found the building, now a Middle School, with its mellow sandy grey and white stonework opposite a hospital. It was a Saturday afternoon, but the school was open and college students were poring over their notes before exams. No one stopped us as we entered the building and wandered along class rooms on three floors. So much remained from the past and looked to be as Minoru remembered it.

Minoru at his old school in Shanghai

Outside we wandered round the back and found the Suchow Creek. Minoru took me to a bridge to tell me how he used to swim in the dirty waters of this creek. In defiance of Japanese school rules he used to leave his Japanese pals and swim here with Chinese boys. It was great fun and he enjoyed it. Now Minoru can see how significant that act was – identifying with Chinese boys, who were just like him.

The house where Minoru used to live was destroyed long ago, but he showed me the approximate location in old Hongkiew (now Hongkou). As he did so he recalled how every day he had gone to the Shinto shrine to pray for victory over the enemy. He was as enthusiastically patriotic as any of his friends and family. War united the whole Japanese community in determination to defeat

America in battle. USA was seen as the demon to be hated and overcome.

During the war period there were ten Japanese primary schools but only one Middle School. Minoru only went there for one term before the war ended, after that they were taught by teachers at home until he was repatriated to Japan in 1946. When Minoru and Yoshiko had visited Shanghai in 2003 they had failed to find this school, which is now in a university campus. On this visit we were successful. The old building still stands, a white institution with a tablet recalling its Japanese architect. We were impressed that the building has been preserved and that its Japanese origin is frankly recorded. Around us students strolled, laughed, played and moved freely past without any concern for us. Only once in the whole day did anyone stop and stare at Minoru, suspecting he was Japanese.

It was time for us now to go to the place where I used to live before the war began. We took a taxi to Xinzha Road. The building still had its old number, 1531, outside the gate. It had never occurred to me that the address could still be the same after all the upheavals of the Maoist period. The place is now a children's hospital. Its six stories were so well built in the 1930's that it has not been pulled down. I showed Minoru the balcony from which I used to drop pellets on the neighbours below! Once again we were free to wander round and even up the stairs.

We still had one more place to go to, and that was to the nearby Grace Church on the old Bubbling Well Road. Thankfully the church has been restored after the ravages of the Cultural Revolution. We stopped to pray and give thanks to God for the amazing day in which we had experienced new depths to the gift of reconciliation. God had taken us a step further. No longer were we meeting in the middle of the bridge between our different nations, cultures and traditions, but we had gone over together first to one side and then to the other, to see life as the other sees it. We had relived the past and shared each other's painful memories.

## China Rediscovered

By retelling our dramatic reunion with Minoru and Yoshiko I have missed out another remarkable reunion. For more than half a century I had nothing to do with China, my second motherland. After 1945 there had been no possibility of visiting China for many years. India had become our home from 1963 – 1983, and even when we did return to England we continued to work with migrants from the Indian sub-continent in Britain. It was only in the year 2000 when I retired from full-time employment and moved to Cambridge that we began to meet visitors from mainland China.

By 2000 there was an increasing flow of students coming to Cambridge from various parts of China. Some of these were visiting scholars and university lecturers on a year's study leave, many more were Ph.D. students. We began to discover how China had changed and was changing. Shirley helped some students with their English and we enjoyed welcoming Chinese to our home.

In 2003 we decided to visit China. Our trip was made possible by all the Chinese friends we had made and their warm invitation to visit them in their home cities. Other factors also encouraged us. In 2000 the British government had launched a plan to compensate former British prisoners of war in Japanese held territories. To begin with we thought this would only be for military personnel or for civilian adults, but then it was clarified that even those who had been children in Japanese civilian camps could apply. So my sister and I applied for these grants, and we were astonished to receive £10,000 each. This made me think that I ought to use some of this gift to visit China. At the same time we could travel by the Trans-Siberian railway and visit Carol and Patrick, Lawrence and Deborah in Yekaterinburg across the Urals.

The leisurely journey by train through Russia and Mongolia helped me to leave Europe behind, but did nothing to prepare me for China. I had wisely warned myself that nothing would be the same after more than fifty years and I would recognise nothing. How wrong I was. On arrival in Beijing our friend, Zhang, took us to his home. Lunch was being prepared, as his mother-in-law made more than one hundred *jiaozi*. Suddenly the north China food I love and have missed so much was there in front of me; not only *jiaozi* but *tofu*, *muer* (a type of crinkly mushroom or elephant's ears as we used to call them), Chinese green vegetables and much more. The smells and tastes and sounds of childhood came flooding back. Yes, this was home, and the heart of China was still the same.

For nine years from the age of 2 to 11 I had lived in Sichuan, Shandong and Shanghai. The first of these places that we visited was Shandong. Revisiting my old school in Yantai was quite overwhelming. When I lived in coastal Chefoo (Zhifu), as we called it, the population could not have been much more than 100,000. Now Yantai is a city of 6 million. Surely everything I had known would be buried under ubiquitous blocks of concrete, nothing could be the same. Imagine my joy when I looked out over the bay from our hotel window to see all the old landmarks shining in the sun. There was First Beach, the Bluff and Lighthouse Island looking brighter and nearer than ever before.

A naval academy now uses the buildings of the old Chefoo international school. Despite the best efforts of our local guide we were not permitted inside the premises. So we had to peer over the wall from a side road and take pictures from a boat out in the bay.

I went to Chefoo School in 1939 when I was five. My sister, five years older than me, had been there from 1936. Chefoo was a boarding school, so we stayed there all year except for the winter holidays. For the holidays of Christmas 1940 we sailed back to Shanghai. Journeys were by ship, usually via Qingdao, sometimes also calling in at Dalian, known then as Port Arthur. That winter was very cold and even Shanghai had heavy falls of snow. In December 1941 Japan's attack on Pearl Harbour changed our situation dramatically. The school was put under Japanese guards. The headmaster was imprisoned and holidays were cancelled. A year later all the children and teachers were removed from the school and taken to a camp in Temple Hill, Chefoo. With this move began my three years in Japanese POW camps or civilian internment camps as they were called. After ten months the Japanese moved us by ship and train to Weihsien (now Weifang). The most famous inmate of this camp was the Olympic gold medallist, Eric Liddell, but I hardly met him as I was transferred to Shanghai with my sister to join my parents in Pootung (Pudong), as recorded in the first part of this book.

One of the consequences of being at an international school and then in Japanese POW camps was that I lost all my knowledge of Chinese. Up to the age of five I had played with Chinese boys and used a child's language. Admittedly my Chinese would have been simple and limited, but at least it was fluent and natural. I regret now the loss of facility in Mandarin, which would have been so useful now.

After Yantai we visited Weifang and Qingdao. In Weifang we were generously welcomed for a feast by the headmaster of the No. 2 Middle School, because this was the site of the Weihsien Japanese POW camp, where I was for two months. In 2003 the memorial to Eric Liddell, which had been set up between the school and the old hospital was being restored in preparation for the sixtieth anniversary of Eric's death in 2005.Eric died in the camp of a brain tumour just six months before the end of the war.

From Qingdao we flew to Xi'an and then on to Sichuan. The ancient city of Langzhong on the Jialing river in East Sichuan was my home town from 1936-39. In 2003 we had no friends in Langzhong, so we went to Chengdu and Chongqing. My diary records: "Sichuan at last! The country where I first became conscious. The place of my first memories. How will I feel?"

Our friend Huang took us to a traditional Sichuan opera and tea house, and then to a meal of proper Sichuanese food. Despite being used to chilli hot food in India, *mapo tofu* was too much for me! Perhaps I did not have such a dish as a five year old.

The bus trip from Chengdu to Chongqing enabled me to see Sichuan again. The scenery was one long sequence of little valleys, hills rising and falling, and rice in the paddy fields at the valley bottom. Sichuan may be called the rice bowl of China, but it is not a flat bowl but a dish full of ridges. I had forgotten how many hills my father must have climbed as he trekked across the province on his travels.

In Chongqing we stayed in a hotel close to the junction of the Yangtze and Jialing rivers. It was down the Jialing river that I came by boat from Langzhong in 1939, when my parents brought me out of Sichuan to Shanghai. That must have been quite a slow river journey by sailing boat, and would have taken about ten days, as the Jialing bends so many times on its way to Chongqing. I have always been fascinated by boats and rivers, so we had to make the tourist trip down the Yangtze to the Three Gorges dam and Ichang. In the old days my parents would have gone this way to Shanghai. In 1939 China was cut in half by the Japanese invasion, which began in 1937. Instead we had to take a long circuitous route by Red Cross truck from Chongqing to Kunming, then over the border into what is now Vietnam and by rail to Hanoi and Haiphong. In Haiphong we boarded a ship for Hong Kong, where we changed to a steamer for Shanghai.

In 2003 we were able to cut the journey short and fly from Wuhan to Shanghai, and so to find the third of my childhood homes. I remembered the address where we used to live – 1531 Sinza Road (now Xinzha Lu), but it never occurred to me that this would still be the number outside my old home. So we set out to search for this building believing that the address had changed and that the building was no longer entered from Xinzha Lu but from a parallel street. We knew that the old mission headquarters, where my father lived and worked, was now used as a hospital, so we asked the taxi driver to take us to a hospital on Xinzha Lu. He dropped us at a hospital, but it was clearly not the one we were looking for. Peering at houses as we walked along, a Chinese man came up to us and asked in perfect English, "What are you looking for?" After we had explained, he took us to Grace Church nearby, where we met an elderly teacher we had been told to meet. He guided us along Beijing Road and so to the back of the six storey mission building, which was now the main entrance. There I could see to my joy the balconies I remembered so well. After a nostalgic wander round, we walked through the compound to the back entrance on Xinzha Lu. Our way was barred by a locked back gate, but looking through I could clearly see the house number on the wall outside. It said "1531". I should have believed that things do not change that quickly even in the Maoist era.

Our five week trip round China concluded with four days each in Guilin and Hong Kong. The trip had shown us long before most in the west had realised what was happening, that China was on the move. Even then, five years before the Olympic Games, the whole nation was getting ready and the country was one large construction site with everything from stadia to shopping malls being built in readiness. As we all know now, the giant has awoken.

# Remembering the Pain of Two Massacres

## Hiroshima

In 2007 Shirley and I returned to Japan to visit our two daughters and to see Minoru and Yoshiko. This time we not only had Carol in Osaka, but also Rebecca in Tokyo. So this time we went straight to Tokyo to stay with Rebecca and family and have more time to visit Minoru's home and university. I realised that if I was to pursue the theme of reconciliation there is one place I would have to go to in Japan and that is Hiroshima. Yoshiko was living just outside Hiroshima when the A bomb was dropped. The black rain from the mushroom cloud fell on her white school dress leaving an indelible mark on her memory of that fateful day. It was important that we went with her to her city.

On Sunday 11 November, Armistice Day, we flew with Yoshiko and Minoru to Hiroshima. In the morning I took part in a Remembrance Sunday service at the Hodogaya

Commonwealth War Cemetery outside Yokohama. After the Last Post and two minutes' silence, wreaths were laid by ambassadors, the military and others. I was astonished that a Japanese veteran representing the Japanese Burma Veterans Association laid a wreath. Afterwards he showed me his card with his name, Suichiro Yoshino, representing the All Burma Veterans Association of Japan. A wreath was also laid by Yoshiko Tamura on behalf of the Burma Campaign Society, which includes both British and Japanese veterans who fought in the Burma war, and met mostly in London. Yoshiko and Taeko Sasamoto have pioneered the POW Research Network of Japan, investigating the POW camps that were set up in Japan holding allied prisoners. Graham Fry, then British ambassador, told me that on his recommendation they had both been awarded the MBE for their services to British POWs.

Looking back on that day I can see how appropriate it was that we should fly on Remembrance Sunday from that service to commemorate British POWs who had died in Japan straight to Hiroshima to witness the pain inflicted by the atom bomb. This coincidence was not planned, it just happened, and added poignancy to the commemoration of war's victims on both sides.

Drawing back the curtains the next morning on the ninth floor of our hotel we were stunned by the beauty of Hiroshima. The setting of the city, ringed by an arc of mountains with seven rivers flowing from the hills, is spectacular. You would never have thought that such a beautiful city could have risen out of total devastation, but, as we were soon to see, in the city centre there are reminders everywhere of the awful day the Bomb exploded in a fireball and mushroom cloud.

The two museums of the Peace Centre, the new and the old, record for posterity what nuclear war means. To visit these museums is itself a gruesome experience. The destruction recorded by one exhibit after another is immense, but much worse are all the details of what happened to human beings. I went round the old museum with Minoru. Here are many artefacts showing the effects of the Bomb. The clothing of the children who were clearing the streets that morning for a fire lane in case incendiary bombs were dropped is carefully displayed. You see the stone with a human shadow imprinted on it – all that remains of a person who had been sitting by it. The story is told of the girl who survived only to fall victim five or six years later to leukaemia. Because she tried to make 1,000 origami cranes believing that would bring her blessing, school children still make these origami cranes, and long columns of them hang everywhere.

In the afternoon we were taken round the Peace Park by a *hibakusha*. He had survived as a 13 year old, because his teacher had decided his class should go that morning to weed the sweet potato fields outside the city centre, 2.2km from the epicentre where the bomb exploded. His face had been burnt on one side, but he survived. All the younger 11-12 year old children in the first two classes of the Middle School were killed. Now that he is retired, he said he devotes four days a month to taking people round and sharing his story. He wanted to do his part in keeping the eyewitness account alive and warning the world to ensure that no nuclear bomb is ever dropped again.

There are many significant sites in the vicinity of the Peace Park. The most visited site is the Memorial Cenotaph for the A-Bomb victims, a concrete arch over a granite stone with a perpetual flame burning till all nuclear weapons are destroyed. It contains the names of all the known victims of the bomb. The A-Bomb Dome is the most prominent symbol of the city's destruction. Formerly the Industrial Promotion Hall, it stands as a reminder of the moment when the bomb exploded almost directly above it. Later we walked into what remained of an elementary school, still preserved as a museum, where we saw the messages parents had written on a wall for the children and teachers they had lost that morning – all painstakingly restored from under plaster in later years. We were impressed to see the recently relocated Korean A-Bomb Memorial for the approximately 20,000 Koreans who were killed. Most of these were labourers who had been shipped under compulsion to Japan to work in factories during the war.

Yoshiko pointed out for us a small memorial outside the Peace Park to the Christian mayor of Hiroshima in 1945 on the site of his residence by the river. He and his house and family were all destroyed by the bomb. Though not commemorated or mentioned in the museums, he was famous for an incident during the war when he opposed the military and insisted that they should obey the police and traffic rules like everyone else. Outside the Peace Park conference centre we were pleased to see the Coventry statue of Reconciliation with its two kneeling figures embracing and supporting each other. We had last seen this in the ruins of the old Coventry cathedral in England.

Stephen Lieper, the director of the International Cultural Peace Centre, was another person we met. It was strange that an American should be holding this post in Hiroshima, but his role was to raise international awareness of the Peace Movement and to lobby for the removal of nuclear weapons in the UN. He was most successful in promoting the Mayors for Peace project, which was then led by Hiroshima Mayor, Tadatoshi Akiba. There are now an impressive number of cities involved in this programme, including mayors from more than 6,700 towns and cities from 160 countries in all continents, especially Europe and Asia each with more than 2,500 cities. The Mayors for Peace movement aims to abolish nuclear weapons by 2020, and also works to eliminate poverty and protect the environment.

The horror that was Hiroshima has burnt itself into human consciousness the world over. Despite more than forty years of the Cold War between the Soviet Union and America, and countless wars, no country has dared to use a nuclear bomb against another for seventy years. At least 140,000 died because of the bomb. The death toll though great was not what horrified most; it was the way people died, some obliterated without a trace and others left to die of their injuries and from radiation sickness in the days and months and years that followed. Kenzaburo Oe was himself transformed by his first visit to Hiroshima in August 1963, as he witnessed the silent suffering of victims and the heroic labours of doctors at the A-bomb Hospital. In his book *Hiroshima Notes,* he records his visits to the city from 1963-1965 and the reflections he wrote after each visit. In the 1995 Introduction to his book he wrote:

"In the A-bomb survivors' view, Japan's rapid modernization, with its many distortions, led to Japan's wars in Asia, which in turn led to the atomic bombings of Hiroshima and Nagasaki; thus they hold the Japanese state responsible for their sufferings. While they also criticize the United States for dropping the bombs, they have long sought compensation for their sufferings from the Japanese government."

In 1994 Kenzaburo was awarded the Nobel Prize for Literature. He said in his Nobel Lecture:

"After the end of the Second World War it was a categorical imperative for us to declare that we renounced war forever in a central article of the new Constitution. The Japanese chose the principle of eternal peace as the basis of morality for our rebirth after the War. I trust that the principle can best be understood in the West with its long tradition of tolerance for conscientious rejection of military service. In Japan itself there have all along been attempts by some to obliterate the article about renunciation of war from the Constitution and for this purpose they have taken every opportunity to make use of pressures from abroad. But to obliterate from the Constitution the principle of eternal peace will be nothing but an act of betrayal against the peoples of Asia and the victims of the Atom Bombs in Hiroshima and Nagasaki. It is not difficult for me as a writer to imagine what would be the outcome of that betrayal."

Minoru and Yoshiko have made it their practice to go on a peace pilgrimage every month, whenever possible, in their mountain retreat near Fujimi. The pilgrimage routes they take follow old paths in the mountains and lead to sacred sites along the way. They walk with a few friends. There is no publicity, simply the determination to pray as they walk for peace.

## Nanjing

Our plan had been to visit Nanjing together at the end of November 2007 to visit the museum dedicated to the massacre of Chinese in 1937. This however proved impossible as the Museum in Nanjing had been closed and a new memorial to the massacre was being constructed. I did however go with Shirley to Nanjing in December 2007. This proved to be a worthwhile visit as we met Prof. Liu Cheng of Nanjing University History Department. He has pioneered courses in Peace Studies both at undergraduate and MA levels.

*Reunion!*

It was not until November 2010 that Shirley and I were able to visit the new Nanjing Massacre Museum. Prof. Liu Cheng and his wife, He Lan, generously welcomed us to stay with them and gave us several days to take us round Nanjing. Although they had not been to the new museum they kindly took us there. The new museum has a forbidding black stone appearance like a long dark wall. The grimness is enhanced by gruesome statues recalling the agonies of Nanjing residents in 1937. In the main building the full extent of Japanese atrocities is fully recorded. Impressive sections are also given over to showing the efforts of John Rabe and many other foreign civilians and missionaries in setting up the Nanking Safety Zone to rescue Chinese civilians. Fortunately the museum does not end here, but goes on to call for peace and friendship between the Chinese and Japanese peoples.

The horror of what happened in Nanjing from December 13$^{th}$ 1937 when the Japanese entered the city till the end of January 1938 is hard to comprehend and harder still to convey in words. Iris Chang's bestseller, *The Rape of Nanjing,* has a chapter on 'Six weeks of horror'. She was instrumental in locating the diaries of John Rabe, which were later translated and published under the title, *The Good German of Nanking.* In Rabe's diaries we gain a first-hand eyewitness account of the atrocities committed. These need to be complemented from the Japanese side by Honda Katsuichi's detailed investigation printed first in Japanese, in *Nankin e no Michi,* and then in an English edition, *The Nanjing Massacre: A Japanese Journalist Confronts Japan's National Shame.* We are indebted to Honda for showing that the slaughter in Nanjing was not a momentary aberration but the culmination of a policy that the Japanese invading army had pursued from the moment that its forces landed in Hangzhou Bay in November 1937. The troops who landed

## *Two Pilgrims Meet*

in the bay south of Shanghai pillaged village after village on their way inland, carrying out the so-called 'three-alls', of 'loot all, burn all, kill all'. When they came to Nanjing they simply continued this war of annihilation on a massive scale. By then they had lost all restraint in bayoneting babies, raping women, looting the poor, burning buildings, and killing all who stood in their way.

John Rabe witnessed the mayhem as the Japanese marched into Nanjing. His hopes that disarmed, surrendering Chinese soldiers would be treated with humanitarian care were immediately crushed as thousands who threw away their arms and uniforms were hunted down and killed like animals. He had his work cut out to protect civilians in the International Safety Zone. Repeatedly he found Japanese troops invading his house and garden in search of loot and of women to rape, and had to force them out waving his Nazi swastika. In his property alone he kept 600 or more Chinese, whilst the Safety Zone was the only hope for 200,000 civilians. Not that they were safe there, as Japanese military kept entering in search of soldiers and girls to carry off and rape. Houses were systematically burnt down till half the city was razed to the ground.

The tragedy of Nanjing is often obscured by the argument about the numbers killed. There is however no doubt that all Chinese soldiers who surrendered or were subsequently captured were killed, often in gruesome ways. This figure of mass executions may account for most of the 50,000 Chinese troops in Nanjing. The number of civilians killed is much harder to compute. Honda Katsuichi prefers to treat all the three months from November to January of the assault on Nanjing as 'a single phenomenon'. In this case he concludes: 'no one can deny that the victims of the massacre numbered in the hundreds of thousands'.

The sad fact today is that the voice of the victims is hardly heard. Very few survivors are alive today. There is no equivalent in Nanjing to the *hibakushas* of Hiroshima. We are left with recorded interviews from those who were there but have since departed, and with pictures. These pictures speak volumes. A picture of a different sort is a sculpture outside the Nanjing Memorial Hall of a mother in agony. She is holding in outstretched arms the crumpled body of her dead child with her head thrown back in hopeless lament. The black, doomed figure cries out to us, and if we have any heart we cry back, "No more Nanjings".

Iris Chang notes that survivors of the Nanjing massacre vanished from public view during the Mao years. Then in the 1990s the city saw the demolition of its ancient landmarks, including many of the massacre sites. By the summer of 1995 when she visited the city she was shocked to find most survivors living in such poverty that even a minimal sum of compensation from Japan would have greatly improved their lives. The Massacre Museum records the fate of some of the noble foreigners who saved so many lives by organising the Nanking Safety Zone. Sadly these include John Rabe, who was arrested by the Gestapo after he returned to Germany and only released on condition that he never spoke again about the Japanese atrocities in Nanjing. His condition became even worse after the war ended, when he lived in poverty. In 1948 news of his dire condition reached Nanjing and people raised money and sent him food supplies. He died of a stroke in 1950. His diaries in six volumes were only recovered in 1996 and published later that year. They at least give a neutral viewpoint and eyewitness record from a German ally of Japan, and they bear eloquent witness to the cry of the victims, especially the women. The heroine of the Safety Zone, Minnie

Vautrin, the acting head of the Ginling Women's Arts and Science College in the university campus, refused to leave Nanjing with other foreign staff. So it was left to her to care not just for her students but for the women and children who poured into the Safety Zone. The sheer numbers of women eventually overwhelmed her. Time and again she confronted Japanese soldiers seeking girls to rape. The mental torture wore her down and she was forced to return to the United States in 1940 after suffering a nervous breakdown. On 14 May 1941 she committed suicide. We should also note that Iris Chang suffered from depression and committed suicide in November 2004, in part due to the trauma she had experienced through researching the horrifying massacres that took place in Nanjing in 1937.

# Japan and Prisoners of War[1]

## Introduction

We have recounted our personal experience of reconciliation to ground our discussion of reconciliation in reality not in theoretical armchair exercise. But our concern is not limited to or primarily for the sake of our own story but rather for reconciliation between our countries and especially between Japan and China.

In this chapter we will consider what steps have been taken to further peace and friendship. In particular we will point to what has happened to improve relations between Japan and British Prisoners of War (POWs).

## POWs

Brian MacArthur tells the story of British, Australian, Dutch and American soldiers who were captured and imprisoned by the Japanese between 1942 and 1945. This is a forgotten story of unbelievable suffering and bitter memories (Brian MacArthur: *Surviving the Sword: Prisoners of the Japanese*, 1942-45, London, 2005).

According to the Tokyo War Tribunal Japan took 132,142 Allied prisoners, of whom more than a quarter did not survive.

"The most striking commentary on the treatment of the Far East Prisoners of War (Fepows) is provided by the death rate in Japanese prisoner-of-war camps: 27 per cent of Japan's prisoners died in captivity, compared with 4 per cent of Germany's" (MacArthur op.cit. p.2).

---

[1] This chapter and the three that follow were written by Basil

*Two Pilgrims Meet*

Those who returned to Britain felt not only forgotten but forsaken. Generally speaking when they arrived by ship at Southampton or Liverpool there were no guards of honour and no bands to welcome them. Worse still their own families and friends did not understand them or care to appreciate the tortures they had endured. As Eric Lomax memorably recorded in his fine book, *The Railway Man,* he wanted to tell his fiancée when they met and after they married about his experiences, but she brushed this aside saying they had both had a hard time and should forget it. "The hurt I felt silenced me," he wrote, "as effectively as a gag." MacArthur quotes another Fepow, Ian Watt, who said: "Old friends hadn't really changed, but I had and they didn't know it. But I did."

In another telling comment, Ronald Searle, whose stark sketches of the skeletal frames of tortured POWs speak louder than words, called Fepows members of the world's 'most exclusive and impenetrable' club. MacArthur comments: "This is not as silly as it might sound. When one has touched bottom, become the lowest of the low and unwillingly plumbed the depths of human misery, there comes from it a silent understanding and appreciation of what solidarity, friendship and human kindness to others can mean. Something that is difficult to explain to those unfortunates who are on the outside of our 'club', who have never experienced what it means to be dirt and yet be privileged to be surrounded by life-saving comradeship" (MacArthur, p.7).

The privilege of being rescued from the depths of misery by life-saving comradeship is the theme of Ernest Gordon's well known book, *Miracle on the River Kwai.* First printed in 1962 this account of the suffering of the POWs on the Thai-Burma railway was translated into Japanese by Kazuaki Saito (a friend of Minoru and graduate of ICU, Tokyo) and published in 1976. It had an immediate impact in Japan, as did the visit of Ernest Gordon himself later. The treatment of POWs was so severe that 12,399 out of 61,806 sent to work on the Thai-Burma railway died. The prisoners were driven to depths of degradation, but out of that abyss of despair sprang spiritual renewal through the examples of self-sacrifice. Captain Gordon himself was saved by the selfless heroism of a young soldier, Dusty Miller, who washed his wounds day after day till he recovered. Gordon was suffering from diphtheria, malaria, dysentery, beriberi, and blood infection. Every night Miller came to wash him and massage his paralysed legs. Self-sacrifice not only saved Gordon's life but also revived the dehumanised prisoners. Death no longer had the last word.

Only after thirty years did many POWs start to tell their stories. In the bibliography for MacArthur's history 127 books written by Fepows are listed. Of these 83 were published after 1980; most came out in the 1990s and even between 2000 and 2010 there were 22 books written by Fepows. On the other side of the world Japanese soldiers were also telling their stories, and again many memoirs were published in the 1990s. From this we can understand that what was suffered in the war has not disappeared and has not been forgotten. There remains much bitterness and sorrow, which is being passed on in families to succeeding generations.

One of the Japanese who recorded their memoirs was Yoshihiko Futamatsu, a professional engineer, who helped to oversee the construction of the Thai-Burma railway. His book, originally published in Japanese in 1985, has recently been reproduced in English with a translation by a former POW who knew him under the title: *Across the Three Pagodas Pass: The Story of the Thai-Burma Railway* (Folkestone, 2013). Futamatsu graduated in engineering at Kyoto University in 1936 and joined the Japan National Railways head office in their construction department. In 1942 he was responsible for surveying the route of the projected Thai-Burma railway and became the professional adviser on the construction of the railway on the Thai side of the border. He took pride in the achievement of the completion of this daunting project through jungle terrain in eighteen months. But he was unable to come to terms with Japan's responsibility for the enormous death toll of 90,000 Asian coolies and 12,399 prisoners of war.

The British POWs have long requested an apology from the Japanese government, but nothing official has been forthcoming. In the immediate post-war period, according to John Dower, Japan was overwhelmed by the pain and suffering of defeat. Remorse was felt for the futile loss of so many young Japanese recruited for the war, who died far from home. But there was little appreciation for the suffering of civilians and soldiers brutalised by the Japanese armies in the Asian countries they invaded, whether those were western or Asian nationals. Few in the post-war generations of Japanese young people have known what happened to POWs during the war. To many Japanese the history of the Second World War does not cast a shadow over Japan's relations with Britain. Nobuko Kosuge points out that, "Generally speaking, post-war Japanese people cherish a certain rather hard to define family-like feeling towards the people of the United Kingdom, who similarly live on an island and, like the Japanese, have a monarchy with a long history and tradition ….. These feelings of familiarity and trust towards the British, arising from what the Japanese have seen as similarities between the two countries, have played a central role in the way the Japanese have built up their image of post-war Japan-UK relations"(*Britain and Japan in the Twentieth Century*, ed. P. Towle & N. Kosuge, p.167, London & New York, 2007).

Instinctive British attitudes to Japan, on the other hand, have been affected by the treatment of British POWs on the Thai-Burma railway. The fact that Sony, Toyota, Honda and many other Japanese products are so popular in Britain has not cancelled out the memory of wartime atrocities. It was therefore to be expected that Emperor Hirohito's visit to London in 1971 aroused vitriolic comment in the British tabloid press, whilst papers in Tokyo were stunned by the reactions. To the British public the Emperor was not seen as a benign, traditional monarch, but as the symbol of the Japan in whose name military outrages had been committed. Even his successor, the sympathetic Emperor Akihito, was treated with hostility by Fepows, when he visited London in 1998.

Unlike Germany there has been no government led national determination in Japan to condemn the conduct of the wartime military regime and to pursue reconciliation with China, Korea and other East Asian countries invaded by Japan. Even in August 1995 at the 50th anniversary of the end of the Pacific war attempts to make a united apology in the Diet, Japan's parliament, were scuppered by Japanese opposition parties. Since then there have been some official statements by the Japanese government specifically acknowledging the suffering of allied POWs. In January 1998 Tony Blair visited Japan and it was stated by the Japanese spokesman that Prime Minister Ryutaro Hashimoto expressed to him Japan's deep remorse and heartfelt apologies to the people who suffered in World War II, but did not specifically mention POWs. In 2001 the Japanese Minister for Foreign Affairs, on the occasion of the 50th anniversary of the Signing of the San Francisco Peace

Treaty, said: "We have never forgotten that Japan caused tremendous damage and suffering to the people of many countries during the last war. Many lost their precious lives and many were wounded. The war has left an incurable scar on many people, including former prisoners of war." In 2009 the Japanese government apologised through its ambassador in the U.S. to former American prisoners of war who suffered in the Bataan Death March. This led to six American POWs being invited to Japan in 2010 at the expense of the Japanese government, when they received an apology from the Foreign Minister, Katsuya Okada. In 2011 Foreign Minister, Seiji Maehara apologised to a group of Australian POWs who were visiting Japan as guests of the government for the ill treatment they received whilst held captive by the Japanese army. These specific apologies since 2009 would have been welcomed by British POWs, most of whom died long ago.

There have however been statements of regret and apology at a less official national level. For example, Sadayuki Hayashi, the Japanese Ambassador to Britain, said on August 15, 1999, during an address from the pulpit of Coventry Cathedral marking the anniversary of the end of the Second World War, in the presence of Fepows and Burma veterans: "The experience of those people who suffered during the war against Japan will remain forever etched in their minds. We Japanese feel deeply remorseful about what happened and sincerely apologise for it" (quoted from an obituary to Masao Hirakubo, The Times, 2 April 2008). Recently the Mitsubishi Corporation gave a public apology for using American POWs as forced labourers at four mines during the war. This very public event at a ceremony in Los Angeles in 2015 is thought to be the first such apology given to POWs by a Japanese company.

Many individual Japanese have not only expressed their apologies and profound regrets for what happened to POWs but have dedicated themselves to acts of repentance and to work for reconciliation. We will refer to some of these. One example comes from Eric Lomax's well known book, *The Railway Man*, published in 1995.

Nagase Takashi had worked for the Kempeitai, the notorious Japanese military police, as an interpreter in Thailand during the construction of the Burma railway. After the war ended he travelled with allied soldiers in search of abandoned war graves, when he also saw the countless abandoned mounds of earth marking the graves of Asian labourers who had died in their thousands constructing the hated railway. After 1963, when restrictions were lifted and travel outside Japan became easier, Nagase went with his wife, Yoshiko, to Thailand as an act of penance for the atrocities of the Imperial Japanese Army. On that first visit he recalls visiting the war cemetery at Kanburi and laying a wreath before the white cross that dominates the scene surrounded by the graves of 7,000 officers and soldiers. As he folded his hands in prayer he felt his body emitting beams of light. "At that moment", he wrote, "I thought, 'This is it. You have been pardoned.'" His concern to make reparation for the past became a way of life and he went back more than sixty times. He opened a temple of peace on the bridge over the River Kwai and did charitable work for the surviving Asian labourers who had worked on the railway and had been unable to return to their homes in Malaya, Indonesia and other neighbouring countries. He wrote several books in Japanese about the war, one of which was republished in English in 1990 with the title, *Crosses and Tigers*, in which he exposed the atrocities of the Japanese army and attacked militarism. Nagase identifies 'the cult of absolute obedience' as being to blame for the way the military implemented the plan to build the Thai-Burma railway, whatever the cost, even though one prisoner should die for every sleeper laid on the line. From 1963 onwards he courageously spoke out against militarism and worked for reconciliation between former enemies. In 1979 he protested publicly against the installation in the Yasukuni shrine of the first steam locomotive to pass along the Burma Railway.

Eric Lomax tells the incredible story of how after 40 years he came in contact with Nagase, the man he most hated, because he was the interpreter and voice of his torturers when he was subjected to fierce interrogation for over a week, culminating in the dreaded water treatment. If there was one Japanese whom Lomax fixed all his desires for revenge upon, it was this interpreter, Nagase. In his book, *Crosses and Tigers,* Nagase recalling the week of torture that Lomax endured, wrote: "I still cannot stop shuddering every time I recall that horrible scene." Eventually in 1992 Lomax and Nagase met by the bridge over the River Kwai. Nagase was trembling, in tears, saying over and over, 'I am very, very sorry ....' In the moving climax of Lomax's book he tells how he finally laid to rest the bitterness and hatred that torture had generated in a quiet Tokyo hotel room, where he met Nagase alone and assured him of his total forgiveness. Nagase had won his respect by his sincerity, suffering and courageous stand against militarism and for reconciliation. On 5 August 1995 Nagase and his wife were among the organisers of the first memorial service sponsored by Japanese held at the Hodogaya Commonwealth War Cemetery in Yokohama.

Eric Lomax was not the only POW to meet his most hated Japanese torturer and to become friends with him. Peter Rhodes tells the story of his effort to find the one he called The Pig in *To Japan to Lay a Ghost.* Twenty years after the war he decided that the hating must stop and he must try to meet his 'enemy'. With the help of the Japanese Embassy in London he was able to find the address of Chuzo Maeda and write to him. As a result Peter Rhodes met Maeda-san on 22 March 1970 near Fukuoka. The welcome he received at Maeda's village hall was quite overwhelming with 150 people present. There followed a visit to the old mine where he had worked as a POW and then on to Maeda's home. It was only on the drive back to the airport that the two former enemies had a chance to talk to each other. But this reconciliation did not take place unnoticed by the media. In Japan their meeting was reported in virtually all major newspapers and by all Radio and TV channels. Maeda's welcome for Peter Rhodes was turned into a thirty minute video by the Japan Broadcasting Corporation in 1984, which enabled Rhodes to tell the Japanese viewers about the brutal treatment of POWs in the war. A young woman schoolteacher who saw the programme was horrified to learn what had been done in the war and thought the video should be screened every year as a reminder of the past, so that it should not be repeated.

One of the most influential Japanese emissaries for reconciliation was Masao Hirakubo. During the war Hirakubo fought as an officer in Burma with the Japanese 31$^{st}$ Division on the Kohima front. He experienced the horrors of that campaign, in which half of all the Japanese troops in Burma were killed or died of wounds or disease. On returning home he found that his family home in Yokohama had been destroyed by bombing. His former company re-employed him and eventually sent him to Britain as its representative in 1967. After retiring in 1982 he remained in Britain and began his mission of reconciliation with his former enemies. He translated *Burma – The Longest War* by Louis Allen into Japanese in the belief that the book would help Japanese veterans and younger generations to understand the plain truth about the Burma war, because the book was based on interviews with soldiers from both sides. In collaboration with British veterans the Burma Campaign Fellowship Group was formed in 1991, and later became The Burma Campaign Society. Although the primary focus was on bringing veterans together from both sides of the Burma campaign, there was also an attempt to include former prisoners of the Japanese who had suffered on the Thai-Burma railway. Hirakubo believed in the importance of dialogue between former enemies and was instrumental in organising visits of Fepows to Japan, and in 1984 he brought a party of Japanese veterans to meet with the Far East Prisoners of War Association of Britain. In 1989 British Burma veterans visited Japan. The party toured around Japan, being met everywhere with warm hospitality by the Zen Biruma Senyukai (All Burma Veterans' Association of Japan). His obituary in The Times for 2 April 2008 records that: "Ever mindful of the suffering of British prisoners of the Japanese in captivity, Hirakubo helped them whenever he could, particularly in their contacts with Japan." Along with the members of the Burma Campaign Fellowship Group he believed that hatred should not pass from generation to generation and that reconciliation should follow when a war ends. Their motto: *Yesterday's Foe is Today's Friend* adorns the plaque unveiled by Hirakubo at St Ethelburga's church, Bishopsgate, London, in 2003. In his quest for reconciliation he was clearly motivated by his Christian convictions, for he had become a Roman Catholic after the war as a result of his experiences in Burma. It is therefore not surprising to learn that he took part in services of reconciliation at Westminster Abbey, Canterbury, Coventry and other cathedrals, and at

Kohima and Imphal in India. As a result of his efforts he was honoured by his Emperor and was presented with an Honorary OBE by Lord Caithness at the British Foreign Office in 1991.

A British veteran of the Burma campaign, Philip Malins, worked with Masao Hirakubo and became the Deputy Chairman of The Burma Campaign Society. Philip Malins did a great deal in the last twenty years of his life to promote reconciliation with Japan through the International Friendship and Reconciliation Trust, of which he was the founder. Although he had not been a prisoner of war, he was acutely aware of those who had suffered, for example, on the Thai-Burma railway and strove to help them. In 1998 he initiated a campaign which resulted in the British government giving an ex-gratia payment to all British citizens who had been imprisoned in the war by the Japanese. He also inspired the placing of the Hiroshima Stone in the Anglo-Japanese Garden at the National Memorial Arboretum on 15 August 2012. This stone from the ruins of Hiroshima is a memorial dedicated to the millions who died and suffered in the Second World War. The Japanese ambassador, Keiichi Hayashi, said on this occasion: "I am sure that this monument will keep reminding all the visitors to this site of the importance of post-war reconciliation."

## Keiko Holmes and Agape

No Japanese has done more to atone for the atrocities suffered by British POWs at the hands of the Japanese military than Keiko Holmes. I met Keiko in Japan in 2007 on one of her pilgrimages with POWs, when I took part in a memorial service at the Hodogaya Commonwealth War Graves Cemetery in Yokohama. For one of the POWs present that was an important day, as he could see the grave of one of his close comrades for the first time. It was also his 88th birthday. Denis had been imprisoned in Hong Kong and torpedoed on his way to Japan. Never had he told his wife, children or grandchildren anything about his wartime tribulations. He had vowed never to have anything to do with Japan or to eat rice ever again. But on that day at the end of the pilgrimage experience he said: "All that hatred has gone. I love Japan."

Keiko grew up in Kiwacho district of Mie prefecture, south of Osaka. In 1970 she married an Englishman, Paul Holmes, who was working for a Japanese trading company when he was killed in a plane accident in Bangladesh in 1984. Her concern for prisoners of war was sparked off when she returned to Japan in 1988 and saw a memorial for 16 POWs who had died at a copper mine six miles from her home. She had visited the grave before, but this time it had been transformed with a beautiful marble monument, a memorial flower garden and a large copper cross. Amazed at the care and generosity of the villagers who had constructed this memorial, she wanted to tell the British families that their loved ones were honoured and remembered in this corner of a foreign land. But she had no idea how to contact these families. Back in England in a remarkable way she was put in touch with Joe Cummings in Northumberland, who had worked in that mine as a POW. She also got in touch with Japanese who had been compelled to work in the copper mine during the war when they were 15 year old school children.

Keiko says: "I began to think that God was calling me to do something for the POWs." In 1991 she went to the Far East POWs (Fepows) national conference in London. Being Japanese she got a predictably hostile reception and was refused admission. But she persisted and showed her photos of the POWs' memorial and told them she was looking for Kiwacho POWs. Eventually they sold her a ticket and she went in. It was the beginning of her battle to overcome hatred and bitterness with the love of God.

The first great achievement was to take a group of 26 POWs, including two wives, back to Kiwacho in 1992 to see the memorial at Iruka (now Itaya). To do this she had to raise £40,000. With the help of a Japanese national newspaper the money came in at the last moment. Many of the POWs were apprehensive even in the plane on the way to Japan, not knowing whether they were doing the right thing, because their friends accused them of being traitors. However the reception given to these men, whom Keiko calls the 'Iruka Boys', was overwhelming. The main memorial service for the 16 POWs who died was attended by about 300 people from all walks of Japanese life, from the Mayor of Kiwacho to a hundred year old lady. One of those who went wrote to Keiko on returning to England: "for us, it was much more than a pilgrimage; it was the removal of the cancer of hatred from our inner beings."

Since 1992 Keiko has taken more than 400 POWs and their families on pilgrimage to Japan. The pilgrimages, like the first one, have received widespread media coverage in Japan. As a result many of the post-war generation have learnt what really happened during the war. The pilgrims have also visited Tokyo, Hiroshima and Nagasaki and other areas of Japan. They visited their comrades' graves and met Japanese people, often spending a night with a family sharing their wartime stories. They also visited Japanese schools and universities and found people were very eager to know about their experiences. They also met former Japanese soldiers who apologised to them, bringing healing to the memories on both sides. Reconciliation has been promoted by all these events and by memorial services. Since 1996 Keiko's organisation has been known as Agape, a Greek word meaning unconditional love.

Keiko's work is an example of what can be achieved by an individual. In Japan her impact can be gauged not only by the media interest but also by government recognition. In 1995 she was honoured by two prestigious Japanese awards. In London the Japanese Embassy has arranged an Annual Reunion for peace and friendship with POWs and others, which began in 1997 and continues to be held to the present. The Embassy welcomes invitees "to promote further friendship between Japanese people and British former Prisoners of War, Civil Internees, their families and people engaged in reconciliation activities." For eleven years the Japanese government helped to finance Keiko's tours. In May 1998 she met Emperor Akihito and his wife on several occasions during their visit to London. She spoke to them several times and they expressed their thanks for what she is doing. Partly as a result Keiko met Empress Michiko, when she was next in Tokyo, and had a long private interview with her about her work with POWs. It may not be totally unconnected with Keiko's work that the most specific apology made by the Japanese government to those who suffered in the war was issued by Prime Minister, Tomiichi Murayama in August 1994 and repeated in August 1995. He expressed his "profound remorse for these acts of aggression ....(which) caused such unbearable suffering and sorrow for so many people ...."

In Britain Keiko was invited to Windsor Castle where she received the award of the OBE at a private function, where the Queen and Duke of Edinburgh expressed their approval of the work she was doing. After the ceremony the Queen also met nineteen POWs, who had just been with Keiko to Japan, to acknowledge the importance of her reconciliation work. During Emperor Akihito's visit she was invited to the state banquet for the Emperor and there met royalty and government leaders, including the prime minister. The British Embassy in Tokyo has been very supportive of her pilgrimages and has invited POW groups to the embassy on every visit to Tokyo. One of the diplomats told me that he had seen how POWs had been profoundly changed by coming to Japan on pilgrimage with Keiko.

Many examples could be given of the impact of Keiko's reconciliation ministry on individuals both British and Japanese. Here are two examples.

Jack Caplan became famous, and a hero for the POWs, when he burnt the Japanese flag at the parade to welcome Emperor Akihito on his visit to London in 1998. Many POWs were outraged at the welcome given to the emperor, though the national federation of Far East POWS did not want to be rude to the Queen's guest. It so happened that Jack heard about Keiko and invited her to visit him. He told her that his parents were Lithuanian Jews, who had escaped to Glasgow, where he was born. He volunteered for the war in 1939 and was sent two years later to Singapore, where he was captured and suffered for the rest of the war. He eventually agreed to go with Keiko to Japan. He agreed with her that, 'we should understand each other.' So in 2002 he went in a wheelchair to Japan when he was 87. He was overwhelmed with the love shown to him. At the end of his visit he confessed: "I have really been through a revolution."

Hiroshi Abe was a soldier on the Thai – Burma railway. After the war he was tried for his treatment of POWs and was imprisoned as a war criminal. Keiko first heard of him during the preparation of a BBC documentary programme. When she asked him some questions over the phone about the treatment of POWs, he said that they were all treated well and that the Japanese soldiers had fought with a righteous heart. Keiko met Mr Abe in 1996 for the first time and then met him quite often whenever she was in Tokyo. Abe was moved by her booklet *LITTLE BRITAIN*, which she sent him after the telephone interview. One day he told her that he wanted to tell her everything, and he did. He wanted to apologise. So he came to the British Commonwealth War Cemetery in Hodogaya and confessed what he had done in the war, and apologised to the nine Fepows who were there. These Fepows had told Keiko before they left Britain for Japan, 'We will not meet any former Japanese soldiers; we will never forgive them.' But immediately they met him they forgave him, saying, 'You are forgiven…..You are brave….. We admire you.' Abe said that he looked forward to meeting Fepows each year, and that it was the only thing he really looked forward to in his old age. He attended POW receptions and came to the Hodogaya Cemetery almost every time Keiko's pilgrimages visited Japan. "I cannot deny the fact," he said, "that I am partly responsible for the deaths of many POWs and I apologise sincerely for what we did during the war." He made many British friends. He wanted to visit London and meet Fepows there to apologise to them, but died before he could make the journey.

## POW Research Network

Another group that have sought to make the Japanese public aware of the sufferings of Allied POWs during World War II are the POW Research Network Japan. I met two of their remarkable workers in 2007 at the Hodogaya Commonwealth War Cemetery. Mrs Taeko Sasamoto and

Mrs Yoshiko Tamura have spent more than 30 years independently researching the history of POWs in Japan.

Mrs Sasamoto helped to found the POW Research Network in 2002. The purpose of the Network was to bring to light the history of the Allied POWs in Japan. Their aim in doing so "is to know the facts correctly, and hand them down to the people, especially to the young ones, and to talk about them with the former enemies beyond the barrier of the nationalities, to enhance mutual understanding, and further to think together about the ways in which we will be able to prevent a recurrence of such tragedies in the past" (POW Research Network Website).

The research carried out by the Network shows that there were about 36,000 POWs imprisoned in Japan, of whom 3,559 died as a result of starvation, disease, accidents or mistreatment. The mortality rate in Japan was 10%, much less than the overall rate of 27% for all Allied POWs held by Japan. This may reflect the somewhat less harsh conditions in some parts of Japan as compared to the terrible brutality on the Thai-Burma railway and in the Philippines.

A full list of the camps in Japan, and a list of POWs who died in the camps are given on the Network website. There is also a full list of the 1,700 names of those who are buried at the Commonwealth War Cemetery at Hodogaya. I was impressed that Mrs Sasamoto and Mrs Tamura were able to show the POWs present at Hodogaya in 2007 the names of those who died in their camps and the causes of death. These were often listed as cardiac failure, beri beri, bacillary dysentery, acute pneumonia, and less frequently as mining accidents.

The activities of the Network include welcoming POWs returning to Japan, and helping them to locate the site of the camps where they were held prisoner, as well as making friends with local Japanese. As a research facility the Network have published books, organised seminars and workshops, and through TV broadcasts and national newspapers they have sought to disseminate information so that the Japanese public are more aware of what happened to POWs during the second world war, especially in Japan.

Significantly, the British Government have recognised the contribution of Mrs Sasamoto and Mrs Tamura to relations between the UK and Japan. In May 2006 they were both presented with the honour of the MBE at the British Embassy in Tokyo. In the official citation it was noted that in 1992 Mrs Tamura helped to make a TV documentary *"The Truth After 46 Years – Testimony of ex-British POWs of Iruka POW Camp."* Mrs Sasamoto published the results of her seven-year research in 2004 in *The Epitaph of the Allied POWs*.

## Professor T. Muraoka

Professor Takamitsu Muraoka left Japan in 1964 to study at the Hebrew University of Jerusalem on an Israeli government scholarship. After receiving a doctorate in Jerusalem he was appointed to a lectureship in Semitic languages in Manchester University in England, where he taught for ten years, before moving to Melbourne, Australia. In 1991 he was appointed to the prestigious chair of Hebrew at Leiden University in the Netherlands. In both Britain and Australia he became aware of the bitterness of those who had suffered at the hands of the Japanese in the Pacific War, but it was only when he moved to the Netherlands that he decided to do something about this and find out more.

Contact with an elderly Dutch lady who had long battled with her bitter memories of being imprisoned in a civilian internment camp set up by the Japanese army in Indonesia led him to meet many more Dutch returnees from Indonesia. Some had succeeded in overcoming their bitter feelings. Others told him bluntly of their burning animosity. In 2000 he and his wife and friends organised a conference for about 60 Dutch returnees and their relatives and some 20 Japanese residents in Holland, in order to face their shared history of three and a half years of Japanese occupation of Indonesia and its consequences. This conference has been held every year since then.

Prof. Muraoka had not been taught at school about the damage inflicted by the Japanese military on other Asian countries, but he had been taught about the suffering caused by the atomic bombs dropped on Hiroshima and Nagasaki and the civilian casualties of systematic carpet-bombing of Japanese cities at the end of the war. He began to realise that serious attention needed to be given to the relationship between Japan and her Asian neighbours. The damage inflicted by imperial Japan as a colonial power in the first half of the 20$^{th}$ century was not caused by the military alone. Confronted with this national history, he was forced to ask: 'Where do we stand as Japanese nationals and Japanese Christians?'

Muraoka says: "Firstly, I fully and honestly admit that during the first half of the last century my country inflicted an inestimable amount of damage, loss, destruction and suffering, not only on POWs of the allied forces, but also and far more seriously on the lands and peoples of Asia and Pacific islands. I offer no excuses; I can only belatedly express my sincere sympathy for all those countless victims and their relatives and friends.

"Secondly, I express my serious concern over the fact that my country, its successive post-war leaders and the great majority of the population, have not yet faced the modern history of Japan honestly and sincerely. For us, sixty years on, the war is not over yet. I feel responsible for this situation. I shall not remain idle or sit back on the side. I am determined to act, not just say things."

Consequently when Prof. Muraoka officially retired from Leiden University in 2003, he acted. He decided to spend one tenth of his time, or five weeks every year, sharing his knowledge and expertise with academics and students of those countries in East Asia which suffered under Japanese imperialism and military aggression during the first half of the 20$^{th}$ century. He chose to teach and lecture at universities and seminaries as a volunteer, free of charge.

From 2003 Prof. Muraoka and his wife have visited a different Asian country every year. They began by going to Korea in 2003. He taught Greek, Syriac and Biblical Hebrew from 9 a.m. to 5 p.m. During his 30 years' career as a university teacher he had never taught so intensively. On the last day, he addressed nearly 2500 staff and students. But he did not only give lectures. He spent time with Koreans to apologise to them and did not indulge in tourism, but went to places of significance for the relations of Japan and Korea. Since 2004 Prof. Muraoka has visited Taiwan, Hong Kong, China, the Philippines, Singapore, Malaysia, Indonesia, Burma (Myanmar), Thailand and Vietnam. In 2015 he returned to Taiwan.

In Hong Kong there was a revealing moment when Prof. Muraoka visited the Hong Kong Museum of History and learnt that during the war the Japanese military administration compelled all Hong Kong residents to exchange their local currency, the Hong Kong dollar, for special yen denomination bank notes. At the end of the war the Japanese reneged on the pledge on the back of the notes and declared them to be invalid and worthless rendering thousands of residents bankrupt. The Hong Kong Reparation Society still campaigns for compensation for this fraudulent deception.

*Japan and Prisoners of War*

In Taiwan there was a different atmosphere. With its fairly pro-Japanese stance, Taiwan differs from other Asian countries. However intense anti-Japanese feelings came to the surface in 2008 when a Taiwanese fishing boat was sunk off the coast of Taiwan by a Japanese Marine Security Patrol. As far as the history of Japanese-Taiwanese relations are concerned the Pacific War has not been consigned to the past.

In 2008 Prof. Muraoka visited mainland China and lectured in Nanjing, Shanghai and Beijing. It was traumatic for him to visit Nanjing, where his father had served as a lieutenant-colonel, though he was relieved to know that his father was not posted to the city till after the massacre in 1937-1938. Their host took them to the Memorial Hall for the Nanjing Massacre. It was a shattering experience to stand in front of a large fenced space exposing a burial ground where mutilated corpses were dumped or victims were just hurled in alive to be covered up with a heavy layer of earth. He rightly says: "Since the end of the Pacific War the Japanese have kept shouting, and are still shouting, 'No more Hiroshima!' This call, however, will keep falling on deaf ears outside of Japan, unless the Japanese learn to shout as loudly, 'No more Nanjing!'"

Sometimes Prof. Muraoka is asked whether he has already obtained Dutch citizenship. He used to say that he would not do that as long as his mother is alive, as he is the only son and eldest child of four children. His mother died in 2008, but now he has an additional argument: "I am determined to remain Japanese until my country, its leaders, including its symbolic figure-head, and the majority of its citizens resolve squarely and honestly to face this past legacy of ours, deal with it adequately, and begin to translate this resolution into tangible deeds." He looks forward to the day when he can stand in public to address an audience and lift his Japanese passport boldly and wave it with pride.

# Signs of Hope in Japan and China

Two of the most contentious issues from the Sino-Japanese War that resurface again and again in relations between China and Japan are the Nanjing Massacre and the Yasukuni Shrine. Both issues concern memories of the war and the ways its history are seen in both countries. To these may be added many other incidents such as the Manchurian invasion, the Marco Polo Bridge affair, the bombing of Chongqing, and the Japanese military use of 'comfort women'. China has not been satisfied with the apologies that Japan has given at the official level and has been critical of the lack of information given in Japanese school textbooks concerning the military invasion and occupation of China. Japan has invested billions in China since 1980, but this has not altered the hostility of many Chinese people to Japan for wartime atrocities. Despite these tensions there are signs of hope in China and Japan, where individuals and communities have sought to work for peace between their countries.

## Hopeful Signs in Japan

### Writers

No Japanese has worked harder than Honda Katsuichi to discover exactly what happened in the Nanjing Massacre and to record the details. His book *Nankin e no Michi* published in 1987 was republished in English in 1999 as *The Nanjing Massacre: A Japanese Journalist Confronts Japan's Shame*, edited by Frank Gibney.

Honda Katsuichi traces the advance of the Japanese army from their landing on Hangzhou Bay on 5 November 1937 to the capture and destruction of Nanjing in December 1937. He shows that from the moment the army landed on Chinese soil the policy of the army was to pursue the practice of the 'three alls' : 'burn all, kill all, loot all.'

Gibney in his Introduction gives the following information. Katsuichi was a top reporter for Japan's leading newspaper, *Asahi*. He had first gone to China in 1972, as reported in his earlier book, *Journey to China.* It was only from 1972 when diplomatic relations with China were restored that Japan's military record in the Sino-Japanese war of 1930-1945 began to be uncovered. Honda reported on the atrocities committed by the army, including biological warfare, forced labour, the "Three All" campaign and the Nanjing Massacre.

In 1986 Asahi asked its readers to write some of their recollections about the war time. They received an unprecedented flood of letters – over 4,000 – some 1,200 were printed later in a book of 2 volumes. By the end of the 1980s almost 20 books had appeared in Japan exposing the Nanjing atrocities. Honda's book about the Massacre in Nanjing was written in response to the 1982 textbook controversies, when liberal journalists complained about the Japanese Ministry of Education's attempt to whitewash the atrocities committed during the invasion of China. It was not until 1979 that a textbook for the first time mentioned the Nanjing Massacre by name.

Over the past few years, middle and high school textbooks have been issued that convey to students a correct if underplayed statement of the wholesale killing that went on. Most middle school textbooks in current use give the figures for the Nanjing massacre as 150,000 –

300,000 killed. Honda's estimate of the numbers killed is a bit over 100,000 but not nearly as much as 200,000.

Why did the Japanese kill and rape so many? Honda gives the broad answer by showing that the policy of the "three alls" was carried out from the moment the troops came ashore on Hangzhou Bay in November 1937, and they carried this out right up to the capture of Nanjing and in the city itself. "They thought them (the Chinese) a mass of inferior people, to be handled as they wished." "With the arrogance of a conquering army, they were out to teach the Chinese a lesson." The military were eager to loot and pillage – and rape followed suit.

The Nanjing Massacre was only part of the brutal invasion and occupation of China by the Japanese Imperial Army. It is estimated that 20 million Chinese civilians and soldiers were killed by the Japanese in the years 1931-1945. How can such a legacy of bitterness be atoned for or overcome?

For a recent discussion of the evidence concerning the Japanese attack on Nanjing, see Daqing Yang's chapter, "The Nanjing Atrocity", in *Toward a History Beyond Borders* (Harvard, 2012, pp. 178-204).

## Chukiren – the Association of China Returnees

One of the most remarkable associations formed by ex-Japanese soldiers was the Chugoku Kikansha Renrakukai (The Association of China Returnees), known by its acronym, Chukiren. The group was founded in 1957 by about 1,000 Japanese war veterans, who had been repatriated from China in 1956. After the war most of them had been captured by the Russians and deported to labour camps in Siberia. Stalin chose to return 969 of them to China in 1950 as a good will gesture to Mao. They were then held for six years in a new prison created for them at Fushun in Liaoning province of north-east China. Expecting the worst from their former enemies, they were amazed to be well treated, given good food and freed from any forced labour. Although some had belonged to the kempeitai most were rank and file soldiers, but this also meant they had been taught to be brutal to Chinese. The Japanese army in China had not only killed soldiers taken prisoner, they had indulged in atrocities against civilians including torture, rape, use of poison gas, vivisection and much more.

The lenient treatment given to these Japanese soldiers was not a generous whim, but a deliberate policy of the Chinese Communist Party, overseen by the Chinese Premier, Zhou Enlai. To begin with the detainees were angry when they were told that they were being classified not as prisoners of war but as "war criminals". They protested that they had no choice but to obey the orders of their superiors. However the Chinese authorities insisted that they must accept responsibility for their actions. This was to be a key part of their treatment.

On the other hand the prison staff had great difficulties in implementing a generous regime. Many of them had lost parents and relatives at the hands of the Japanese. They found it difficult to accept that the prisoners were being given three meals of white rice a day, when their families could not afford such luxury. The official policy of the Chinese Communist Party was: 'Even war criminals are human beings, and as such their human dignity ought to be respected.' One young guard wanted to leave when he discovered that one of the Japanese had killed his father. The warden said: "I know perfectly how you feel…. But if you give up on these detainees now and walk out, they will pick up guns and invade China again. This means that there will be many more deaths like your father's." Realising the importance of his part in re-educating the Japanese prisoners, he worked harder than ever. Later when his "enemy" suffered an acute appendicitis attack in the middle of the night, he carried him on his back to the medical room to save his life.

Seeing many incidents of kindness like this, the prisoners began to change their hostile attitude to their guards. But more was needed. Since they had nothing to do but amuse themselves, they eventually began to hold study meetings. They also engaged with the education programme run by Korean Chinese officers who were fluent in Japanese, and so began to understand the war from the perspective of the victims. Some began to confess the atrocities that they had committed against Chinese. Some told how they had used live peasants for bayonet practice, how they enjoyed chopping people's heads off or what they did to kill women and babies. One of the prisoners, Yasuji Kaneko, recalled: "China's generous treatment gradually melted our hardened minds. We started thinking how the victims felt, and realised we have to repay their generosity."

In 1956 special military tribunals were opened to try the Japanese prisoners in Fushun. By then they were expecting to receive the maximum penalty for war crimes. They were amazed when they were told that almost all were to be released without any charge. Only 45 prisoners were sentenced, and none of them were given the death sentence or life imprisonment. This was also shocking to the prison officers, who believed that at least the high-ranking Japanese officers should be executed. They protested to Zhou Enlai, whose response was: "You will understand the correctness of our decision in 20 years' time. Suppose these people who committed crimes in the war of invasion reflect deeply on their wartime actions and tell other Japanese about their experiences in

China. I am certain that this is a far more effective way of making Japanese people aware of the facts about the war of aggression than being told by us Chinese Communists." Zhou Enlai's view was not his personal policy only but in line with a resolution of the First Plenary of the Chinese People's Congress passed in April 1956, which ordered lenient treatment of Japanese war criminals (*The Search for Reconciliation,* Yinan He, p. 150).

What happened when the prisoners returned from Fushun to Japan in 1956? It may seem surprising to us now that after being given a warm-hearted send off by the Chinese at Fushun railway station and the port of Tianjin, they received a cold reception in Japan. Only one official was there to receive them, who gave them a little cash, a blanket and some old clothing. Worse was to come. They were accused of being brainwashed, treated as communists, put under police surveillance and found it difficult to get jobs.

One year after their return they formed the Chukiren association and published a book in 1957 entitled *Sanko* ('Sanko' referring to the Three Alls, 'burn all, kill all, loot all'), containing testimonies about their horrifying deeds during the war years in China. The book sold 50,000 copies in twenty days, but the publishers were put under such right-wing pressure that no more editions were printed. In 1960 at its members' second general meeting, they scrapped the original aims of the association for pursuing compensation from the Japanese government and for promoting mutual help and friendship among themselves. Instead they adopted new aims, to deepen their sense of remorse for their part in a war of aggression against China, to tell their countrymen what they were guilty of having done to Chinese, and to work for Sino-Japanese friendship.

The Chukiren members never forgot what happened to them in the Fushun camp. In fact, many of them only began to grapple with the significance of their experiences at Fushun after they settled down again to life in Japanese society. As they enjoyed normal family life again they recollected how destructive their wartime brutality had been to countless families in China. Their respect for their Chinese guards deepened. Reflecting on the feelings of the victims of Japanese aggression, they were motivated to tell their stories and admit their individual or collective guilt. They spoke at public meetings, visited schools and published their periodical *Chukiren*. Members in Hiroshima had the courage to speak about their victims to an audience in the Hiroshima Peace Museum. The association supported lawsuits brought by Chinese war victims and opposed revisionist historians who wanted to whitewash Japan's war record.

From 1965 onwards Chukiren began to send delegates to China, and later to encourage reciprocal visits to Japan. To begin with this process was severely restricted by the Cultural Revolution in China and the fact that relations between the two countries were not normalised until the Peace Treaty of 1972. However on the first visit in 1965 headed by Chukiren president, Fujita Shigeru, former general commanding the 59$^{th}$ division, he was surprised to be called for an unscheduled meeting with Premier Zhou Enlai. In 1984 eight former prison officers from Fushun, including Jin Yuan, the former chief warden in charge of the re-education of prisoners, were invited to Tokyo and many members had the chance to meet them again. It was an emotional reunion. The Japanese media could not understand why these former enemies could embrace each other with tears of joy. Jin Yuan said: "We were your governors and you were the governed. That the two groups so separated from each other have been able to maintain this relationship of friendship is uncommon in the history of mankind. It might justly be called a miracle." Perhaps from this date people began to talk about the 'Miracle of Fushun.'

In 1988 the Chukiren were permitted to put up a monument of apology in the grounds of the Fushun prison. The inscription in Chinese on the monument reads (when translated) as follows:

*"We took part in the 15-year long war of aggression against China, committed heinous crimes of burning and robbing, and after the war we were detained in the prisons in Fushun and Taiyuan, where we were treated in accordance with the revolutionary principle of the Chinese Communist Party: Hate the crime, but not the criminal. This helped us recover for the first time our conscience and humanity. Totally contrary to our expectation we were released through the generosity of the Chinese people and all allowed to return home without a single execution.*

*Now that Fushun Prison has been restored, we see it right to set up here a monument as a token of our sincere apology to the martyred Chinese anti-Japanese resistance fighters and renew our vow never to allow a war of invasion to happen, and to dedicate ourselves to the cause of peace and friendship between China and Japan.*

*22 October 1988, Chukiren."*

In Japan the veterans have urged the government to apologise for crimes committed during the war and to atone for them. One of the issues that has resurfaced again and again is the issue of the so-called Chinese and Korean 'comfort women'. Until the 1990s the use of Korean and Chinese 'comfort women' for Japanese troops was denied. It was left to a Japanese historian, Professor

Yoshiaki Yoshimi, working on his own, to track down the paper trail proof in the Defence Research Library in 1992 that showed that their procurement was official Japanese Army policy. In 2000 the Women's International War Crimes Tribunal on Japan's Military Sexual Slavery was held in Tokyo to deal with this issue. Two old veterans of Chukiren participated in the tribunals as witnesses. They testified as perpetrators of wartime rape in China to support the plaintiffs' accounts. The judges praised the old soldiers for speaking out and confessing their own involvement.

In 2006 the Chukiren Peace Memorial Museum was opened in Saitama prefecture, near Tokyo. The core of the museum's collection is the testimony of about 300 Japanese veterans who confessed to atrocities committed in China. The main purpose is to provide the resource data for historians who wish to research the history of the Sino-Japanese war. The museum is designed primarily as a place for scholars and researchers, as well as providing the facilities for people who want to read what veterans have recorded for the future.

Chukiren was dissolved in 2002, as war veterans were dying out, but has been succeeded by an organisation called *Fushun no Kiseki wo Uketsugu Kai* (The Committee to Pass on the Miracle of Fushun). Formed by young people the continuation committee aims to gather more testimonies and to promote friendship with China. Their activities include holding meetings to publicise the miracle of Fushun and the stories of the returnees. They plan to arrange an annual study tour to Fushun and to continue publishing the quarterly journal *Chukiren.* For a more detailed historical account of the Fushun story see *Men to Devils, Devils to Men* by Barak Kushner, Harvard, 2015.

The Miracle of Fushun is extremely significant for the task of achieving reconciliation between Japan and China. Some of the crucial points that emerge are the following: understanding the brutalisation process that affects combatants in war, reversing this process by treating the victimisers as human as well as the victims, creating the possibility of reconciliation by treating enemies as friends, feeling the enemy's pain, and studying history from both sides of war.

There are also other Japanese war veterans associations working for peace. The Veterans for Japan-China Friendship was founded in 1961 by army general Endo Saburo. He visited China in 1956 and saw the need to encourage friendship between Japan and China. The biggest challenge for their group was that of acknowledging history and learning from past mistakes. They see August 15, 1945 as the day when Japan began to reflect on losing a war of aggression and moved on to the creation of the peace constitution. In 2011 the Veterans celebrated their 50$^{th}$ anniversary and changed their name to "Japan-China Friendship Society of August 15$^{th}$." Veterans want to tell their stories rather than carrying them to the grave. They want the young generation to realise the horrors of war and not to repeat them, so publicise their stories through their monthly magazine and by giving public lectures. To promote friendship with China they invited one to three Chinese students a year to attend Waseda University and stay in members' homes. In addition they also send a delegation of about ten members to China every year to visit different parts of the country for two weeks or more. Veterans believe strongly in Article 9 of the Japanese constitution and share with conviction the determination that Japan should never again take up weapons of war.

A more recent association, Pacifist Soldiers and Civilians, was founded in 1988. Veterans who were writing letters to *Asahi Shimbun* started the group. One of the leaders was Shiro Oishi, who was injured in the Philippines and became a Christian minister after the war. The main purpose for founding Pacifist Veterans was to tell people about the horrors of war and what it was like to experience a living hell. Their purpose is to tell the following generations how the war began, how inhumane war is, and how countless citizens became victims of a surrender delayed by the personal egos of the country's leaders. To counter militarism they have a three point policy: first, to resolve international disputes peacefully through discussion; second, to seek world peace in the spirit of Article 9 of the Japanese Constitution; third, to oppose all ideologies that reject government of the people, by the people, and for the people.

These associations are concerned about the role of the emperor in the war and the destructive effect of emperor worship on the behaviour of the military. Any brutality could be sanctioned by army officers invoking the authority of the emperor. The part played by Emperor Hirohito in the period 1930-1945 remains a matter for historical debate. Liberal opinion in Japan has yet to determine the future role of the emperor in the event of war.

## Peace Museums

The peace movement in Japan has many branches. One of the important bodies is the Peace Studies Association of Japan (PSAJ) founded in 1973. The aim of the PSAJ is to study conflicts between nations, to carry out research on the causes of conflicts and the conditions for peace, and to contribute to academic progress in related fields of study. According to a survey in 2005, 42 Japanese universities offer a course entitled 'Peace Studies'. Thirty percent of Japanese universities provide peace related courses. But there was no department of peace studies at any Japanese university. As far as Japan's war responsibility is concerned, there is an important organisation set up in 1993, called the Centre for Research and Documentation on Japan's War Responsibility (JWRC). This organisation is not only concerned for research but also for taking action in support of Asian victims of Japan's aggression. It publishes a quarterly journal, in which research findings are made public. In 1993 it submitted its investigations of the sex slave issue to the Japanese government and as a consequence the government was forced to admit that these so called 'comfort women' had suffered at the hands of the Japanese military.

There are more peace museums in Japan than in any other country. In 1998 out of 100 peace museums worldwide, 52 were in Japan. By 2009 the number of peace museums worldwide had risen to 204 and those in Japan to 66. Not surprisingly the first two museums were established in Hiroshima and Nagasaki in 1955 to record the horrors of the atom bomb and to protest against any more war and especially against nuclear armaments. The great majority of the peace museums were set up in the 1990s, when every year saw one or more new centres opened and a total of 27 museums came into being. These new museums began to focus not only on the bombing of Japan but also on the effects of Japanese military aggression in Korea, China and South-East Asian countries. Now more than ten museums in Japan honestly display wartime atrocities. The Kyoto Museum for World Peace established in Ritsumeikan University in 1992 is a good example of how aggression can be shown objectively. The text of their website says: during the Fifteen Years War with China, *"Japanese military forces carried out indiscriminate bombing and used poison gases and biological weapons against China and other countries. In war zones, they killed and tortured soldiers and civilians alike, their operations aimed at totally destroying areas that put up resistance."* The museum includes sections on the Japanese army, colonisation of other countries, and determining responsibility for war crimes. In the latter, reference is made to the role of the emperor and the use of vivisection by the notorious Unit 731 in China. In October 2008, the International Conference of Museums for Peace was held in Kyoto and Hiroshima. Three duties of peace museums were highlighted. First, peace museums must convey the misery of war, and cultivate a respect for human dignity in the face of war, violence, and inhumane acts. Second, they must deepen historical awareness to enable people to understand the causes and the reality behind the undermining of peace. Third, now more than ever, peace museums must educate people who will take action to resolve the challenges of war for humanity through research and by laying a path to reconciliation and coexistence that will lead to a sustainable peaceful society. The Kyoto museum is interactive and takes the role of education seriously. Another notable museum is the Oka Masaharu Memorial Nagasaki Peace Museum, which has had a partnership with Nanjing Museum and has raised funds every year to send Japanese students to China. Oka Masaharu, a Protestant minister and civic assembly leader, was determined to reveal Japan's wartime responsibility for invading other Asian countries. In particular, he worked hard for the Korean victims of the atomic bomb.

The Osaka International Peace Centre is the only publicly owned peace museum in Japan, established by the Osaka municipality. It has three sections. The first shows the bombing of Osaka which destroyed the city in 1945. The second exhibits the destructive effect of Japanese military expansion in Asia. The third concentrates on the future for world peace. In the middle section the exhibits deliberately seek to inform visitors about atrocities in China, such as the Nanjing Massacre.

Another centre founded in 1989 is the Kochi Grassroots House, a private peace museum focusing on issues related to peace education and the environment. It is located in Kochi City, Shikoku, and was founded by Shigeo Nishimori. One of the functions of the museum is to pass on an awareness of the reality of war and the value of peace to the next generation. Pertinent artifacts and materials are collected, classified, and exhibited in order to accomplish this. The museum also produces materials on peace education and distributes them to a wide audience. The aim is to learn from nature and create lifestyles which harmonize with it, believing that nature is the best model for peace. Activities include the collection, preservation, study, and exhibition of artifacts and materials relating to war. The Grassroots House is a community based peace museum working to achieve world peace. They organize visits to war sites and peace trips in Japan and China, and hold community events.

The Japanese Network of Museums for Peace was formed in 1998 to counter attacks by revisionists and right-wingers who sought to attack peace museums like the one in Osaka for exhibiting the atrocities by the Japanese army. The Society of Correcting One-Sided Exhibits was founded in 1997 to attack peace museums like the one in Osaka, apparently unconscious of the anomaly that Peace Osaka presented both sides and refused to be one-sided. Sadly the government sided with the revisionists and the Prime Minister in 1996 ordered local governments to investigate public peace museums. The ensuing report criticised the Osaka Peace Museum for being based on "one-sided ideology". Subsequently the nationalistic group of the Association for Correcting One-Sided War Exhibitions held a conference on 23 January 2000 entitled, "The Biggest Lie in the 20th Century: Complete Verification of Nanjing Massacre." Using a room of the Osaka International Peace Centre, a lecture was given denying the existence of the Nanjing Massacre, which aroused protests in China. This only serves to show that the history of what happened in the war with China is still a very hot issue.

## Japanese History Textbooks

Controversy over history textbooks used in Japan gained international publicity in 1982. This was revived in 2000 by the publication of the *New History Textbook* for use in Japanese schools. Written by right-wing scholars, it was approved by the Ministry of Education in 2001. The text downplays the military aggression of Japan's invasion of China and of other countries during the Second World War. It raised a storm of protest not only in China and Korea but also from Japanese historians and educationalists. However in the four years after its issue it was only used by 0.039% of Japanese schools. Nevertheless it caused further controversy in 2005 and demonstrations broke out in China and Korea in protest against the revisionist tactics of Japanese right-wingers. In China some of the demonstrations became violent and damage was done to Japanese businesses and some individuals were injured.

*Two Pilgrims Meet*

Despite the diplomatic outcry over the *New History Textbook,* the controversy led to some positive developments. Major changes were made in the way textbooks were treated in Japan. In 2005 the Ministry of Foreign Affairs published sections of eight approved middle school textbooks dealing with modern international history. These were translated into Chinese, Korean and English, so that the international community could see what was said about Japan's military past. Japanese textbooks do contain information on Japan's wartime history. For example, middle school textbooks describe the invasion of China after the Marco Polo Bridge incident in July 1937, the attack on Nanjing, the millions of victims of Japan's occupation of Asian countries and the deportation of Chinese and Koreans to Japan for hard labour. Japan's sense of superiority toward other Asian nations is noted.

The textbook controversy also led to meetings between historians from Japan, Korea and China. In 2001 academics and educationalists from China, Korea and Japan met to protest and decided to create a textbook together. The textbook was called in Japanese, *Mirai o Hiraku Rekishi,* meaning 'History that Opens the Future'. This first attempt at publishing a trilateral supplementary textbook was published in all three languages in 2005. It has not been used as a textbook in any country, and has been read more by adults than young people. Most copies were sold in China. The Chinese and Japanese governments agreed to launch their own Joint Historical Research project in 2006. In January 2010 the final report was issued online in Japan. The result was a compromise with academics from China and Japan presenting separate views of the war and not a joint account. A production of a different kind is *Toward a History Beyond Borders.* Distinguished Japanese and Chinese historians have worked together to discuss *Contentious Issues in Sino-Japanese Relations.* The resulting volume was published in Chinese and Japanese, and then in English in 2012.

The attempt to produce joint history publications has resulted in a number of benefits. First, the authors have had to reflect on the different attitudes to past history in the three countries and have had to record these different perspectives, especially in writing on controversial issues like the Nanjing massacre. Second, they have had to come to terms with the different way history is taught in East Asia. Japanese record the facts, Chinese interpret the facts in provocative language, and Koreans prefer narrative and simple language for mass appeal. Third, scholars have come to question the way history is written in their own countries. A Chinese historian, Bu Ping, commented that "narrow-mindedness exists in the textbooks of all countries." Fourth, a transnational collaborative network of scholars in East Asia has developed, which is significant for the future.

Finally we should note that however objectionable the notorious right-wing Japanese textbook might have been the real problem lies elsewhere. The general perception is that Japanese of the post-war generations know little or nothing about what their military did during the Fifteen Years War with China and subsequently in the invasion of South-East Asian countries during World War II. We have already noted that when POWs told their stories on visits to Japan young people were horrified to know what had been done by their soldiers in the war. It is shocking to read that the highly educated lecturer in peace studies, Kazuyo Yamane, knew nothing about the atrocities committed by the Japanese military until 1998 when she read Iris Chang's *The Rape of Nanjing*. This shows that a few references in a school textbook are no substitute to an in-depth exposure to what happened in the war period. Everyone in China knows about Hiroshima and Nagasaki and the devastation caused by atom bombs, but how many in Japan know about the Nanjing Massacre and the 15 - 20 million Chinese who died in the war between 1931-1945?

## Apologies

Demands for apology and compensation from the Japanese government have been a recurring theme in China both at the official level and from ordinary citizens. As far as China is concerned the right to compensation from the Japanese government was renounced in 1972, when diplomatic relations were restored between the two nations. China declared "that in the interest of friendship between the Chinese and the Japanese peoples, it renounces its demand for war reparation from Japan."

In September 1972 after the signing of the Joint Communiqué between China and Japan, Prime Minister Kakuei Tanaka said: "The Japanese side is keenly conscious of the responsibility for the serious damage caused in the past to the Chinese people through war, and deeply reproaches itself."

In 1982 Kiichi Miyazawa, the Chief Cabinet Secretary, made a statement on the History Textbooks controversy. "The Japanese Government and the Japanese people are deeply aware of the fact that acts by our country in the past caused tremendous suffering and damage to the peoples of Asian countries, including ... China."

In 1992 the Heisei Emperor, Akihito, became the first Japanese emperor to visit China. In the course of his six day visit he said in Beijing: "In the long history of relations between our two countries, there was a tragic period when my country caused great suffering for the people of China. We have rebuilt our country and strongly resolved to pursue the path of a peaceful country on the basis of our deep regret and desire that this kind of war should never be repeated." Although this statement is somewhat vague and was not an official apology, it was nevertheless of great significance, as was the visit of the Emperor to China when western countries were still boycotting China for the 1989 crackdown in Tiananmen Square.

The most quoted apology by a Japanese Prime Minister was made by Tomiichi Murayama on 15 August 1995, on the occasion of the 50$^{th}$ anniversary of the end of the war. "During a certain period in the not-too-distant past, Japan through its colonial rule and aggression, caused tremendous damage and suffering to the people of many countries, particularly those of Asia …. I express here once again my feelings of deep remorse and state my heartfelt apology." This statement was drafted with the full support of the cabinet.

In 1998 in the Japan-China Joint Declaration on Building a Partnership of Friendship and Cooperation for Peace and Development, Prime Minister Keizo Obuchi said: "The Japanese side is keenly conscious of the responsibility for the serious distress and damage that Japan caused to the Chinese people through its aggression against China during a certain period in the past and expressed deep remorse for this."

On the 60$^{th}$ anniversary of the end of the war, in August 2005, Prime Minister Junichiro Koizumi reaffirmed Japan's apology to all who suffered at its hands in wording that was almost identical with that used by Murayama.

On August 14 2015 Prime Minister Shinzo Abe issued a lengthy statement commemorating the 70$^{th}$ anniversary of the end of the war on the basis of a report by a panel of Japanese experts on the history of the 20$^{th}$ century. The statement was primarily designed to gain the approval of the domestic audience in Japan, including right-wing spokesmen. Abe regrets Japan's error in taking the road to war, but blames colonialism and economic blocs for this. As a result apology for what Japan did to China and other East Asian countries is not as forthright as in the Murayama and Koizumi statements. As so often Japan laments and names its own losses, including Hiroshima and Nagasaki, but does not mention atrocities committed by its own military. There are three references to China's sufferings, of which the most specific mentions, "what great efforts must have been necessary for the Chinese people who underwent all the sufferings of the war." There is nothing here to convince China that Abe sincerely wants to express real sorrow for Japan's invasion and occupation of China.

As can be seen from the above statements Japan has expressed regret for the past, but these statements are given in general terms and there is little detail added to official apologies. Chinese people would like some official acknowledgement of the Nanjing massacre and other events such as the occupation of Manchuria and the invasion of mainland China. Actions by Prime Minister Junichiro Koizumi and other Japanese premiers in honouring the Class A war criminals at the Yasukuni Shrine have made China doubt the sincerity of Japan's apologies. Nevertheless Japan has expressed more than mere regret and has repeatedly reaffirmed her commitment to peace and her determination not to become a military power in future.

## Peace Constitution

The Peace Constitution and particularly Article 9 is still strongly supported by many, especially of the war generation. Article 9 states under the title 'Renunciation of War':

> *Aspiring sincerely to an international peace based on justice and order, the Japanese people forever renounce war as a sovereign right of the nation and the threat or use of force as means of settling international disputes. In order to accomplish the aim of the preceding paragraph, land, sea, and air forces, as well as other war potential, will never be maintained. The right of belligerency of the state will not be recognized.*

Former career soldiers are among those who strongly support Japan's peace constitution, as already noted above. For example, Kaneko Kotaro of Veterans for Japan-China Friendship said, "August 15, 1945, the most significant moment in Japanese history, is the day that we began to reflect on losing a war of aggression and the creation of our peace constitution. We want to take this to heart and pass it on to our children and grandchildren." He and his association will continue to campaign against the removal of Article 9. Another old soldier, Inokuma Tokuru representing Pacifist Soldiers and Civilians, says: "War is a murderer. Nothing but a ruthless murderer." He is worried that the new generation has no memory of the war. "Article 9 of our constitution is the product of the grief, hatred and suffering of countless citizens in that war." Takahashi Tetsuro of Chukiren says, "Article 9 is the most pressing concern, but I think the problem is the

Japan-U.S. Security Treaty, placed above Article 9. I think we must widely discuss the issue of the subjugation of Article 9 to the Security Treaty." He urges young people to have "a clear awareness of the reality of war."

# Hopeful Signs in China

## Chinese care for Japanese war victims in China

We have noted the remarkable example of the Chukiren association of ex-Japanese soldiers, who on their return to Japan sought to atone for their past by acknowledging their atrocities. What is not so well known is that some Chinese in the Japanese colonies of Manchuria and Mongolia showed compassion for Japanese victims at the end of the war. Barak Kushner records two examples in his book, *Men to Devils, Devils to Men* (Harvard 2015). Near Harbin, in the county of Fangzheng, local Chinese erected a monument recording the names of the Japanese colonists and soldiers who had died in their retreat after Japan's surrender in 1945. Kushner records the story in the words of a recent Chinese newspaper article: "When Japan surrendered in 1945, about 15,000 Japanese settlers were still in Fangzheng where many had lived for more than a decade. A full third of them, mostly men, had died or been killed. After the armistice the people of Fangzheng seemingly buried their hatred and adopted more than 5,000 Japanese orphans and allowed widows to settle as equal neighbours." The newspaper then added that, "almost 100,000 local people with Japanese relatives have lived and worked in Japan and 38,000 Fangzheng residents now live there permanently" (*Men to Devil, Devils to Men,* p. 317).

That this response by Chinese civilians to Japanese war victims in the Manchuria area was not unusual can be seen from the following story. Tadao Ono left home at the age of 14 to escape his abusive step-father and joined the Japanese Pioneers in Manchuria, around early 1945. When the Russians invaded they rounded up all the

Japanese. He stood in a line with many others and the Russian in charge told him he was too young and let him go to fend for himself. There were a few others who were sent off too. He had to go through streets with dead bodies all over the place, and finally took refuge in a barn, with several other Japanese. But there was nothing to eat. It is not certain how long they were there, perhaps a day or two, after which local Chinese came and took off each member. Tadao went with a family to a farm, where he lived and worked. Eventually he got the last ship transporting returnees to Japan around 1951 or 1952. Many years later Tadao worked at a travel agents where he specialised in taking Japanese who were brought up in north-east China back to re-visit the places where they and their parents had lived. He spoke excellent Mandarin and was respected by the Chinese. He did not believe the local Chinese ever treated the Japanese as former 'enemies'. The title of the book he wrote about his youth is: *Gekidou no tairiku to shonen (*which could be translated as: 'Youth on a continent in ferment'*).*

Barak Kushner also cites the example of a poor Chinese family in Henan Province, who cared for a disabled Japanese soldier after the war and looked after him for more than forty-five years. These farmers found Ishida Toshiro wandering around wounded and semi-paralysed following the end of the war. They took him in, looked after him and cared for him as part of their family for more than four decades, till he was finally repatriated to Japan in 1993. Here we have an impressive case of Chinese benevolence despite the malevolence of war. Though unusual this cannot be the only village in China which behaved in this way to Japanese soldiers.

## Nanjing Massacre Museum

The Nanjing Massacre Memorial Hall was opened in 1985. An important enlargement and renovation took place between December 2005 and December 2007. The relatively positive tone of the new hall reopened on 13 December 2007 reflected the Beijing government's desire to improve relations with Japan. The People's Daily, mouthpiece of the Communist party, noting the sensitivity of the 70th anniversary of the massacre, commented: "Correct treatment of history can help people calmly and rationally deal with the contradictions in ties between the two countries." Officials in Nanjing also said that the new, enlarged memorial embodies an appeal for peace.

The museum has a forbidding appearance with a dark grey wall resembling a massive grave. Inside the memorial hall are recorded the brutal details of what happened in Nanjing from 13 December 1937 to the end of January 1938, when up to 300,000 Chinese were killed. Impressive sections display the help given by Germans and Americans to rescue civilians by establishing International Safety Zones. The work of John Rabe, well known after the publication of his diaries in 1998, is prominently displayed. The dedication of less famous foreign businessmen and missionaries in saving thousands of Chinese from the massacre is also exhibited.

After emerging from the main hall visitors cross a wall and a space covered with rocks and stones – suggesting the thousands who died. A passage way leads into a silent memorial area for meditation. Here words are inscribed on the opposite wall, ending with the lines:

*"Let war be abolished,*
*Let peace be for all nations."*

In the next section there is a wall below which coloured paper chains have been laid. Some have been made by Chinese children, but there are also Hiroshima style crane bird paper chains made by Japanese children from the Japanese school in Shanghai. Above the chains are these words:

> "May there be friendship between the Chinese and Japanese peoples."

The final section is a garden with a border of yellow flowers. A plaque shows that the garden was donated by a Japanese businessman. The garden leads up to a monument to Peace in the form of a mother holding a dove aloft in her right hand. On the back of the statue is the following inscription:

> *"The statue Peace ... expresses the Chinese people's abhorrence of war and massacre, their pursuit of peace and development, and their strong wish for a better future for all mankind ..... The 9 steps in front of the statue symbolize the progress by human beings toward permanent world peace."*

Like all the inscriptions in the museum the wording is in three languages: Chinese, English and Japanese.

The Museum does not want to foster hatred but ends with a strong plea for world peace, for friendship between Chinese and Japanese, and for the abolition of war. The curator of the museum, Zhu Chengshan, said at the re-opening of the memorial in December 2007: "In the past it was just about the Great Nanjing Massacre – now the peaceful content is more important." Zhu has been the curator since 1991 and his influence in the transformed museum is significant. He has been to Japan more than forty times and met many Japanese politicians and historians. He has said, "This memorial hall was not built to fan anti-Japanese sentiment. Its purpose is to help ensure that our memories of the war do not fade, not to condemn the Japanese people."

Every year Japanese peace activists make a point of coming to the museum on 13 December, the anniversary of the fall of Nanjing. Other groups come during the year, such as the Japanese Tree-Planting group linked to the Japanese-China Friendship Association. They come to commemorate the victims of the massacre by planting trees as a way of expressing their remorse. A more unusual visitor was Ishikawa Yoshimi, a manga artist, who came on 15 August 2009 to attend the opening of his exhibition by Japanese manga artists. The symbolic date of 15 August was deliberate as he exhibited cartoons describing the wartime suffering of the Japanese. To hold such an exhibit at the Nanjing massacre memorial was as unlikely as arranging for a Chinese massacre exhibit in the Hiroshima Peace Museum. It took three years hard work to persuade the authorities to allow it to take place. Ishikawa however had the support of Zhu Chengshan. He accepted that this sharing of war memories was consistent with the fundamental purpose of the museum to promote peace and not hatred of the Japanese.

## John Rabe House

John Rabe's diary was published in Japan with the title, *Nankin no Shinjitsu (*The Truth about Nanjing), and quickly became a best seller in the late 1990s.

The John Rabe Research and Exchange Centre for Peace and Reconciliation, opened in 2008, welcomes students from around the world to come and take part in activities at the centre and to pursue their own research. Students have come from Japan, including volunteers from the International Christian University in Tokyo. Prof. Yang Shanyou is the director of the Centre. He has written a number of papers concerning John Rabe and the work that has developed from his former residence. The purpose of the Centre is to promote peacemaking and peace studies.

## Peace Studies in China

The first steps towards introducing peace studies as an academic discipline in China were made in 2000 when co-operation between the World History Study Section in the History Department of Nanjing and the Centre for Peace and Reconciliation Studies at Coventry University was established. After Professor Liu Cheng completed a graduate course in peace studies at Coventry University in 2003, he initiated the study of peace related issues in Nanjing University. He was able to introduce courses for undergraduates and post-graduate students and to write the first major original textbook on peace studies by a Chinese scholar. Peace research in China was launched through an International Symposium on Peace Studies in March 2005, with extensive coverage in academic circles. More recently in May 2011 another conference was held in Nanjing University called, "Peace Studies: Perspectives on Religion, Peace and War."

Peace researchers in China and Japan plan to have regular dialogue meetings beginning with a forum in Beijing, which took place in November 2015. Prof. Liu

Cheng established the first peace studies website in China in 2014 (www.peacestudiesinchina.org).

China has emerged with many bitter memories from its turbulent passage through the twentieth century. War and peace are subjects of deep-rooted emotional history. China's past is still too close for unbiased research and assessment. Present stability seems to have been won by military victories and prowess. However peace does not grow out of a barrel of a gun. On the positive side the Chinese government wishes to promote a harmonious society and to maintain peaceful international relations. Realism suggests that conflicts will arise and that these may increase as China's powerful economic expansion continues apace. How then can peace studies contribute to conflict resolution?

Prof. Liu Cheng believes that Nanjing's past must be remembered, but the memories of the 1937 massacre must not be used to perpetuate bitterness and hatred. As a historian he knows that history is a treasure house of lessons for the future of humanity. But he knows too that unscrupulous people can manipulate the past to promote their own agendas. The challenge for educationalists is to enable students to study history with a view to learning what makes for peace and how to achieve peaceful solutions. For this to be successful students should apply peace principles to their own lives, in order to understand that the pursuit of peace is both practically possible and vitally important to human beings.

In 2009 the Nanjing Publishing Company published a set of three books for use in Schools at elementary, middle and high school levels, edited by Liu Cheng. Subsequently this set of school textbooks was awarded a prize for being in the top 100 new books published in China in 2009-2010. With government approval Nanjing High School became the first school to order and use the textbooks. If this example is followed there could be a breakthrough for peace studies in China as a whole. Importantly each book has an introduction by Professor Qian Chengdan, who is one of China's most distinguished historians. Currently at Beijing University, he was formerly at Nanjing, where he supported the development of peace studies. In his introduction Prof. Qian emphasizes that peace is not merely the absence of war, but includes struggles for justice and human rights, and this peace can only be achieved through non-violence.

In tackling the legacy of the Nanjing massacre the textbook for High Schools states that the aim of the course is to help the young generation to avoid repeating the Nanjing tragedy, to understand modern Japan correctly and to actively pursue the goal of world peace. In relations with Japan this raises a number of questions. How can China and Japan develop normal relations without the psychological tensions that lurk in the memory of a brutal 15 year war? How can China and Japan avoid emotional reactions when conflicts between them erupt? When the whole school engages in special activities during the week of December 13, the aim is to inspire a rational, non-violent response.

More recently Liu Cheng and Egon Spiegel have produced an unusual, illustrated book in Chinese and English, entitled, *Peacebuilding in a Globalized World*, published in Beijing in 2015 by the People's Publishing House.

Unlike Japan and western countries peace studies and peace museums are not popular in China. In Japan, the peace constitution adopted after the war and the demand for nuclear disarmament following the destruction of Hiroshima and Nagasaki by atomic bombs have generated a powerful desire for peace. In the west the campaign for nuclear disarmament also inspired peace studies. By contrast modern China was born out of the military campaigns of the PLA and Mao gloried in the power of his army. Never again will China allow the country to be subjected to military occupation by western or Japanese powers. The backbone of Chinese foreign policy is and will continue to be its overwhelming military budget. Though current Chinese leaders espouse the policy of harmonious international relations, they have not abandoned the belief that power grows out of the barrel of a gun, or more harshly out of nuclear deterrents.

So what can peace studies achieve in China? The answer to this question may not be so difficult to define since the Chinese government is also committed to achieving a harmonious and peaceful world order. The practical challenge for peace studies is to show how conflicts can be dealt with in a non-violent manner to China's benefit.

## Liu Xiaobo

Liu Xiaobo is well known as the 2010 Nobel Peace Prize Winner. Less is known about his contribution to peace. He has taken a strong stand against the use of force and believes that any changes in China should come about through gradual change and peaceful means. Revolutions in China have always been achieved by the use of force, but these have not only cost millions of lives but have been harmful to the ongoing development of the nation and its people. So although Liu Xiaobo is well known for his criticism of the massacre of students and civilians at Tiananmen Square in 1989, he has rejected protests which make use of force in order to achieve their ends. But he goes further than simply adopting a policy of non-violent action to obtain political ends. Violent responses are usually prompted by bitterness and the desire for revenge. So he has sought to rid himself of hatred and revenge, and at his trial in 2009 he told his judges and guards that he did not think of them as his enemies and wished to treat them with respect. The English edition of his Chinese articles, published in 2012, is entitled *No Enemies, No Hatred*. In taking this peaceful stand he has been greatly influenced by Mahatma Gandhi, Martin Luther King Jr. and Vaclav Havel, and above all by Jesus Christ, who overcame overwhelming force through boundless love and forgiveness.

In relation to reconciliation between China and Japan, Liu Xiaobo's writings are of great significance. In searching for a peaceful way forward for China both domestically and in her international relations, he emphasises the importance of treating everyone with respect whatever their status or race. The principle of human dignity is the basis on which all should be treated whether they are our friends or opponents. In particular this applies to China's relations with Japan. He is particularly scornful of the brash, patriotic outpourings of invective against Japan, which pour forth from the Chinese media from time to time. He traces the rise in anti-Japanese propaganda to the policies of Jiang Zemin and Hu Jintao. This continues to affect the young generation of Chinese students and professionals, who tend to express anti-Japanese slogans. The periodic attacks on Japanese homes, businesses and cars is abhorrent to him and a symbol of thoughtless behaviour which is not worthy of free human beings. For him Japan is a neighbour to be treated with dignity and appreciation. Harmonious relations should extend to Japan. Freedom enables people to disagree with others, but not to denounce and defame.

# Relations between the governments of China and Japan

In August 1945 at the time of Japan's surrender, Chiang Kai-shek broadcast to the Chinese people calling on them to be benevolent towards Japanese and not to indulge in acts of revenge. He declared his policy to be one of "returning virtue for malice" toward Japan, and refused to dwell on Japan's past wrongs, for he held the Japanese military clique to be China's real enemy. Even before the war ended the KMT (the nationalist government) had initiated a policy of treating Japanese POWs well, to turn them against their own government. Therefore when the KMT drew up a list of Japanese military leaders to be put on trial as war criminals, the focus was on judging the generals responsible for the Nanjing massacre. When the Communist Party defeated Chiang Kai-shek they adopted a similar policy repatriating thousands of Japanese prisoners of war and pursuing informal trade links with Japan. From this we can see that the broad outlines of China's policy toward Japanese responsibility for the war bore similarities under both the KMT and CCP.

Despite Mao's policy of promoting friendship with Japan, it was not until 1972 that diplomatic relations were established between the People's Republic of China and the Government of Japan. The joint communiqué issued in September 1972 contained nine clauses, including a preamble, in which the Japanese government acknowledged responsibility for the serious damage caused to the Chinese people through war. For its part, China renounced its demands for war reparations from Japan. In a substantial statement the two governments agreed *"to establish relations of perpetual peace and friendship between the two countries on the basis of the principles of mutual respect for sovereignty and territorial integrity, mutual non-aggression, non-interference in each other's internal affairs, equality and mutual benefit and peaceful co-existence. The two Governments confirm that, in conformity with the foregoing principles and the principles of the Charter of the United Nations, Japan and China shall in their mutual relations settle all disputes by peaceful means and shall refrain from the use or threat of force."* For a detailed account of the negotiations which led to this agreement and for an analysis of how both sides understood the provisions, see Yang Zhihui's chapter in *Toward a History Beyond Borders* (op.cit., pp. 372-410).

In 1978 after the Cultural Revolution Deng Xiaoping became the first top Chinese leader to visit Japan and signed the Treaty of Peace and Friendship with the prime minister of Japan, Fukuda Takeo, which enabled trade to blossom and flourish between the two countries. However in the 1980's the Deng regime chose to reverse Mao's benign attitude to Japan when he reactivated a patriotic desire for revenge and denounced the Japanese attitude to its wartime military atrocities. It was Deng who set the tone for the present Chinese use of the history card against Japan. On the other side Japan never made the most of the benevolence of Chiang Kai-shek and Mao Zedong by facing up to its wartime record and rejecting not only war but the leaders who destroyed Japan's reputation in the East Asian countries they had invaded.

Nevertheless trade has flourished between China and Japan. After 1978 Japan invested trillions of yen in the Chinese economy, which helped China's industry to take off in spectacular fashion in the 1980's and 1990's. China became Japan's largest trading partner in 2009 and Japan is China's second most important partner after the USA.

In 2012 Japan had 23,094 companies operating in China, which was much more than any other country. Total bilateral trade in 2013 amounted to $312 billion.

In 1998 President Jiang Zemin became the first Chinese head of state to pay an official visit to Japan. This was followed ten years later by an important state visit from President Hu Jintao, which reaffirmed the desire for friendly relations between the two powers. In May 2012 China, Japan and Korea agreed to continue talks toward framing a detailed trilateral trade agreement. Though subsequent events have delayed progress, this project should not be forgotten. Recently, on 1st November 2015 after a 3 year gap, the leaders of China, Japan and Korea agreed in Seoul to completely restore the trade and security ties between the three countries. Chinese Premier Li Keqiang, Japanese Prime Minister Shinzo Abe and South Korean President Park Geun-hye said in a joint statement that "trilateral co-operation has been completely restored on the occasion of this summit meeting." They also maintained their goal of "denuclearising" North Korea.

Apart from official visitors it is worth noting that the two-way flow of visitors between China and Japan has been increasing rapidly. In 1972 there were only 9,000 visitors, by 1980 the figure was 90,000, and this had multiplied tenfold by 1993 to 900,000. Of greater importance is the number of long term residents in both countries. In 2006 there were nearly 115,000 Japanese long term residents in China and nearly 520,000 Chinese residents in Japan, which had increased to 649,000 by 2013. This figure is likely to increase as will the flow of Chinese tourists to Japan. In 2014 Chinese tourists to Japan increased by 83% to 2.4 million.

In March 2011 Japan's earthquake and tsunami shook the world. China's rapid show of support and solidarity with its Asian neighbour in distress contrasted sharply with the noisy anti-Japanese demonstrations in some Chinese cities after the Diaoyo/Senkaku Islands dispute of September 2010. After the earthquake, officially sanctioned editorials talked about shared pain and what China can learn from Japan's orderly response to the disaster. A commentary from the official state-run news agency, Xinhua, recalled how Japan had aided China in 2008 after the Sichuan earthquake, when many ordinary Japanese lined up to make donations and a Japanese rescue team helped recover victims. *"The willingness and readiness to help each other is just a natural reflection of the time-honoured friendly bond between the two neighbouring Oriental civilizations. The virtue of returning the favour after receiving one runs in the blood of both nations,"* commented Xinhua.

# Vision for Reconciliation

Reconciliation is a journey in which we travel from being enemies to becoming friends. Every journey has its story. We have told our reconciliation story, an ongoing journey which is not yet complete. Nations too have their stories, as their people interact with their neighbours. They too can travel on the path, which leads from conflict to the exploration of friendship. China and Japan committed themselves in 1972 to pursuing this path. Despite this commitment barriers like mountains remain between China and Japan, posing a perpetual question: What can be done to bring about reconciliation between the two countries and their people?

The barriers between China and Japan are well known. They can be viewed as divisions relating to the past, present and future of both countries. All serious international conflicts have a long history. They cannot be solved unless both parties are willing to address their history.

## Past, Present and Future

The past century has been a painful one for both countries, but in quite different ways. For China the period from 1895 to 1945 was one of humiliation at the hands of Japan, starting with the loss of Taiwan, annexed by Japan in 1895. More humiliation followed in the indemnity paid to Japan after the Boxer Rebellion in 1900, the Japanese occupation of Qingdao in 1915 and the invasion of Manchuria after the Liutiaohu Incident in 1931. What weighs most in the Chinese memory now is the Sino-Japanese War of 1937-1945, in China commonly called the War of Resistance against Japan, and the Nanjing Massacre (December 1937). China sees herself as the victim of Japanese aggression, an aggression that must never be allowed to happen again.

Japan looks back on the past century with a mixture of pride and pain. Both before 1940 and after 1960 Japan achieved astonishing industrial and technological advance in modernising itself to compete on the level of equality with western powers. In between, the country suffered total defeat in 1945 with the occupation by American forces and the abyss of nuclear destruction inflicted by atom bombs at Hiroshima and Nagasaki.

Attitudes play a major part in shaping national identities. Both sides see themselves as victims. Yet this identity is not reciprocal, for China inflicted no war damage on Japan. Japan was the victim of the west, but China was the victim of Japan's war machine. China does not forget the past and is determined never to be so weak as to be invaded again. Both sides are proud and confident, but China suspects that Japan continues to see herself as culturally and technologically superior. This suspicion is a serious matter of concern, because lack of respect for their Chinese neighbours gave rise to Japanese atrocities inflicted on civilians in their occupation of China.

As far as the present is concerned relations are marked by friction, cooperation and the changing world order. Friction has increased since 2010 with the dispute over the Senkaku/Diaoyu Islands threatening to escalate. The dispute over these islands is one aspect of China's maritime expansion, which can be seen in the attempts to enforce claims to the ownership of many islands in the South China Sea and in the increase in Chinese naval power. Tension also continues over the following issues: the numbers killed in the Nanjing massacre, the Yasukuni

Shrine, claims to oil and gas reserves in the East China Sea, compensation for 'comfort women', Japanese school textbooks and Taiwan. Nevertheless economic cooperation remains the dominant feature of relations between the two countries. In 2009 China became Japan's largest trading partner and Japan is China's second most important partner after the USA. The relative change in world league tables is unsettling for Japan. China overtook Japan as the world's second largest economy in 2010. Japan is no longer the dominant world power it was in the 1980s and is losing its technological superiority, even though China is still behind in this respect.

Looking to the future, new problems arising from the unresolved conflicts in the past and the rising power and wealth of resurgent China can be expected. Japan fears what China will do when it becomes all-powerful as a world super-power. China fears that Japan will revert to a military regime, abandoning its peace constitution and aligning itself with other world powers against China. These fears will unsettle attempts to build harmonious cooperation between East Asia's major powers.

## Forgiveness, Apology and Reconciliation

In discussion of longstanding conflicts between countries and attempts at peace building three terms are often prominent: forgiveness, apology and reconciliation. These three words have been given more attention in literature since 1990 when they were popularised by the events in South Africa that led to the removal of apartheid without bloodshed. The definition and understanding of these concepts is of critical importance.

## Forgiveness

The most prominent example of forgiveness in South Africa was the action of Nelson Mandela himself. He went into prison in 1963 an angry man, committed to fighting the wrongs of apartheid with violence. Twenty-seven years later he walked free from prison, a transformed person with a forgiving spirit. Because Mandela was the leader of the African National Congress (ANC) his actions and those of the South African government were of immense importance and had profound repercussions. If Mandela had not forgiven his captors, South Africa would have been plunged into bloodshed and civil war. Instead he forgave his political opponents and his warders, and invited his former jailer to be a VIP guest at his presidential inauguration. Mandela's peaceful revolution is the most powerful endorsement of Desmond Tutu's book entitled *No Future Without Forgiveness.*

Forgiveness concerns wrongdoing in the past, and is a way of undoing the hurtful consequences of what has been done without excuse or cover up. It can be seen to operate most clearly at the interpersonal level, when two parties interact in dealing with an injury done by one party to the other. Here the forgiveness process must have at least four phases: the wrongdoing is acknowledged, both parties change their view of the other and of themselves, the victim forgoes revenge and in contact between the parties forgiveness is requested and given. This process took place when Eric Lomax met Nagase Takashi again nearly 50 years after the war, as recounted in an earlier chapter. In the moving climax of Lomax's book he tells how he finally laid to rest the bitterness and hatred that torture had generated, when he met Nagase alone in a quiet Tokyo hotel room and assured him of his total forgiveness. Nagase had won his respect by his repentance and his sincerity.

True forgiveness is costly for both parties, as it was for Lomax and Nagase, because it exposes the abuse, the pain, the hurt and the truth. The injured person has to be willing to give up his/her resentment and desire for revenge, whilst the wrongdoer must acknowledge that they were responsible for the injury, express their sorrow and repair the damage where possible.

Forgiveness is not forgetting. Memory is essential if the wrong is to be acknowledged and dealt with. It is important for both sides to remember, so that atrocities do not recur. The Preamble of the 1995 Act which set up the South African Truth and Reconciliation Commission puts it well when it states that, *it is deemed necessary to establish the truth in relation to past events as well as the motives for and circumstances in which gross violations of human rights have occurred, and to make the findings known in order to prevent repetition of such acts in future.*

Forgiveness is not condoning or excusing evils that have been committed. Forgiveness differs from mercy, or pity, where the well-off care for the weak, for in forgiveness both parties are equals. Nor is forgiveness a judicial act of pardon. Forgiveness is not being sentimental, for though it deals with emotion it requires deliberate action.

In Gandhi's commitment to *ahimsa* (non-violence) we find a different, Asian view of the importance of forgiveness. Gandhi believed, in stark contrast to Mao and Stalin, that power does not grow out of the barrel of a gun. He opposed the British not with the sword but with unflinching adherence to the truth, whatever the cost. The truth, or reality, is that beneath appearances all is one. Therefore in reality there is no enemy, and no "other", who is against us. From this perspective vengeance inspired by hatred is folly and forgiveness of all who act against us is an essential virtue. Forgiveness has to be extended to rulers who impose unjust laws, even when the *satyagrahi* (non-violent protester) is penalised for disobeying the oppressor.

Liu Xiaobo, drawing on a different understanding of the nature of the world, came to the same conclusion. He said to his judges at his trial: *I have no enemies, and no hatred. None of the police who have watched, arrested, or interrogated me, none of the prosecutors who have indicted me, and none of the judges who will judge me are my enemies......Hatred only eats away at a person's intelligence and conscience, and an enemy mentality can poison the spirit of an entire people......I hope that I can answer the regime's enmity with utmost benevolence, and can use love to dissipate hate* (Liu Xiaobo, No Enemies, No Hatred, Harvard, 2012, p. 322f.).

Writers differ on whether they believe the forgiveness process can take place between nations. Some define forgiveness as essentially an interpersonal interaction and therefore not possible between countries. Desmond Tutu has famously argued for the necessity of forgiveness in politics, citing the experiences of South Africa. He notes that whereas previously when he had visited Israel and Palestine he had not gained a hearing, after the transformation of South Africa and the inauguration of the Truth and Reconciliation Commission there was a willingness to listen to what he had to say about forgiveness between divided peoples. Tutu believes that leaders are persons representing communities, who can turn from revenge and view their former enemies differently.

However Long & Brecke in their study of conflict resolution found that whilst the forgiveness process was effective in civil conflicts like South Africa, it was not so evident in conflicts between countries. Nations do not usually engage as individuals do in a reciprocal interaction where one side says 'Sorry' and the other side responds with unmistakeable acceptance (for example, as in the fourfold process mentioned above). Nevertheless elements of forgiveness are at work as we shall see in political apology and in steps toward reconciliation between countries which have been in conflict.

Many victims of war atrocities are unable to escape the bitterness they justly feel without any apology from or contact with their wartime enemies. Concerning this predicament Desmond Tutu writes: "If the victim could forgive only when the culprit confessed, then the victim would be locked into the culprit's whim ..." The evidence of some participants in the South African Truth and Reconciliation hearings supports this view. Take the example of Beth Savage who had been shot and blown up by a grenade. She said, "What I really want is to meet the man who threw the hand-grenade. I would want to do it in a spirit of forgiveness, in the hope that he, for whatever reason, will also forgive me." In that spirit she was able to forgive her attackers, even if they were unwilling to meet her.

Christians following the example of Jesus Christ hold that the victim can take the initiative in renouncing revenge and anger and express forgiveness for the torture they suffered at the hands of their attackers. They also believe that when Jesus prayed on the cross for his killers and when he sacrificed his life for the sins of humanity, this did not mean automatic pardon for all, but requires confession and repentance in response from anyone who wishes to receive forgiveness from God. The example of Jesus as the victim who took the initiative to forgive before his enemies showed any sign of remorse opens up new possibilities for victims even in the conflict between

China and Japan. In 1940 German bombers destroyed the English city of Coventry. The city's medieval cathedral was burnt to ashes. The next morning, the Dean in charge of the cathedral wrote in chalk on a blackened wall the words of Jesus as he died on the cross, *Father, forgive.* We all need forgiveness. In war both sides need to forgive and to be forgiven. After the war Coventry sent people to Germany to help rebuild Dresden, which had been annihilated by British bombers. Out of that action developed the International Centre for Reconciliation based at Coventry cathedral, which now has centres all over the world. Andrew White, a former director of the Coventry centre, now a peacemaker in Baghdad, writes: "So often, in reconciliation talks, I am presented with a long list of the hurts that the other party has caused to that person or nation. Stored-up pain causes immense conflict and division. Yet, the principle of 'Father, forgive' provides a way out of this trap ..... Forgiveness releases people who are trapped in the past to become all they were intended to be, now in the present and in the future" *(Father Forgive,* p.26, Oxford 2013).

Simon Wiesenthal in his anthology *The Sunflower,* deals with a related question, whether the living have the right to forgive on behalf of those who have suffered and died at the hands of their foes. This dilemma is faced by communities where atrocities have taken place and especially by those whose relatives have been killed. The living can hardly presume to act on behalf of those who suffered so grievously. If their relatives and countrymen are to begin to forgive it can only be on their own behalf, being willing to let their resentment and hostility go, if their former enemies acknowledge their guilt. Another writer goes further and says forgiveness is in the power of the victims. It is their initiative and their prerogative. Forgiveness does not require any conditions when it is born of love, for love is free (T. Gorringe, *God's Just Vengeance,* Cambridge 1996, p.267).

## Apology

This brings us to the meaning of apology and its place in international politics. Apology can only take place when the guilty party is willing to say 'Sorry'. In any language the most difficult words to say to your enemy are, 'I am sorry'; indeed some languages do not have such a word or expression, instead the thought has to be expressed more obliquely. Politicians and national leaders find it even more difficult to admit to any fault. To his great credit the former president of South Africa, F.W. de Klerk, fervently apologised for the policy of apartheid and for the pain it had caused when he appeared before the Truth and Reconciliation Commission in 1997.

The importance of apology is clearly recognised in conflicts between states. To be effective a national apology should state clearly that wrongdoing has occurred, accept responsibility for this and express respect for the honour of the offended country. Griswold notes that as a public statement apology puts truth on record as a narrative, and in doing so draws attention to the place of narrative in a meaningful apology. The people of both sides have stories to tell, not only of their sufferings but of how they are beginning to view their opponents differently, even though there is no unanimity in their accounts. At the national level there may be an attempt to come to a consensus about their joint history as is currently happening in the meeting of Chinese and Japanese historians of the war period. Apology gives rise to the quest for a new narrative embracing the past in order to liberate the future.

On the importance of apology Ignatieff has this powerful appeal:

> "What each side, in the aftermath of a civil war, essentially demands is that 'the other side' face up to the deaths it caused. To deny the reality of these deaths is to treat them as a dream, as a nightmare. Without an apology, without recognition of what happened, the past cannot return to its place as the past. The ghosts will continue to stalk the battlements. Of course, an apology must reflect acceptance of the other side's grief ..." (M. Ignatieff, *The Warrior's Honour*, London, 1998, pp. 189-190).

Apology is more than regret. Mere regret only expresses the idea that it would have been better if the unfortunate events in the past had never happened. It is no better than saying, 'Let bygones be bygones', only for the bygones to remain. An apology takes responsibility for the harm that has been done and addresses the other party with the aim of restoring relations. So a country that has attacked and invaded its neighbour has to be truthful in admitting its past actions if it is to issue a true apology to its former foe.

## Reconciliation

Reconciliation is more complex than either forgiveness or apology, and unlike these two actions it is not in the power of anyone to give or to achieve. No one can give or grant reconciliation, except God himself.

Reconciliation sounds a peaceful word but it raises difficult questions in the very nature of the word. The use

## Vision for Reconciliation

of 're' before 'conciliation' implies a return to a desirable state before conflict occurred and poses the question 'what do we want to return to?' This in turn implies questions about the future: 'what exactly is the goal of the reconciliation process?' In the case of China and Japan we can look back in history and see that before 1500 the two countries were part of the same cultural family, where with the exception of the planned attacks by the Mongol fleet in the thirteenth century the two countries were friendly neighbours. As the Chinese Premier, Wen Jiabao, pointed out in 2007 in a memorable speech to the Japanese Diet, China and Japan had enjoyed centuries of friendly relations dating back to the Tang dynasty when Jianzhen, a Chinese monk, brought Buddhism to Japan in the $7^{th}$ century. The Japanese writer, Kanzo Uchimura, acknowledged in words Chinese can appreciate: "The country of Japan is only a part of China extended into the Pacific Ocean. It is true to regard Japanese civilisation as a kind of advanced Chinese civilisation." The preamble to the 1972 Japan-China Joint Communiqué affirmed that, "Japan and China are neighbouring countries, separated only by a strip of water with a long history of traditional friendship." Now, the future has to be addressed by both sides, for both have fears concerning the ambitions of the other and the possibility of threatening rivalry. All attempts to deal with the memories of past aggression will fail if there is no common vision for a harmonious relationship in the rest of this century.

Some will regard the goal of reconciliation as being the peace which follows the end of conflict, guns being silenced and the laying down of weapons. In 1945 fighting stopped and planes no longer bombed the enemy, but we are still struggling to come to terms with the bitterness that war engendered. The division between war-time enemies is not overcome merely by the passage of time.

Others will consider that when people give up thoughts of revenge and no longer plan acts of hostility toward former enemies that all is well. But reconciliation is much more than the absence of hostile action. It requires a constructive change in relationships from those driven by fear to those motivated by friendship and respect.

The idea of restored relationships is fundamental to the way the Bible treats this word. The Greek words translated by 'reconciliation' or 'reconcile' are all derived from 'allasso' meaning 'to change' or 'to exchange' or 'to become another', and this in turn comes from 'allos' meaning 'other'. The words suggest the sense of exchanging places with 'the other' and so overcoming the division between the two. Reconciliation is the process of overcoming alienation through identification with an erstwhile enemy, thus making friends. The Bible sees God as initiating this process and expecting people to treat each other as members of the same human family (*Reconciliation: Restoring Justice,* John W. de Gruchy, 2002, p.51).

In South Africa the meetings of the Truth and Reconciliation Commission caused many in the Afrikaner community to feel that they were all being regarded as guilty and being subjected to a witch-hunt. Desmond Tutu and his fellow commissioners were anxious to avoid a new division between victims and oppressors. The truth does divide as well as heal depending on the response of the hearers. As the truth of the atrocities suffered by so many innocent black citizens was broadcast in the media day after day there was every possibility that the Afrikaners would reject the whole process. Mandela said at the inauguration of the Commission: "The choice we have is not whether we should disclose the past, but how it will be done. It must be done in such a way that reconciliation and peace are promoted." He went on to observe that everyone in the country was a victim and everyone had suffered. Later another speaker pointed out that everyone is guilty. The German philosopher, Karl Jaspers, said bluntly in 1946: "Before God not only a few, or many, or even the majority, are guilty, but everybody!" The reconciliation process between Japan and China will make progress when both sides acknowledge that all were victims in the Second World War and that before God all need forgiveness.

Reconciliation is costly. It involves pain in facing up to the truth of past suffering. It requires honesty in admitting past failures to treat opponents as fully human. It demands justice in responding to the crimes committed. It will only succeed when it is understood that everyone is responsible for their actions in the past and for their contribution in the future to the wellbeing of all. It is not only governments and the powerful who are responsible for future harmony; every individual, every group, every part of society in every country has a vital contribution to make to a new world order.

Reconciliation can best be viewed as a journey, a journey from the past into the future. Where nations are concerned it is always a long journey, in which recovery from conflict takes decades not years. It is not a technique requiring better skills, processes and strategies for success, nor does it stop when the fires of conflict have been extinguished, for that is when the call to move on together is needed by both sides.

The journey of reconciliation is inspired by the voice of lament from the victims of violence. The cries of the victims come from both sides, from both Hiroshima and Nanjing. None are unaffected by the brokenness of this world, for what is broken is our relationship with others and ultimately with God, the source of life itself.

The journey is a long trek, because healing takes time. Healing of the heart takes longer than healing of the body. The ravages of war, the scars of Hiroshima and Nanjing and the trauma of torture are never forgotten. Countries need healing as much as individuals. A profound purpose of the Truth and Reconciliation Commission led by Desmond Tutu was to heal the wounds of apartheid and bring hope to a bitterly divided nation. Just as wounds may need to be exposed to fresh air, so all parts of society needed the fresh wind of truth to blow away the fog of government secretiveness. All sides need healing, though for different reasons.

The quest for reality sees both sides as human and rejects the view that the other side are monsters and to be treated as beasts. However, in the brutality of the Sino-Japanese war both aggressor and victims were dehumanised. This shocking degeneration has to be admitted and healed. Despite the depths to which humanity sinks in war and the barriers this creates seeds of hope are being sown. Out of sight and beneath the surface the divine spirit is ceaselessly at work in ways that are least expected. Sometimes these shoots of new life come to light and the evidence is seen in individuals who bridge the gap between old enemies. Through listening to the bitterness of victims, welcoming strangers and crossing racial and cultural boundaries reconciling work brings healing and transformation.

Political scientists have generally ignored reconciliation, seeing this as a process which does not apply to dealings between nation states. However two political scientists, a Chinese and a Korean, have recently argued for the possibility and importance of states engaging in deep reconciliation after being separated by a history of bitter warfare. Yinan He claims that her book, *The Search for Reconciliation: Sino-Japanese and German-*

*Polish Relations since World War II (2009)*, "is the first comprehensive treatment of the understudied subject of interstate reconciliation." The Korean academic, SH Heo, notes that the existing literature on cases where deep reconciliation has been achieved mostly deal with intrastate situations following conflict within a country, as in the case of South Africa. She focused in her book, *Reconciling Enemy States in Europe and Asia (2012)*, on international relations, believing that in politics relationships are all important and that national leaders like individuals can forgive or hate. Both writers are able to use the examples of the remarkable change in relations between Germany and France and between Germany and Poland in the past fifty years to show that reconciliation between states which have been bitterly divided by war is possible. The role played by Adenauer and De Gaulle, Brandt and Gomulka in the peace process was of supreme importance for their nations.

Kim Dae-jung provides an Asian approach to reconciliation in the Korean context. Though a Catholic Christian, he appealed to the Confucian virtues of coexistence and cooperation, which had long been honoured in Korean history, in his pursuit of peace. Like Nelson Mandela and Mahatma Gandhi, he had spent many years in prison and under house arrest. However this did not motivate him to seek revenge, instead like Mandela, he embodied forgiveness and reconciliation as the mainspring of his political platform. His bold outreach to North Korea through his 'sunshine' policy has been likened to the *Ostpolitik* of Willy Brandt. Both leaders took the initiative in reaching out to neighbouring countries with which they had been at war, risking their reputation in the pursuit of peace.

In international relations, as Liechty and Clegg point out, a true understanding of reconciliation has to be "built on the inter-locking dynamics of forgiveness, repentance, truth and justice, understood in part as religiously-rooted virtues, but also as basic dynamics (even when unnamed or unrecognized) of human interaction, including public life and therefore politics" (J.Liechty & C.Clegg: *Moving Beyond Secularism).* One of the means by which countries can promote reconciliation is by the use of what Long & Brecke call 'signalling', that is using a public event to signal their desire for a closer relationship. Signals may be given by means of a public event, which symbolises a desire for reconciliation, involving a leader of a country. Sadat's visit to Israel (1977), the first by an Arab leader, and his speech at the Knesset, the Israeli parliament, is a well known example, as is the action of Willy Brandt in kneeling before the memorial of the Warsaw ghetto (1970). Signalling in the context of international relations is the result of a unilateral initiative taken by one party, not the outcome of a joint deliberation between two countries in conflict. Such signals are effective when they are unexpected and costly for the initiator. Apology through signalling may be of practical importance if Japan and China are to journey further on the path to resolving their differences (*War and Reconciliation: Reason and Emotion in Conflict Resolution,* W.J. Long and P. Brecke, Cambridge MIT, 2003).

# Preparing for Partnership

## Reconciliation and International Relations

The context in which any discussion of Sino-Japanese relations takes place is the field of international relations. Countries, like individuals, are guided by their perception of their own self-interests. Also, like individuals, they do not exist as isolated entities but interact with other states. In this interaction which we call international relations, some principles should be recognised for the good of the nations concerned, just as principles guide the interaction of citizens in any society. What should these principles be?

The first principle, as in any law abiding society, is the principle of justice. All countries have laws, which are there to prevent lawlessness for the stability of the government and the benefit of the citizens. The purpose of the legal system should be the administration of justice for the benefit of all. It is possible to have laws without justice, but where laws are framed with the intention of being just they commend themselves to the people. Similarly in international relations if there is to be a legal framework, such as that provided in treaties or trade agreements, this will be more likely to be accepted if its provisions are seen to be in accord with the principles of justice.

From this point of view, justice requires governments to pursue right dealings with other nations in their quest for wealth and security. This in turn means that countries should be opposed to imperial domination by any nation. Consequently as noted in the *Jubilee Manifesto* (ed. M. Schluter & J.Ashcroft, p.260): "Unjust regimes forfeit their legitimacy by their actions against their own people and against other nations."

A second principle is partnership. Effective partnership is based on trust and fidelity. Diplomatic relations and treaties between states depend on a measure of trust between the partners. For this to be truly effective between several nations in an area, such as East Asia, a supra-national vision is needed to which all can concur. This would not require uniform goals for the partners, but would include respect for cultural and national differences. Japanese political scientist, Kensuke Takayasu, commenting on Japan's need to "figure out what kind of international order is preferable for itself," notes that, "Japan's influence will increase in global affairs through multilateral partnerships" (Asahi Shimbun January 11, 2013).

A third principle could be termed harmonious growth as opposed to war. Where there has been conflict the restoration of broken relationships becomes of supreme importance. For Japan and China this is the crucial element that could enable the two countries to overcome the legacy of the past. A commitment to mutual harmonious growth would pave the way for both sides to face the memories of war and find solutions acceptable to both countries. True reconciliation would then become a possibility.

We turn now to the specific question: What can be done to bring about reconciliation between Japan and China?

## What has already been done?

During the past seventy years a great deal has been done to normalise relations between Japan and China. There is a free flow of trade and visitors between the two countries. It is worth recording how much progress has already been made before discussing what could be done to address the obstacles that remain from the past.

We have noted the outstanding work done by some individuals in both countries. In Japan the members of the Chukiren association have spoken out with great cost to themselves to inform their countrymen of the inhuman treatment inflicted by the Japanese military on China. Peace museums, like the one supported by Kazuyo Yamane in Kochi City, graphically depict what happened in the Sino-Japanese war in a bold attempt to communicate with young people. Journalists like Honda Katsuichi have put their lives on the line to investigate and record the atrocities caused by the practice of the Three-Alls (*Sanko),* 'kill all, loot all, burn all', which led to the Nanjing massacre. Prof. Muraoka is one of many Japanese who have sought to apologise for war atrocities by pilgrimage to China and other neighbouring countries invaded in the war, to offer restitution by deeds as well as words. In China many unknown individuals promote peace with Japan, especially those who have studied in Japan or worked there. We have noted that in Nanjing there are signs of hope. Zhu Chengshan, the director of the Nanjing Memorial Museum, has shaped the new museum to be a symbol of peace not a sign of revenge. The John Rabe House has become a centre for reconciliation. Prof. Liu Cheng has established peace studies in Nanjing University. These are only a selection of the many individuals who could be named.

For our purposes here cooperation at international level by the governments of China and Japan is most significant. Here the main events have been the 1972 establishment of diplomatic relations for the first time between the Communist government of the People's

Republic of China and the government of Japan. This was followed by the Treaty of Peace and Friendship signed in 1978, which enabled trade to grow between the two countries, aided by massive investment from Japan. Japan has issued apologies, of which the most often quoted is the one given by Prime Minister Murayama in 1995. There have been important visits by leaders including those of China's presidents to Japan in 1998 and 2008. Crises that have arisen, such as the dispute over the Diaoyo/Senkaku islands, have not been allowed to escalate into conflict. China responded positively to Japan's assistance at the time of the Sichuan earthquake in 2008 by condolences and prompt action after the Fukushima earthquake and tsunami of 2011.

The most significant and unexpected action by China was taken by Zhou Enlai in his decision in 1955 to treat the Japanese war criminals imprisoned in Fushun with respect not revenge. We may never know why Zhou Enlai decided to adopt such a remarkable response to war crimes, but the example he set is pregnant with meaning for any who wish to see reconciliation between China and Japan. First, he totally rejected the policy of revenge. Second he understood that even war criminals should be treated as human beings. This understanding went to the heart of the matter, because it eventually helped the prisoners to realise that they had been dehumanised by their own war machine. It was not just that they had treated their Chinese victims as less than human, they had themselves stopped behaving as human beings in the war. Zhou wisely insisted on them accepting responsibility for their actions, despite their protests. No doubt fearing the consequences of being labelled 'war criminals', the soldiers had argued that they were only obeying orders. But these orders had made them do things they would never have dreamt of doing at home. On reflection they came to see that the imperial orders they had obeyed had also dehumanised them. Zhou chose to treat them well, giving them the best food, ordering his guards to help them when they fell ill, and saving them from the hard labour they had suffered in Siberia. As a result they began to confess the atrocities they had committed. Amazingly Zhou decided not to convict the great majority of any crimes and to release them without charge. Even the few who were charged with war crimes were released within five years. Believing that this treatment would mean that the prisoners would return to Japan to work for peace not war, Zhou was proved right by the actions of the Chukiren. Although as far as we know, words of forgiveness were never spoken by the Chinese, Zhou's policy was forgiveness in action. If Zhou Enlai's example were to be followed today by both sides reconciliation would not be a distant dream.

# What could Japan do to bring about reconciliation with China?

## Apologies

As has already been mentioned in a previous chapter, Japan has apologised for the damage inflicted on her Asian neighbours by her aggression during the war. Questions still remain whether these apologies have been adequate and whether anything more needs to be said.

In the most well known Apology issued by a Japanese Prime Minister, Tomiichi Murayama chose to make his statement on the fiftieth anniversary of the end of the Pacific War, on 15 August 1995. He addressed those who mourned for all victims both in Japan and other countries, who had suffered "following a mistaken national policy". He acknowledged that Japan "through its colonial rule and aggression, caused tremendous damage and suffering to the people of many countries, particularly to those of Asian nations."

This statement is honest in so far as it goes, but those who suffered from Japan's aggression want more specific acknowledgement than this. There is no mention here of China despite the 20 million or more Chinese who were killed in the war, the great majority of whom were civilians. No Japanese prime minister has explicitly apologised for the massacre in Nanjing.

It is true that Japanese school textbooks do give details about the slaughter in Nanjing, and do give some details of the invasion of north-east China following the Manchurian Incident and the Marco Polo Bridge affair, which led to all-out war with China in 1937. But more needs to be done by the government to officially acknowledge these events both within Japan and China. A recent estimate of war casualties in China concludes that: "All told, in eight years of war in China, Japan suffered 410,000 killed and 920,000 wounded. Although no reliable figures are available for Chinese losses, perhaps as many as 10 million Chinese soldiers died during the fighting, and civilian casualties certainly were as high if not double that figure ...... It must always be remembered that between July 1937 and September 1945 China endured enormous suffering on a scale so great that no one has yet captured its totality" (*The Battle for China*, ed. M.Peattie, E.J.Drea & H.van de Ven, Stanford, 2011, p.46f.).

As we have already seen, to be effective a national apology has to state what wrong has been done, must take responsibility for this and should express respect for the invaded country. If Japan were to issue a statement to

China condemning the military aggression which led to the Nanjing massacre and millions of deaths of Chinese victims, this would mark a new milestone on the way to reconciliation. The issue of 'comfort women' in China also has to be officially admitted and addressed, since there are still right-wing Japanese writers who refuse to admit the plain evidence of Japanese army policy tracked down by Yoshimi Yoshiaki.

On the other hand for China to demand yet another apology from Japan would be counter-productive. An apology has to be freely given, otherwise it is worthless. Japan believes that it has issued more than twenty official apologies. In addition to these official government statements many Japanese have given their own individual or group apologies, which have been very specific and have gone far beyond the language of their political leaders. We note that a former editorial writer for the Beijing People's Daily, Ma Licheng, has urged the Chinese government to desist from demanding apologies from Japan. He believes that the issue of apologies has already been settled, because Japanese leaders have publicly expressed remorse over their nation's wartime past. In his book, *There is No Future for Hatred* (Hong Kong, 2014), he urges China to follow a different path in pursuit of peace with Japan. "Peace and quiet will not be achieved in Asia", he writes, "without reconciliation between Japan and China. The key is to cut the chain of hatred."

## Compensation

In 1972 China renounced all claims for war reparations from Japan. At that time Mao had more pressing matters to think about than obtaining compensation from Japan. China was isolated and needed to establish diplomatic and trade relations with Japan. So China agreed "that in the interest of the friendship between the Chinese and Japanese peoples, it renounces its demand for war reparation from Japan." Subsequently China and Japan signed a Treaty for Peace and Friendship in 1978, which established trade links between the two countries and also paved the way for Japanese assistance in promoting China's economic development. This provision of goods and services has been the means by which Japan has provided non-compensatory aid to East Asian countries attacked by Japan in the war. China's economy has benefited in this way from Japanese aid by billions of dollars since 1980. The cumulative amount of aid given to China by Japan has been calculated as 3.66 trillion yen.

However the issue of compensation for individuals has not disappeared. From the late 1980s Chinese started to write to the Japanese embassy in China claiming compensation for war damages. In addition petitions were submitted to the National People's Congress asking for compensation from Japan for individuals on the basis that the 1972 renunciation of reparations only concerned government losses. In the 1990s Chinese war victims began to file claims in Japanese courts against the Japanese government and some Japanese companies, demanding monetary compensation for the injuries they suffered in the Japanese invasion of China. Attempts by Chinese to obtain legal redress in Tokyo courts against the government of Japan have failed, despite support from some Japanese veterans groups, because the courts have ruled that China renounced its demand for reparations in 1972. However there are two claims against Japanese companies that have been successful. One was the claim by Hanaoka victims representing 986 Chinese labourers who were deported to Japan and forced to work on a river project in north-eastern Japan run by the Kajima construction company. This was successfully concluded in November 2000 and resulted in compensation being paid to the victims or their families. The Hanaoka Reconciliation was the first case in which a Japanese corporation agreed to compensate foreign wartime victims through a fund set up for that purpose. Kajima agreed to pay 500 million yen into this fund. The second example that can be cited is the Nishimatsu Yasuno Reconciliation for Chinese victims who were forced to work at the Hiroshima Yasuno Power station during the war. The agreement included a written apology and funds for the construction of a memorial, as well as compensation money for the victims and their families. For details see the article by Li Enmin in *Rekishi and Wakai* (History & Reconciliation) by Kurosawa Fumitaka and Ian Nish (Tokyo, 2011). Recently, Mitsubishi Materials announced in July 2015 that the corporation will pay compensation to Chinese victims of forced labour brought to Japan during the Second World War to work at their mines and construction sites. Their spokesman said the company will express "deep remorse" and "sincere apologies" to the victims and build a monument to honour them. This is a welcome move to mark the 70th anniversary of the end of the Pacific War. Mitsubishi have now announced (in 2016) that they will pay about 3,700 surviving victims and their next of kin 100,000 Yuan each, and build a memorial statue for the victims.

The Chinese government has not actively supported the claims of its citizens to monetary compensation, nor has it opposed the rights of individuals to file legal suits in Japan. It continues to uphold the 1972 agreement. Ma Licheng believes that Japan has more than compensated the Chinese government through substantial economic aid, which was particularly important from 1980 – 2000. For a thorough examination of this issue see Yang

Zhihui's presentation, "From War Reparation to Postwar Reparation" in *Toward a History Beyond Borders* (pp. 372-410).

Some western sinologists believe that even at this late stage opening an avenue for legal redress would give Chinese families, who lost parents and children through wartime atrocities, the recognition they crave. However now that nearly 70 years have passed since the end of the war, it seems unlikely that such claims will be successful without a change of heart by the Japanese government.

In addition to Chinese families, whose members were killed by Japanese soldiers, there are at least two other Chinese groups who have an understandable claim for compensation.

Chinese 'comfort women' compelled to serve the Japanese military as prostitutes are one group. Although Japan set up an unofficial "Asia Women's Fund" in 1995 to give material compensation and to provide each surviving 'comfort woman' with a signed apology from the then prime minister, Tomiichi Murayama, many 'comfort women' have rejected these payments and continue to seek an official apology and compensation, because of the unofficial nature of the fund. The fund was not endorsed by the Japanese Parliament and the payments given were not the equivalent of legal compensation.

A very different, yet specific claim, is that of the Hong Kong Reparation Society. During the war the Japanese military administration compelled all Hong Kong residents to exchange their local currency, the Hong Kong dollar, for bank notes issued by the Bank of Tokyo. At the end of the war the Japanese government announced that all these yen denomination notes were invalid and worthless. At the time this was an unimaginable loss for Hong Kong citizens, who have never been compensated for their losses. Again time seems to be running out on this issue, and there is not much appetite for pursuing it in Hong Kong today.

## Dramatic Action

In a previous section we drew attention to the findings of Long & Brecke that a form of reconciliation event, which has proved effective, is a dramatic signal by one country that conveys more than mere words could do in helping to heal past wounds. Famous incidents of this kind include Sadat's visit to the Israeli Knesset and Brandt's act of kneeling before the commemoration memorial of the Warsaw ghetto. Willy Brandt's action was not a publicity stunt, but a humble expression of sincere contrition and a longing for reconciliation with Poland. By kneeling before the memorial to Jews murdered by German SS units in 1943 he conveyed the clear message to the Polish nation that Germans offered their heartfelt repentance. In a speech in honour of Brandt in 1989, President Richard von Weizsäcker said to Brandt:

> *Power without morality is a dead-end street, because it finds no trust. You have found trust and used it.*

On 12 August 2015 Yukio Hatoyama, former Prime Minister of Japan, fell on his knees in silent prayer on the site of the former prison in Seoul, where thousands of Koreans were tortured under Japanese rule between 1910 – 1945. If he could do that how much more effective it would be if the current Japanese Prime Minister were to do the same and also kneel before the Nanjing memorial to Chinese massacred there in 1937.

**The Emperor** represents Japan in a unique way. His action in broadcasting to the Japanese people for the first time in August 1945 brought the war to an abrupt end. An apology by the Emperor would have dramatic effect. Some Japanese believe that Emperor Akihito should apologise for actions taken by his father, Emperor Hirohito, in leading his country into war. There are other actions that the Emperor could take in expressing friendship with China, which would also have a dramatic effect, but to be effective they cannot be prescribed or suggested by a third party.

**Hiroshima and Nanjing.** A different event could bring the victims of Hiroshima and Nanjing together to remember all victims of war, especially civilians in Japan and China. This has been done in other parts of the world, for example bringing together Dresden in Germany and Coventry in England, both destroyed by bombing in the Second World War. The cries of the dead will be magnified when the victims of both sides cry out together. There were rumours of reciprocal visits by President Hu Jintao (to Hiroshima) and by Prime Minister Hatoyama (to Nanjing) in 2010, but they did not materialise. However that such an exchange was considered shows that this is a real possibility in the future. The dates for such an event should be both 6 August and 13 December, bringing citizens together from both Hiroshima and Nanjing. There are other dates that also need to be remembered, including 9 August (Nagasaki), 18 September (Manchurian Incident) and 7 July (start of Sino-Japanese war). Erecting monuments as common memorials for both sides is a powerful unifying symbol. The Okinawa Cornerstone of Peace commemorates all who died in the battle for Okinawa. The names of those who died are inscribed on the stone, regardless of their nationality or status, including Japanese, Korean and American victims.

**Yasukuni.** In 1978 fourteen Class A war criminals, hanged by the Allies, were secretly enshrined in Yasukuni. The enshrinement upset many Japanese and caused outrage when it became known in China and Korea and other countries of East Asia. Subsequently, the annual visits by Prime Minister Koizumi to the Yasukuni shrine from 2001 to 2006 undermined relations between Japan and China. Proposals have therefore been put forward to adopt a different approach to the honouring of war dead which could bring the countries together. The suggestion that a new, non-religious site for honouring the war dead in Japan, which was supported by Koizumi, might be a way forward to resolve this contentious issue. If such a site was free from imperial ideology and embraced all who died during the war, including civilians and not just the military, and had a place for honouring the war dead of other countries including China, then even Chinese representatives might be able stand alongside Japanese leaders on 15 August (see *Yasukuni, the War Dead and the Struggle for Japan's Past*, ed. J. Breen, London, 2007). Helmut Schmidt appreciated the Park of Peace in Okinawa, because it is dedicated to all the people who died there, enemies and friends, soldiers and civilians, Japanese and Americans, and all their names without distinction are engraved there. All of them were victims of that war. Recently in 2014 the Fukuoka branch of the Japan War Bereaved Families Association passed a resolution calling on the Yasukuni authorities to "dis-enshrine" the 14 war criminals. Similar proposals have been made before, but not by such a powerful association representing ultra-conservative bereaved families. Many people are not aware that after 1978 Emperor Hirohito ceased to visit Yasukuni and his heir, Akihito, has not been there since either. So this proposal if acted on would not only please China but would heal a rift with the Japanese royal family.

## Education

Reconciliation must be built on truth. The part history has to play in reconciliation has been examined in a book edited by Fumitaka Kurosawa and Ian Nish published in Japanese in 2011 under the title, *Rekishi to Wakai,* meaning in English, "History and Reconciliation". The history of Japan's wartime aggression in China became a controversial issue when the Japanese textbooks controversy first erupted in the 1980's. Prof. Kurosawa argues that this led to the 'politicization of history', which became an obstacle to reconciliation between China and Japan. The misuse of history should be overcome by a retelling of the past free from distortion, which he calls the 'historicization of history'. The book "attempts to approach the issue of 'reconciliation' by making a conscious effort to look at history through academic historians' eyes." The minimum requirements for the protagonists are that they face up to the history of the conflict, accept these facts and where appropriate apologise for them, and make the historical facts known to the next generation. Since the memory of the war is the root cause of Chinese distrust of Japan, the key to reconciliation lies in the history itself. For reconciliation to take place both sides must share historical facts and the historical materials that support them, so that they sincerely face up to their past history. Ian Nish adds: "Reconciliation has to be evidence-based; and this means history-based. Historians are therefore important in generating mutual understanding and overcoming misapprehensions about the past which create ill feeling." He quotes Funabashi Yoichi, editor-in-chief of *Asahi Shimbun,* as saying that it is "deepened historical consciousness" that is necessary for reconciliation: more apologies "would make the current young generation resistant and obstinate. What is important is not an apology but the historical consciousness of why we have to apologize."

Young Japanese react with dismay and disbelief when they are told about the atrocities committed by the Japanese military in China, Korea and South-East Asia. Sadly they do not discover this from their own government, schools, universities and media. Helmut Schmidt, in a speech in Tokyo in 2005, commented on the fact that after more than 40 visits to Japan, he felt that relations with China were not as good as they should be and that this was due in part to the media and the political literature, including the books to be used in schools. As if to confirm his fears, the critical parts of his speech were not reported in the Japanese media. In Germany in 1979 the televising of the American mini-series *Holocaust* had enormous repercussions. The showings broke the taboo on discussing the Jewish massacres and awakened the moral conscience of the nation about Germany's disgraceful past. This media event also enlightened school students who knew little about Nazi history. By the end of the 1970s more than five thousand school groups were visiting the Dachau concentration camp each year, compared to only 471 in 1968. No such media event has ever occurred in Japan featuring the slaughter of innocent civilians in Korea, China and South-East Asia.

Since the country is largely run by the same elite families who led the country in the war, there may be an unwillingness to reject what their kith and kin did. Japan has a lot to be proud of, so it should be possible for the country to reject what was evil as well as to honour what was good in the past century. Japanese are not insensitive, but many of the post-war generation are ignorant. When they come to know what happened in China between 1930 and 1945, they are likely to feel guilty and will want to put things right. For them there should be no shame or loss of face in acknowledging the evils of militarism, but only praise for facing the truth and promoting understanding with China.

Germany has shown what can be done to inform and educate the nation about her Nazi past. With the same determination the Japanese government can set the record straight and aim to educate her people about the history of the China war. Important progress has been made by Japanese and Chinese historians in recording the events of the Sino-Japanese war. Examples of this are the recently published essays on the military history of the Sino-Japanese War of 1937-1945, entitled *The Battle for China (op.cit.),* in which seven Japanese and seven Chinese historians are among the contributors. The cooperation of historians on both sides is essential to a holistic understanding of the war. As noted in the previous chapter the book, *Toward a History Beyond Borders: Contentious Issues in Sino-Japanese Relations,* written by eleven Japanese and Chinese historians is another notable example, which covers issues from 1871 to the present. Kawashima Shin calls for a historical perspective that is more inclusive than that of the nation state and aims to be – for example – not "pro-Chinese" or "anti-Chinese" but "knowing about China" (op.cit. pp. 411-433).

## Future reconsideration

An observation that is sometimes made is that Japanese political leaders have habitually given *ad hoc* attention to issues as they have arisen with China. Despite the rapprochement with China in the 1970's, the leadership failed to face up to the legacy of Japan's bitter wartime history. They left the problems of the past to fester. Ian Nish quotes the metaphor used by Dr Hirano: "Japan has kept the bandages on its wounds too long. It has sought to protect the wounds. But wounds need exposure to the air at a later stage in order to heal."

What is necessary is a fundamental reconsideration of the past in order to shape future direction. Kenzaburo Oe is famous for his advocacy of the victims of Hiroshima and for his commitment to Japan's peace constitution. For the Nobel Prizewinner the Fukushima disaster confirms the menace of nuclear power. The country has gone down the wrong road by using nuclear technology for the sake of productivity. The pursuit of prosperity has led Japan astray. "The way Japan had tried to build up a modern state modelled on the west was cataclysmic." It was not merely the pursuit of wealth that led Japan astray, but the creation of a nation state fired by nationalism and modelled on the West that impelled Japan to seek power by militarism and imperial expansion. Kenzaburo is therefore willing to acknowledge that the people and state of Japan "has been stained by their own past history of invading other Asian countries." This opened his mind to acknowledge that there are other victims besides those who died at Hiroshima, whose blood cries out to be heard. Modernisation, westernisation and consumer cultures are all targets of his attack. Japan needs to step back from the pursuit of industrial, technological and commercial dominance, and rediscover its enduring values. In this process Japan can avoid recourse to military power, and view China again with respect and see her war victims as fellow human beings.

Instead of pursuing a nationalistic agenda, which is bound to conflict with China, Japan's future lies in peaceful cooperation with the international community in Asia and the rest of the world.

# What could China do to bring about reconciliation with Japan?

## A generous spirit

The example of the miracle of Fushun should influence China's policy toward Japan today. With hindsight we can see that Chou Enlai was right, that treating even war criminals as human beings with generosity has resulted in a positive stream of war veterans, who have worked for peace in Japan and have handed on the lessons of Fushun to the modern generation. Their work lives on and testifies to the benefits of replacing revenge with respect even in international politics. It is to this positive message that the Chukiren motto refers: *Forget not the past. Make it your teacher for the future.* To act in a forgiving spirit, as Desmond Tutu has said, is a risky strategy. The risk is all the greater if it is the injured party that takes the initiative to offer a new start. The wrongdoer may be blind or too proud to apologise. China will also feel that her security must never be put at risk again. However Desmond Tutu is right that true security will never be won through the barrel of a gun. China could accept, as Ma Licheng advises, that Japan has apologised many times for the suffering she inflicted on her neighbours in the first half of the twentieth century. Any move by China to appreciate Japan will not be rejected.

## An Integral Relationship

Sun Yat-sen (Sun Zhongshan), who is often regarded as the founding figure of modern China after the collapse of the Qing dynasty, made the following statement on 28 November 1924:

"The Chinese and Japanese nations are intimately related, not only from the point of view of communications but in all other respects as well. There is a saying among the people of both countries that China and Japan are brother nations, whose people are of similar race and culture; that, therefore, they should join hands in common effort."

Kanzo Uchimura, a Japanese Christian thinker, who died in 1930, rejected the westernisation of Japan and objected to the deification of the emperor. Uchimura took seriously the natural geographical, racial and cultural connections between the two neighbouring countries. Being a Christian he saw it as God's design that he should love his neighbour and his country should love their neighbours too. For China to return to the old Confucian ideal would mean renouncing the spirit of nationalism.

Clearly China cannot revert to fifteenth century politics. What Uchimura suggested is that both countries can build on what unites them rather than on what divides them. If this were the aim then it would be possible to reject the war period as a deeply damaging diversion from the close affinity which has been the norm for China's relations with Japan. Such an understanding of the war period, as a temporary divide due to militarism, was affirmed by the 1972 Japan-China Joint Communiqué, which stated: "Japan and China are neighbouring countries, separated only by a strip of water with a long history of traditional friendship." This relationship is not primarily a commercial association of trading partners, as it is at present, but a much deeper bond rooted in common culture, race and history. It is not merely in China's interests to build a strong union with Japan, for the need for this union springs from China's own history and identity.

Ma Licheng pursues this theme in his recent book, *There is No Future for Hatred*. "China and Japan," he writes, "are so interwoven into each other. There are no other two countries in this world like this." He notes that in Kyoto, it is like going back to the Tang Dynasty in China, and so different from walking down streets in America. There are more than 1000 Chinese characters in Japanese, so it is not surprising that on the streets of Japan, you can see some road signs in Chinese characters. When he was a researcher in Tokyo University in 2010, Ma Licheng was impressed with Japanese interest in Chinese poetry and calligraphy. Japanese people have helped Chinese to preserve their own culture through their interest in Chinese art, literature and history. For more than a thousand years the culture and history of China and Japan have been closely intertwined.

## Building a Partnership

Helmut Schmidt acknowledged in his Tokyo speech of 2005 that Germany owed France a debt of gratitude for extending a hand of friendship after 1945 – a welcoming hand that had been conspicuously absent in 1918. As a result the two countries have become the core partners in the European Union. This has transformed Europe from being a battleground of warring nations into a peaceful partnership. What is most striking is that all major EU decisions are taken when Germany and France are agreed. This unity between old enemies is a good example for Japan and China in the 21st century. If China can win the trust and confidence of Japan to work together not only on matters of trade but on matters of regional and international politics, then a real partnership will become possible. This partnership will not follow the pattern of the EU, but will devise its own shape and constitution.

Looking to the future of the 21st century, it is to be expected that China will become a global superpower. China's relations with the rest of the world will be determined by international considerations. Reconciliation between China and Japan will depend not only on a resolution of the divisions caused by the Sino-Japanese war, but on an amicable structure of international relations between the major powers. China is committed to promoting harmonious society not only domestically but on the international stage. Good relations with Japan will depend on China's pursuit of this goal in cooperation with global powers. Peaceful international cooperation will be the best insurance against the danger of China and Japan competing against each other through opposing alliances, especially in Asia and the Pacific.

## Pursuing Security through Non-Violence

The Chinese government has vowed never to allow the humiliations of the past two centuries to be repeated, when foreign armies were able to invade China with impunity and to wreak destruction. So China has acquired nuclear armaments and powerful military forces. After 1980 Deng Xiaoping reduced the size of China's army by a million men, but for the past decade this trend has been reversed. The amount spent on armaments has risen every year and in 2012 was estimated to be as much as $166 billion per year. China is now investing in naval power and using this power to enforce her claims to ever increasing domination of the seas bordering Vietnam, the Philippines, Korea and Japan. However China's security will be most effectively guaranteed not by the quantity of her weapons but by harmonious relations with her neighbours. As JP Lederach observes, "The mystery of peace is located in the nature and quality of relationships developed with those most feared." China has little to fear from Vietnam and the Philippines, but may still be concerned that Japan could once again revert to military nationalism and use its technological superiority to damaging effect.

China and Japan agreed to work together in 1972 and signed a treaty in which both affirmed that: Japan and China shall in their mutual relations settle all disputes by peaceful means and shall refrain from the use or threat of force. This commitment is being tested at the present time by the dispute over the Senkaku/Diaoyu Islands. Of particular significance is the commitment not to use the threat of force to settle disputes. China can make a major contribution to peace in the region by refraining from threatening actions and language. Practical steps should also be taken to defuse present tensions by agreeing with Japan and other governments in the region on what steps should be taken to avoid the outbreak of hostilities if by accident a ship were to be sunk or a plane shot down. Everyone is aware of how a small incident, like the Marco Polo Bridge affair, can be used to start a war. Officials from China and Japan met in November 2014 and again in January and March 2015 to establish a maritime communications hotline to prevent any unexpected incidents turning into open conflict. Peace has been maintained by informal diplomacy and not by reliance on the signing of official declarations. This requires a level of trust on both sides which is being sorely tested at the present time.

# Joint Action

More important than the actions China or Japan can take separately to improve their relations is the question, what can both sides undertake together?

Nations in conflict look back on their past through the stories they tell, stories of triumph and tribulation. Typically these stories depict the achievements of the country and the evil deeds of the enemy. History retold in this way justifies each side in the stand they take in times of conflict. As in personal disputes both sides feel vindicated by their stories. In the conflict between Japan and China both look at the present through the past and feel vindicated by the rightness of their narrative.

The process by which nations in conflict construct their own narratives has been called mythmaking. Yinan He in her valuable study, *The Search for Reconciliation: Sino-Japanese and German-Polish Relations since World War II* (Cambridge 2009), identifies national mythmaking as the cause of prolonged division between China and Japan. National myths, which are the product of government manipulation of history, lead to a distorted view of the past. Pernicious national myths tend to be self-glorifying or self-whitewashing or to denigrate other nations. These symbolic accounts of a nation's past are used to justify foreign policy or to address domestic political agendas. Mythologies use patriotic rhetoric to appeal to pride in one's nation and hostility to others. In the name of patriotism neighbouring countries produce very different accounts of their past. Such myths glorify a nation's virtues, deny guilt for crimes and blame others for tragedies. As a result history, especially history of past wars, becomes a divisive issue between countries who have fought against each other.

This helps to explain why the history issue has become such a longstanding source of division between China and Japan. China, as the victim in the Sino-Japanese war, exploits myths of victimisation and self-righteousness, which appeal to deeply felt grievances from the enormous suffering in the past. These in turn encourage the people to express anti-Japanese sentiments and to demand apologies and reparations. If these are not forthcoming, then China assumes a morally superior position and feels contempt for Japan. On the other hand Japan, as the perpetrator of aggression in the war, feels justifiably misrepresented for its peaceful record over the past seventy years during which it has apologised to China on many occasions and given generous aid for forty years. Japan is understandably frustrated by China's use of the history card and has responded by affirming national pride in its past achievements.

During the Mao era there was no opportunity for the expression of public opinion in China, except in support of government propaganda. In the 1980s as some degree of freedom was permitted memories of the war began to be expressed. When the government itself chose to criticise Japan, then the public were free to do the same. So in 1982 when the textbook controversy began, not only did the Chinese government protest but also public expression of anger against Japanese misrepresentation of war history boiled over. A more dangerous trend then developed, in which Beijing began to foster an appeal to assertive nationalism by depicting Japan as the enemy.

Beijing also protested when Prime Minister Nakasone officially took part in worship at the Yasukuni Shrine on 15 August 1985 - and became the first Japanese Prime Minister to do so on the anniversary of the end of the war. The change in Chinese feelings toward Japan over war memory can be seen from the fact that a government approved publisher produced "The Great Nanjing Massacre" in 1987, which sold 150,000 copies in the first month. The government found it convenient to gain popularity by using the bitter memories of the war to criticise Japan, whilst the public used government approval to express their own prejudices against Japanese militarism in the past.

On the Japanese side, moves toward reconciliation foundered. Whereas liberal intelligentsia in Japan did campaign strongly for a realistic recognition of the damage done during the war to Japan's neighbours, the conservative elites in power attacked any such admission of Japanese responsibility for past atrocities. Since the conservatives retained political power, they effectively eliminated any possibility of Japan officially working with China to face the past and harmonise their views concerning the history of World War II. As a result both governments were free to indulge in historical mythmaking at each other's expense. We are still living with the consequences of this failure to deal with the deep-seated causes of division, especially rooted in the history of Japan's invasion of China from 1931 onwards.

One way of tackling the divisions created by national myths is for China and Japan to undertake joint history research. This was begun in 2006, but this government authorised project has made no progress in recent years. However, as we have already noted under the conflict over Japanese history textbooks progress has been made through cooperation between Chinese and Japanese academic historians. At the same time we note that joint history research faces awkward problems. First, it is not easy to establish facts, and some facts will never be clearly known, such as the number massacred in Nanjing in 1937. Second, facts need interpretation, and all historians have their own values and standpoints from which they judge the evidence. Third, it is difficult if not impossible for two countries to agree on a common account of the war in which they fought against each other. Nevertheless progress can be made, as Yinan He has shown by examining the example of bitterly divided Poles and Germans, who reconciled their differences over the Second World War. One of the best ways of defusing the current tension is for Japan and China to desist from promoting patriotic myths and to renew government authorised joint history research of the past century. For this to be productive both sides can learn from the insights of narrative mediation.

J. Winslade and G. Monk have written a suggestive book entitled, *Narrative Mediation* (San Francisco, 2000). They write: "Stories are we believe the backbone of experience. Out of the stories people construct they take up their stances of opposition and conflict." The process of narrative mediation includes the following steps: meeting the parties, deconstructing the conflict saturated story and constructing an alternative story. The first aim is to create a relational climate in which a respectful encounter can take place. Deconstruction "seeks to undermine the certainties on which the conflict feeds," and invites both sides to listen to and explore different points of view. Conflict stories are always selections that eliminate events that do not fit in. So experiences outside the usual conflict story are a rich source for new insights that encourage respect for the opposition. The alternative narrative that may emerge will portray a different version of the past and a positive view of the future relationship of both parties.

Applying the insights of narrative mediation to the Sino-Japanese conflict would require that both sides listen respectfully to each other's stories. The importance of listening to people's stories was at the heart of the Truth and Reconciliation Commission process in South Africa. Victims who had never been able to open their mouths were able to speak in public. Their voices were heard, their story was told. Their oppressors were not sentenced and imprisoned, instead the victims' experience was made public and their suffering was recorded.

This process takes time, as does all listening to others' viewpoints. Andrew White gives a vivid example of this from Iraq in his recent book, *Father, Forgive* (Oxford, 2013). In his reconciliation work in the Middle East he brought together 12 different religious leaders in a hotel for three days. He set aside a whole day just for the participants to listen to each other's stories and he felt that was a generous amount of time. But the entire three days went in listening and they had to meet again two months later to continue listening. In the end it took nearly two years for him to accomplish what he had thought would take a day for all to be heard. Giving time to listen to your enemy changes your perception; then enemies can become friends.

In the Second World War both sides finished the war as victims. Japan inflicted enormous suffering on Chinese, Koreans and the peoples of South-East Asia. But in the end Japanese suffered the consequences of their own military machine: their soldiers were annihilated and their cities bombed to rubble. Minoru has recorded the misery of post-war Japan and Yoshiko has lived her life under the sinister shadow of the atomic mushroom cloud. In Japan the victims of the atomic bombs dropped on Hiroshima and Nagasaki are never forgotten. Millions visit the memorials at Hiroshima and succeeding generations of children are taken from all over the country by their schools to visit the site. In China millions remember the humiliating invasion by Japanese armies in the 1930's. Streams of people continue to enter the Nanjing museum built to remind the nation of the massacre in December 1937. The victims' stories are part of the patriotic narrative that both governments wish to preserve. For a new narrative to develop the victims of both countries need to be heard by the other side and both sides need to listen to the agonies suffered on foreign soil.

Narrative mediation would become a possibility between China and Japan if both sides visited the places of each other's pain. If the *hibakusha* (survivors) in Hiroshima would visit Nanjing and tell their story there, whilst families of those massacred in Nanjing were to visit Hiroshima, a new movement would be born. Both sides need to visit each other and listen to each other's horror stories, as well as recounting their own suffering. Both might then discover that they have a common enemy – War. Both might also realise that they share something in common – their own humanity. Out of these discoveries it is possible that they would find, as others have, that the one they thought of as an enemy has become a friend.

However this is to leap ahead and forget the topic of narrative mediation. The meeting of the parties is only the first step in mediation. The next is to see what emerges from hearing different points of view. If someone from Nanjing, who has been brought up to hate Japanese because of the massacre in their city in 1937, goes to

Hiroshima and listens to the nuclear bomb survivors (*hibakusha*), how might this change his/her thinking? A great deal will depend on how his story is listened to in Hiroshima. The *hibakusha* I listened to in 2007 was a school boy in 1945. He only survived because his class was sent that morning to harvest crops outside the city. He was not a soldier. He had done nothing to deserve the loss of his home and the terrible fate that befell his classmates in the city centre. A visitor from Nanjing might see that this boy – now an old man – was like him a victim of the same mindless war. What then would happen to someone from Hiroshima who deliberately went to Nanjing to listen to the stories of those whose families had been slaughtered in 1937?

It does not require much imagination to realise that many exchange visits between Hiroshima and Nanjing are needed to bring about a real change in the way the citizens of Nanjing and Hiroshima view each other, let alone change relations between China and Japan. But it would be a start. The example of the Truth and Reconciliation Commission meetings in South Africa shows that such encounters, however incomplete, do diffuse violence and revenge. They open a new path to the future. They bring opponents together.

Something else happens: light is shed on a community's painful past. Although the great majority in China and Japan were not alive between 1937 and 1945, they inherit a remembered history of their nation's past, especially of those events that have shaped or disrupted its story. Painful events, such as Nanjing 1937 and Hiroshima 1945, become by repetition a nation's 'chosen trauma'. The 'chosen trauma' provides justification for the country's actions today against the perpetrators of past pain. When both sides sit together and share each other's traumatic history, both can view the future in a different light.

At present it is unrealistic to think that the initiative for such narrative mediation would come from the governments of China and Japan. But this does not mean that citizens of both countries cannot start their own initiatives for reconciliation. Peacemaking does not depend on numbers. Einstein is quoted as having said, "That which counts can rarely be counted." The few who work for peace may be like yeast. JP Lederach came to the conclusion that focus on quantity may simply be a distraction. It is the courageous and creative few who change the course of events by taking risks. Where there's a will, there's a way. Or, more powerfully, where someone has a dream, as Martin Luther King put it in his famous "I have a dream" speech, a new way opens. Better still is the title of Desmond Tutu's book: *God has a Dream.* Such dreamers sow a seed, which takes time to germinate, but comes to fruition in the end.

# Reflections on Key Issues

*Minoru & Basil reflect on key issues affecting reconciliation between China and Japan*

..........................................

**Introduction to the Reflections on Key Issues**

In the first part of our book we told our stories, recollecting our pilgrimage in search of truth and how we first met in India and were reunited many years later in England and Japan. In these personal recollections we have attempted to share what we have learnt through our experiences. As Minoru likes to put it, what we have received is a pure gift and was most unexpected.

These personal memories were followed by four chapters drawing attention to what has been achieved to bring about reconciliation between Japan and her former enemies in China and elsewhere, and what remains to be done.

To bring this book to a personal conclusion, we met in Cambridge in 2015 to discuss some of the crucial issues in the search for reconciliation between China and Japan. By the kindness of Prof. Toshi Yamamoto we were able to use his peaceful apartment, where we had met again after forty years in 2005. In the Reflections which follow we share our convictions about issues that are important to us both in the search for reconciliation.

# Awakening to the blessed reality

*How is this awakening to Reality the key to Reconciliation?*

Basil: I have to ask you first of all: what do you mean by the "blessed reality"?

Minoru: For me, it is something given, utterly given, and unexpected.

I have discussed with you my situation before I went to America. On coming back to Japan I got to know an older couple who had suffered greatly during the War, because they were accused of being disloyal to the emperor, since they were Christians and also because they were pacifists. They were working as wardens for the hostel where I stayed. I was so blessed to know them, and after work every day to have discussions with them and prayer. On their recommendation I went to International Christian University (ICU). That was an unexpected blessing for me, because I found that the university had just been established as a response to the cries and prayers of the victims of Hiroshima and Nagasaki. The lecturers were dedicated spiritual teachers and very friendly. In my heart grew a burning commitment and a striving for peace, as the only way out of our critical condition.

Then I went to America with a strong commitment to love and justice, as expressions of the Christian faith. But as I stayed there, I became very disturbed by racial incidents, particularly between black and white Americans. At that time Martin Luther King came to the university chapel to preach; that was in 1959. The chapel was packed with students. I was surprised, because usually you would only see a few people there, but on this occasion it was packed with students. Many students were standing, and I was one of them. Fortunately, I was just in front of the pulpit, so I could see Luther King. Hearing him speak, shook me and moved me so much that afterwards, I reflected on what he had said, and then wrote a small essay on segregation.

What Martin Luther King was saying was radically different from my understanding of Christianity at that time. Although my faith was firm and the fire was burning in my heart, I was striving for a kind of futuristic perfection. But in listening to Luther King's preaching I felt this message was for now, not for the future, but for here and now. 'Please be awakened', he seemed to say, 'to the blessed reality. We are brothers and sisters in God's family, so let us be awakened to receive this gift from God, and let us live and walk as brothers and sisters in God's family! Let us be (he kept stressing), liberated, emancipated from the mark of segregation in history, and from anything man-made. So be free, let us be free now!'

I felt that this was not for the future, but to experience the blessed reality right now. To be liberated, here and now. This really moved me and touched me. This was a revolutionary moment for me, to be awakened to the blessed reality here and now. Until then my education in the Christian context was strained. It was very difficult for me at that time to envisage a kind of futuristic perfection, even in religion. Of course, nationalism, capitalism, and Marxism, obviously believe in future perfection, but even in religion there can be a man-made futuristic perfection. But what King was saying was totally different, and that was revolutionary for me. So instead of futuristic perfection, reality is here and now. The task was to live in that reality. That was my response to his preaching.

Then, talking with my friend, I found he had been so influenced by Gandhi and was sustained and inspired by him. But Gandhi was a Hindu man. To me Martin Luther King was a genuine Christian, and I was struck by the love and justice in him, which really inspired me from Japan. Also, he was completely free from bitterness and hatred. I was reminded of Malcolm X, his contemporary. His enemies threatened him, burned his house down and finally murdered him, throwing his body on the road.

Naturally bitterness and hatred and sometimes a revenge mentality are the response. But then, listen to Martin Luther King. There was hardly anything of this hatred in him. He said: be awakened! Let us live directed by God, and not only directed by God, and inspired by God, but be like God. You must become nothing, you are zero. I must confess I was overwhelmed. Yes, I am a Christian, and I burned with zeal for this purpose, but this was something totally new – a revolutionary message. And he was not just speaking as an individual. He had a PhD, a Doctor of Theology, but not out of books. He was living in that reality. So naturally out of this thankfulness, out of wonder, out of surprise, prayer comes naturally. This is real! It was rare to hear such a message, revolutionary and completely new in that sense.

Then there was another thing: my friend - who shared Gandhi's impact and the Hinduism of Gandhi – suggested there must be something strong enough to go beyond racial boundaries and deep enough to be shared even beyond religion. There must be a reality which has not been fully recognised, because our historical experience is still provisional.

So I went to India. For two years we were together. We were shocked by what we saw as we travelled in

North India. We often met refugees from Tibet and we always went on trains by third class. Two were necessary to survive in India; to travel alone was impossible! Stan was instinctively right: he needed me! We slept on platforms twice, at different stations. We saw Tibetan refugees getting up exhausted, dusty and sore, but their smiles really touched us. Stan was so sensitive to the least and poorest. He wondered why they had to face such a fate. It became a serious question for him, so after two years he decided to specialise in cultural sociology and took the suffering of Tibetan people as his topic.

We wanted to see Vinoba Bhave. People said he was a real disciple of Mahatma Gandhi, but he was always on the move. We had to take trains and buses to meet him and then travel on foot. Finally we reached him and had a *darshan* (or view of the great man), and exchanged words with him. We were expected to move with him the next day to another place. But we became very sick and couldn't move, so we gave up. But at least we had experienced a *darshan* of Gandhi's disciple.

Eventually we reached Murray Rogers' ashram and stayed on there. We were particularly touched by the silence at early morning prayer before the day began, and by the silence at evening prayer, which was so meaningful for us, and so different. We had been so exhausted! So in the silence, in our exhaustion, we were waiting. Then we felt God's presence. The silence was so important there

Then I was given some students in Banaras Hindu University, who must have been a gift to me from God. One was Nilekanta Hinimata. A special person. I felt he was the kind of person who witnessed to the reality of *satchitananda* (existence, consciousness and bliss), and not simply *satchitananda*, but also *karuna*, compassion and love. So, in meeting him I experienced Hinduism as a living spirituality. He was my classmate.

Basil: That's very helpful indeed. My next question will be about your awakening to reality, or discovery of it in America through Martin Luther King. You discovered that he was saying that reality is not futuristic perfection, but something here and now. That sounds like a different theology -- theology may not be the right word – but it was a different understanding of history and of where we are now. But later on you talked about reality in experience, and silent prayer, being aware of God's presence. That suggests another question: is reality understanding God's presence? Is it something else? Awakening to reality: is that awakening to the presence of God or is it an understanding?

Minoru: Understanding the reality of God's presence, working with us, living with us, directing us. This is totally given to us, nothing human. That was the blessing given.

Basil: As I understand it, for Martin Luther King and Gandhi this was something given by God.

Minoru: I think from the beginning of the 1920s the American Negroes were inspired by Gandhi's example, because he was facing a powerful colonial government. In those days Great Britain was the most powerful empire in the world, and in that situation non-violent people were raising their voice in protest in India. That moved black people in America to wonder how this could happen. They were so inspired, in spite of their difficulties in America. Politically, it seemed impossible to follow a path of non-violent resistance, or it was much harder than in the Indian context, because in the American context violence followed even passive resistance, immediately. In the 1930s they felt a spiritual yearning to find out more. So in 1936 four black American Christians went to India to meet Gandhi. One became sick so only three could meet with Gandhi. They had such an unforgettable and inspiring time with Gandhi. This was a mutually inspiring experience, for Gandhi was also much inspired by these black Americans. They were living in the reality of the Negro Spirituals. They had been deprived of everything, even spiritually, but in spite of that they praised God. That means there is something of which we cannot be deprived.

Basil: Maybe that's what you meant when you said Martin Luther King said you must become zero, because when you are zero God takes over, and you are liberated. On the other hand you can't be zero when you are in God's presence for there you are liberated by God. But you were saying you need to be zero to be awakened to God's presence. So there is a connecting link.

Minoru: On a spiritual level, they began to understand Gandhi's position.

Basil: And when you went to India you also were reduced to zero!

Minoru: Yes, in many ways! It is a frightening place. Maybe I have visited India a total of seven times and each time I became more comfortable, but the first visit was just such an experience of becoming zero. That experience really changed me. So whenever I was invited to go back to India I thought: may be I will not be able to go back to Japan. That was a traumatic experience!

Basil: This idea of being reduced to zero is so important.

Minoru: That's what I found in America, in 1967, going to Harvard. Prof. R. N. Bellah greatly impressed me. He suffered a lot during the anti-Vietnam protest movement. The final straw for him was that his daughter committed suicide. She couldn't stand it, because the telephone was ringing continuously with people attacking her father. Her father tried to express his opposition non-violently. So the students said that he was betraying their position and many became his enemy. But his daughter knew he was not. He couldn't speak in public for six months after her death. But after six months he spoke in a church conference. His subject was "Reflections on Reality in America." He described his position as one of faith arising out of loss, or 'the faith of loss.'

Basil: This does connect with the fact that in India, you said, you eventually had your experience of meeting Tibetans. These people were reduced to zero. Another question then is this - you mentioned that Martin Luther King said that this understanding of being zero, delivers you from bitterness and hatred. How has that taken place? This is very important for us: how do we get rid of bitterness and hatred? When does it go, or what do we do with it? Does this mean we have to descend to zero, or is it awakening to a new understanding?

Minoru: Basically, I think the reality of new spiritual meaning requires us to be really deeply rooted in God's life. In 1963, on that memorable occasion in Martin Luther King's life, when huge numbers of people gathered in Washington to hear him, he gave his famous, "I have a dream" speech. He was very clear on this point.

Basil: But I think what we need to understand, or help others to understand, is how and why that removes bitterness. Why does this experience of God's presence remove the bitterness of a life time?

Minoru: I think Martin Luther King had been deeply rooted in God. So he was acting as God does, in a sense. In God, there is complete freedom from bitterness. A revenge feeling is so natural in the human world. The person who feels this way is bound to react with aggressive action against the wrong doer. But with God there is no such bondage. There are no conditions to be fulfilled.

Basil: Then we are free, not bound by bitterness.

Minoru: Yes. That is why Martin Luther King said: "I have a dream." Ring the bell and we are free. On mountains and riversides and in towns and villages, we are free. Thank you God, we are free, free, free!

Basil: No president, no political party in a country can remove you, because you are free.

Minoru: That's right. And here he was including all, not only Catholic and Protestant, black and white, but everyone, all mankind. Humanity is a healing family.

Basil: The idea of humanity as a healing family is something we have to discuss later, because ordinarily we don't live like that! So although Martin Luther King, or the awakened person, Gandhi, can see that we are all free, most people cannot see that they are free.

Minoru: Even Gandhi, in his autobiography in the 1920s, in the preface, says I have been always seeking, searching for God and truth, but I have not yet met him! I have had a glimpse, but that glimpse changed me and I even risked my life for this glimpse. And I know, even through a glimpse, that all my being is given, by the grace of God. Even this breath that I am breathing is a gift, God's life.

Basil: So this awakening is beyond borders; it removes the boundaries and restrictions of race, religion, nationality, country, geography and everything.

Minoru: Let us go forward, let us live. And be free from the bondage.

Basil: You were saying, you found in America that this was a very liberating discovery, to realise that this reality is now, not in the future.

Minoru: Here and now. There is tremendous optimism, but at the same time optimistic pessimism, because in actuality the world is darker than ever. People are made stubborn by nationalism, and by all kinds of "isms".

Basil: But Martin Luther King was living in the reality of being free himself. The world is not free but Gandhi and Martin Luther King were living in the present reality, knowing that this is not something for the future but is a gift of God to be enjoyed right now.

Minoru: This has happened even in South Africa, following Desmond Tutu's instruction to the nation to embrace white and black as brothers and sisters. We are brothers and sisters!

Basil: So in your experience, how do we become awakened or receive this reality? Is it through silent prayer, or some other way?

Minoru: In most unexpected moments there comes the total given-ness of blessing. In the case of South Africa, it was a political event, but initiation to the new reality comes out of becoming new beings, black and white brothers. The white brothers are so joyful at being released from the yoke of segregation. In the case of Tutu himself, and in his personal experience, he was deeply awakened to the reality of the human family.

Basil: So, this would connect very strongly with reconciliation, because it is not only an experience of bitterness being removed, but also of more.

Minoru: Bitterness is itself a sign of enslavement.

Basil: Definitely. Once that bitterness is broken, you are aware of something more, that is, of the healing family. It's not just that the bitterness is gone; you are aware of reconciliation.

Minoru: More than that: reconciliation is reality itself, so therefore we experience not just co-existence. Co-existence is a man-made image, but God's creative co-existence is a new reality. Invited by God, we find a new reality. Naturally we become thankful, and after that prayer flows.

Basil: We will come back to the creative part in a minute, but that is a gift of God, and not something that you can contrive or obtain or give to anyone else.

Minoru: That's right. For example, in my case, coming to England this time is not a repetition of the past but is a looking forward to something that is totally unknown. Just meeting with you I am surprised, because there is something of the blessed reality here. So naturally then prayer will flow.

Basil: So anything is possible – we cannot organise it! I think this is a big difference. We are reduced to zero, as we cannot control it. So it is entirely a gift.

Minoru: True, true.

Basil: Let's come back to your phrase of "creative co-existence", which I don't understand! I understand what somebody else might mean, but not what you might mean! Because it does not sound like the way you usually express things. Co-existence is what the politicians think we have to manage, but you are emphasising the creative part, are you not?

Minoru: The creative part – is not repeating the past.

Basil: I see. It is also created by us in this world. I mean by human beings, such as anyone who wants to see the world a better place. We want to be creative, but actually we are not capable.

Minoru: I suspect real artists, drawing, painting, writing and so on, may be creative, when just by painting something creatively that is not devised beforehand, they are guided by the Spirit.

Basil: In that sense, it is something given, because it is not thought about beforehand. But that would be true of many things.

Minoru: Everything. That is the beauty of individuality. Each individual is completely different from the other. But the root is the same: utterly radical diversities, rooted in unity.

Basil: What is the root or the foundation?

Minoru: The root is the truth of God, created by Him. That is life.

Basil: You were saying that your experience in America was a sort of beginning, hearing Martin Luther King.

Minoru: But someone guided me step by step. Previously I had experienced loss when I was returning from Shanghai. On reaching Japan and travelling by train, I saw cities flattened. Hiroshima was just miserable. On reaching Tokyo there were so many homeless children. Complete destruction. That was horrible and I saw no hope for the future.

Basil: That was very disturbing indeed. We are thankful that in different ways that we have been reduced to zero.

Minoru: That is a profound experience!

Basil: Yes, but when you look back you can see we have been reduced to zero and that is when we receive God's blessing.

Minoru: Total freedom.

Basil: Absolutely. In one sense, as I look back on being in that prison camp, I am amazed that the more I reflect on it, the more thankful I am for those three years. I would not wish it otherwise. It would be a profound loss if that had never happened to me, because I received so much in that time.

Minoru: I was struck by reading about your life in the camp; that is what you are describing now. Although I must say that I only have a glimpse of the reality, but it is so powerful.

Basil: It is like you going back to Japan, to your own country and expecting some people to be full of hope. In fact it was terrible. But out of that, something new can be born, which comes from God.

Minoru: Utterly new, but utterly true.

Basil: This is why we see in the poor and suffering glimpses of the reality, more easily than by viewing the rich. That is what Jesus said. Blessed are the poor.

Minoru: The modern world is totally closed to God's reality. Unreality has really become actuality. The reality is not seen in this world, but if someone by God's grace steps into the unknown, confronted with this blessing, then naturally thanks will come, and joy comes, and out of that prayer will come. Let us be free. Let us live together, joyfully, as family!

*Reflections on Key Issues*

Basil: One last point. I should mention that zero comes in the darkness, and we are afraid. You have mentioned this just now and have reflected that in the darkness, if you are not aware of the darkness, you might not be aware of the light. If you say everything is fine you might not see the light. You won't be awakened, unless you see how dark the situation is. How would you explain that?

Minoru: Those who are sensitive to the least are enjoying fullness of happiness. Some are in the midst of the darkness but they are happy; they have such a good position and status but their heart is darkness. The trouble is that people living in that situation cannot see the real reality, because their status and riches and comfort are reality for them. They are insensitive, and they are the most serious cause of suffering and pain for those who are least.

*Two Pilgrims Meet*

# Why is Takamori Soan important as a witness in Japan?

*Takamori Soan is a religious community in the mountains of Japan near Fujimi in Nagano Prefecture. We call it an ashram, using the Indian name for such a spiritual community.*

Minoru: After the war people in Japan were searching for hope, if there was any such thing as meaningful hope. In this context Father Oshida decided to become a Catholic and a member of the Dominican order. The conviction in his heart was that there can only be hope, if there is any for Japan, by really searching for the truth.

At that time his health was not good and he was hospitalised in Fujimi, which is very close to the ashram site. There he had a group of patients like himself, most of them tuberculosis patients. He began having Bible studies and discussions with them. He found that since there were so many patients on the waiting list they could not stay in the hospital and had to leave. But in those days they had no home to return to, so he felt there must be some place for them to live together. In consultation with these patients he built a community house, so that they could stay there.

That was the beginning of Takamori Soan and the first stage in its development. It meant sharing the difficulties of Japanese conditions. Later as the situation changed, the acute need was gone, but Father Oshida felt very strongly the need for a space where they could really listen to the voice of God. So he established a community separated from the Dominican monastery. The monks had their place to stay and live together and so on, but he felt that way of life was not exposed to the harsh reality of Japan.

After that he felt a call from God, to meet with those who wanted to search for a way forward in the midst of this chaotic heart of Japan with no visible hope. Young people began coming to this community, particularly young university students, who had also been tormented, searching for hope for the future. In order to find hope, one must understand the real reason behind hope. They were convinced that hope comes from the real understanding of God. The direction was becoming clear, for a community searching for the truth together and responding to the truth in community.

Then there was a nationwide university student revolt to protest against government control of universities. The academic community must have freedom to search for the truth without being interfered with by the government, otherwise Japan would repeat the mistakes of the past. Strangely, Takamori Soan became the meeting place for students. Coming there, they found real self-understanding, which was most important in order to meet the chaotic situation in Japan. They felt strongly that the country should never repeat the past. There must be new direction and new hope. In that situation there was a conviction, accepted by all who had suffered, that peace is the only way, if Japan is to be reborn.

In Japan students became increasingly divided and did not know what to do. First they started with very idealistic dreams, but then became increasingly political. The student movement had an official position and unless you agreed with that you were anti the movement. In that period I returned from America in 1967-8, and ICU was no exception, but was also occupied by the students and no lectures were being held for the students.

The Soan (meaning 'a thatched hut' or 'hermitage') was surprisingly attracting students, particularly from Tokyo University, the best university in the capital. They were engaged in discussion and dialogue together. But they had to support themselves, so they began to cultivate the rice fields. In this way they were working and supporting themselves and searching for the truth. In all of this what was central in the community was to ask, who you are, and who I am. Father Oshida was increasingly convinced in this critical situation in Japan of the necessity for the search for God.

So the community became known among the circle of students who were seeking for meaning in their lives. Evidently some students were really illuminated, finding God and understanding themselves, and how to respond to these divisive situations. They felt unanimously that interference by the police was the worst thing, which must be avoided at all costs.

Father Oshida's ashram community played a unique role. Some of the students became Christians and pursued that path, becoming firm in their search for the truth, joining this self-supporting community and cultivating the fields. They learnt much more in this way, not simply searching intellectually for knowledge. One of them, Miyamoto, was a student at university, studying philosophy. He came to this ashram. He was really awakened in dialogue with Father Oshida. Now he is the head of the Dominican Society in Japan and fully supports the work of the ashram. There are some others like him in different professions. This was the second stage of the ashram's development, after it had been formed firstly for the sick people, who had nowhere to go.

The third stage the Soan community had to face was the destruction of nature, under the name of the movement for modernisation. In particular the focus was on water. Water has always been necessary, as a lifeline for the peasants to cultivate their fields. But some of the powerful bosses in the local villages were attracted by the economic benefits of selling the rights to use the spring, which was the source of the stream flowing down the mountainside. Their plan to take over the spring was approaching the final stage. The powerful elite in the village council presented their proposal. They were so powerful that they controlled the village. The village people knew in their hearts that the plan was unthinkable, but no-one could speak out against the move. There was only one person standing and arguing against the plan and that was Father Oshida. The village people were pushed out, but they managed to postpone the final decision.

Meanwhile, the village people who had remained silent started coming to Father Oshida. "Your position is right", they said, "and that is our position too". They agreed unofficially to have a second village meeting. There they expressed their opposition to the plan, but the developers had already obtained a contract. It was a difficult situation, so it was taken to court and was debated there. Finally the court decided that the industrial use of the spring was not right, so it was stopped. In this way the people of the village were protected. That was the third stage in the growth of the community.

In 1981 Father Oshida in consultation with us, felt a need to meet with other people from around the world who were working for the poorest and the least, for the sake of justice and out of religious inspiration from different religious backgrounds. There were thirty-five

*Two Pilgrims Meet*

people who came from all over the world, and they had a one-week meeting in 1981. We called it the September Conference. They came from Hindu, Buddhist, Muslim and also Native American backgrounds, and we had discussions concerning the destruction of nature and the environment. When the meeting started there was joy, because the village people had been able to stand against the village leaders and stop the contract. There was joy, but at the same time the need to stand firm for the protection of the environment.

Takamori Soan   September Conference 1981

People came from all over the world. They were eager to learn and share, as we were more or less facing the same questions, concerning being exploited. When the meeting ended, the business contract to acquire the spring was drawn up again with new powers. We had to fight on for ten more years. Soan had to face this environmental threat to the destruction of its mountainside as a result of modernisation. It was a very difficult time. In order to fight the legal battle in court Soan did not have any financial backing. Even for the September Conference they lacked the needed finances. Many people who saw the significance of this meeting and the importance of the community, including many ordinary people, donated gifts and organised collections for us. Consequently Soan's position in the district became a centre for the defence of the environment and against the destruction of nature.

A new trend then began to gather momentum. Some wanted Japan to become a normal country like other countries with its own armed forces. This required the abolition of the Ninth Article, which is the peace article of the constitution. So we had to make clear how important the peace constitution had been after the war in lifting Japan from the ashes. The yearning for peace had been shared by the Japanese people out of their own bitter experiences. But now, because of economic recovery and prosperity there was a change of atmosphere in Japan. In 2006 the new Prime Minister, Shinzo Abe, wanted to change the constitution, but failed in his first term as leader, because this proved absolutely impossible. Japanese sentiment still insisted on keeping the peace constitution, in spite of all the difficulties. Abe's health deteriorated, and he had to resign. But after the Fukushima disaster he returned to power in 2012.

So Soan started a peace pilgrimage and joined other groups in campaigning against nuclear power stations and nuclear weapons, as well as supporting the peace constitution. This could be called a fourth stage in the community's development. A key point in the present situation is that the generation that experienced the wars is now a minority and is less than twenty percent of the population. Their average age is in the eighties and nineties. They are fast disappearing. My wife, Yoshiko, believes that they have kept silent, because their war time experiences cannot easily be described. But now, in this last stage of their lives, they are speaking out and saying, 'no more war'. How they can affect the eighty per cent of the population, who have never experienced war, remains to be seen.

So responding to the question - Why is Takamori Soan the hidden treasure of Japan? - I would say that in my experience the community is really witnessing to the blessing and given-ness of reality. They have adopted a clear position in support of the Ninth Article of the constitution, in spite of the present political situation and the destructive threat of nuclear power stations. In this respect, their position is clearly against modernisation and commercialisation, which threaten to destroy both nature and humanity.

Basil: So where does the Takamori Soan memorial garden to the victims of war fit into that?

Minoru: The memorial garden is a protest against the violence of militarism, which led to Japan invading other countries and suppressing the peoples of those countries. Militarism is very difficult to control. It is totally against the spirit of forgiveness and the blessing of reality. The only way to live in this reality is love and peace. This way to truth and God is totally ignored by militarism. To invade other countries and make them suffer is the expression of a society which denies reality. In the garden there are memorials engraved on stone dedicated to the victims of Japanese aggression in Korea, China, the Philippines and other South-East Asian countries. Each one is placed before a tree. After this in a central place Father Oshida inscribed these words in Japanese characters: *In the sea of infinite, ceaseless tears, I stand for ever.* Therefore, this memorial place says clearly that we Japanese really made them suffer. 'Them' means our brothers in China, our Korean brothers, and our brothers in the Philippines. We really victimised them. But they are our brothers! So we repent and pray for them.

Memorial to Chinese Victims

Minoru beside the Memorial
*In the sea of infinite, ceaseless tears, I stand for ever.*

The garden shows that Japan has been blessed with such an intimate relationship between nature and humanity, which has shown itself in a gentle, fellow feeling. This was expressed by Yasunari Kawabata in 1968, in his speech on receiving the Nobel Prize for literature, entitled: "Japan, the Beautiful, and Myself." His speech depicts the coexistence between nature and man. In this coexistence peace and love and compassion prevail.

Another Nobel Prize winner for literature, Oe Kenzaburo, on receiving the award, entitled his speech: "Japan the Ambiguous and I." He said bluntly that "Japan, the beautiful and myself," the essence of the Japanese spirit, which has cultivated Japanese sensitivity, not only among men but with nature - no longer lives in Japan. There is no space in Japan where we can find meaningful hope. But a meaningful way out is being expressed by the victims of the atomic bombs, through their cries and their prayers. There is a way out: through suffering together with the least, and through prayer.

Despite my limited experience of staying at the ashram, I have met some visitors coming to Takamori Soan. For example, on one occasion I met two Chinese ladies visiting Soan, which was unusual. They were very touched by this special place and asked me to explain the reason for the building of the memorial garden. So I asked Father Oshida why he had built a special memorial sanctuary. In his view the present reality is of a world full of the immensity of tears. The least and lowest are suffering the most. So he inscribed these words on a plaque in the garden: *In the sea of infinite, ceaseless tears, I stand for ever.* Then based on this I explained to the Chinese that the mark of a nation state is violence. The state has no concern for the victims. We must go beyond the nation state. That is why Soan is moving in that direction, always thinking of the least and lowest. One of the Chinese was in tears. It was most unexpected. In another case, a Filipino family also came to the ashram and the man was in tears before the memorial to victims in the Philippines. To a follower of Gandhi from India, I said, this is Gandhi's position: "In the infinite sea of tears I will stand forever." He said, "Yes, that is my position too in India." Hearing the story of Takamori Soan, he said, "I am thankful for this community."

Basil: The message of Soan is complex.

Minoru: But very simple: be emancipated, liberated from violence and the nation state.

Basil: The complication is to see how that position is arrived at by Father Oshida. But anyone coming from China, Korea or the Philippines, who sees the garden, will definitely be touched, because they will see that Japanese are identifying with their suffering. But to move beyond that and see how you arrive at this understanding is to come to the point, where one can realise that this is only possible if one sees and experiences the reality of God's presence, and the fact that we are brothers and sisters with people of other races and nations.

Minoru: It is not simply a formula – we are sent the invitation by God, from God. Responding to this, reality is revealed: to see God, to listen to God, to be God directed and inspired by God and to become as God, so identified are we with him. Then this beautiful reality is given: we are brothers and sisters and so we must go forward together. We should not be enslaved by the past. That's why without forgiving, without going beyond hatred, those miserable realities will remain.

Basil: As you say, the hatred and bitterness go when you see the reality.

Minoru: We go beyond hatred and bitterness. When we do, it is a kind of sign that we have changed from inhumanity.

Basil: For me, Takamori Soan stands for something else. Different things drew me to Soan. The first thing is the memorial garden where there is a clear recognition that people from all these East Asian nations have suffered so much through the Pacific War in their own countries. There is a weeping together with them. Japanese are not only saying we are sorry for it – but rather that we are weeping continuously with the victims and for the suffering our nation has caused. Anybody from China or Korea or the Philippines coming to Soan will be very moved, because there they will see Japanese are weeping with us. The second thing that impresses me is what you said about the struggle to preserve the source of the stream, coming out of the mountain side. That's where you like to go and drink from the spring. That place is the Source: a source for a river, but also a symbolic source. This source is where we receive our life, from God.

Minoru: And it is overflowing.

Basil: Yes, overflowing as a pure gift. Do we want industry to destroy the gift? It is a terrible thing that industry could be allowed to destroy the gift.

Minoru: After two decades the village leaders and powerful industrialists still want to buy it and use it.

Basil: What you are describing is one aspect of the Soan, of a practical struggle to maintain the environment. But the actual picture there is of life coming forth. Where does it come from, from the source? It does not come from anywhere else. What is that source? The source is God, who is the source of nature, also. The third thing that impresses me is the place of prayer, silent prayer, where we can sit in silence. We have the opportunity and the possibility of connecting with reality, otherwise we will be talking too much.

Minoru: In silence we are in the overwhelming presence of God.

Basil: Exactly. To be in the presence, you have to sit in silence. I agree that the rice field is a nice place, where you work together, and you have explained about that. I suppose there is also something else which attracts me, and that is in the garden where there is a memorial of Jesus on the cross. When you enter the ashram, you can only enter by going under the cross on your path. You can't proceed without going through the cross. Why is the cross in that place? It is there because Jesus also identified with our suffering. Without the cross, we are not forgiven and we cannot forgive. Through the cross we receive the spirit of forgiveness.

I think Soan for me, therefore, is a visual demonstration. It is not abstract. All these truths are visualised and can be experienced. They are not concrete or abstract. They are not theoretical. They are not ideological. They are actually made visual and to experience them is a powerful communication. The ashram holds all this together in community, so it is something you can enter into and enjoy.

Minoru: I am so thankful God has given such a place.

Basil: That's why I say it is a hidden treasure. For here in this hidden spot, away from the busy world, we can see everything that you have discovered, and all that you have been talking about.

*Two Pilgrims Meet*

# No More War

*The cry of Japan after the war that led to Peace Clause Nine in the constitution was for "No more war". Is this a realistic aim today for both Japan and China?*

Minoru: "No more war" is my constant and continuous, daily prayer, for both China and Japan. But to explain what this means I have to describe how my conviction was gradually formed through what I have experienced.

When I came back from Shanghai in 1946, just carrying a rucksack, I was hoping to find something better awaiting me in Japan. But after landing I felt very depressed. It became clear to me as I travelled by train from Kyushu in the south, and moved towards my father's home town of Ichinoseki in the northern part of Japan, that this train journey exposed me to the real situation in Japan, without any ambiguity. City after city was literally flat. The people we saw had no vitality. The situation in Hiroshima was just disastrous. As we moved on towards Tokyo my family were puzzled at the sight of women knocking on the windows of the train. The doors were blocked by people who were not supposed to be in the train. So the women were banging on the windows again and again, trying to get us to open the windows, so that they could come in with their bags and food. Because they could not get food in the cities they had gone to the countryside and in exchange for what they had they got food for their families. The numbers increased in Tokyo and the train was full of these women. We had to change trains in Tokyo and had to wait one or two days there before we could get the train prepared for us. We were appalled at the sight of homeless children wandering about the city, enormous numbers of them.

Then we took the train and reached my father's home and my uncle's family. They were astonished to see us. They whole-heartedly welcomed us and we stayed there for one year. The conditions there were very severe. My father tried to get a job but it proved impossible. So my elder sister and brother gave up their studies. My elder sister, fortunately, had a relationship with Shanghai friends and went to work with them in Tokyo. Though we stayed in my uncle's home for one year my father could not get a job.

So we moved to my mother's home in Kyushu. There my mother's father and mother, though so old, received us and cared for us. There again no job was available. Many people were in the same boat. Fortunately my elder brother found a job at the age of eighteen in a remote place, in one of the smallest coal mines. Even forgotten coal mines like that one were kept open. He worked for about six months and then asked us to come to the place where he was working. So we moved there and he worked six months more. Meanwhile he found a job that was suitable for my father and a place big enough for the family.

Through my mother we gradually met people working in this forgotten place. They were always without exception uprooted people, victims of the war. Their houses had been burned down. Nothing remained, and there was nothing they could rely on for support. Some had been soldiers, who had bitter war experiences and found it difficult to work. But around that small coal mine there was a community and we found ourselves very much at home there. Then we could see that what we had endured were not isolated experiences. We all shared in the bitterness of war together. But there was no hope for the future of Japan. The country was destroyed, crushed.

I began to study. I went to high school. It was a remote place. On foot it took one hour to reach the station. From that station to the station where the high school was located took one or two hours. Even at the age of fifteen, I could sense a prevailing feeling of hopelessness. People were longing for a way out and hoping for a future for Japan, in spite of everything.

Then in 1947, on May 3rd, suddenly the new constitution appeared. It was simply written and not difficult to read. Surprisingly that small community of uprooted people were literate people. They had been educated in the past and they could read. When they saw the peace constitution there was a kind of stir among them. It was their common experience that war is just meaningless, disastrous, barbaric and inhuman. So never again would they go that way! That was the common feeling, because they had endured bombing every day. It had been just too much. It was literally hell. Then suddenly in 1947 they were exposed to the peace constitution and shared a common feeling: this is the way out. Here is hope for Japan. I could sense the people's joy, and I also shared with them in the conviction that this is the only way forward.

People say the constitution was something given by America, but content-wise, it really represented the yearning of the Japanese people. They knew nothing of the negotiations that had gone on, so when it was made public it appeared as a gift from Heaven. Actually from America! But we received it in that way. Therefore in spite of the present changes in the international situation the commitment to peace remains firmly embedded in the hearts and minds of the Japanese people. That was what I observed, and what I have found to be true in a much deeper way since then. So "No more War" and the Peace Constitution in the context of Japanese history are identical.

So now coming to the point: how is this to be applied to the relationship between China and Japan? My position maybe exceptional, compared to most Japanese, having been brought up in China. In this respect the two of us are very similar, because we both grew up in China to the age of eleven or twelve or in my case to thirteen. I was brought up by Chinese, eating Chinese food and with constant contact with Chinese. We had adventures in Shanghai with friends and lost our way, so my family had to call the police to find us! Through all these experiences something of China is in my bones and in my being. So my position is probably different from that of most Japanese, but fundamentally I think we still share a fellow feeling with China.

For example, historically speaking, China and Japan are related to an extraordinary degree. During its long history Japan always kept its door open to learn from China and this was repeated over many centuries, as Japanese often went west. That relationship continued from the sixth century onwards, even when Japan closed its doors to the outside world in the seventeenth and eighteenth centuries. The port of Nagasaki always remained open to China. There has been a continuous relationship at different levels.

Most significantly from my point of view we have been united in our search for the truth. That is something which goes beyond national boundaries. For example Dogen, who founded the Soto Zen school in Japan, went to China and stayed for three years. He found truth there, and his teacher recognised that he was the person who would inherit his position, even though he was not Chinese. On coming back to Japan Dogen contributed greatly to the enrichment of Japanese culture, the Japanese spirit and the essence of Japanese aspirations. That is why Yasunari Kawabata quoted first from Dogen in his "Japan, the Beautiful, and Myself" speech on receiving the Nobel Prize for Literature. The Japanese spirit inspires a deep, mutual relationship, not only with man but with nature, and through it we have cultivated a gentle, indescribable care for each other. So in my case, ever since 1968, I have been part of a dialogue fellowship between Zen Buddhism and Christianity.

I found another impressive person in history, not this time moving from Japan to China, but from China to Japan. Jianzhen felt called to Japan to share the truth. So he tried to come to Japan, but in the eighth century it was not easy, because storms threatened to destroy the fragile sailing boats. He set out for Japan, but his first, second, third, fourth and fifth attempts all failed. Finally he was successful, but by this time he had become blind. However he was received reverently and his Buddhist tradition still lives on. His huge temple in Kyoto still stands. These are just two examples, one of a monk going from Japan to China and the other of a monk coming from China to Japan. These two countries have been so blessed and deeply united. At many different levels Japan has learned so much from China, as we have done in the modern period from the West.

Now, coming to the present condition, I must say it looks hopeless. However Ma Licheng argues that Japan has done everything it could in recent decades for China. For the future, both countries should work together in a close, mutual relationship. He has just written an article summarising what he has discovered in his research. For example, he says that Japan has given China huge loans for investment for many projects. He says that many of these things are simply not known in China. Aid has been given not only from the Japanese government but also from private companies and individuals. In the 1960s and 1970s Japanese approved of China more than any other country, even more than the United States! Sadly most Chinese do not know this.

In 1978, Japanese regarded China as the country they were most intimately related to. But now the two countries are divided and Japanese who feel close to China are in a tiny minority. For example, I have just been reading a short article about Japanese going to China from 1970 onwards to plant trees in a desert area. This was done by volunteers going to China to plant trees. Now, it is said that seventy per cent of the trees have grown up and some are up to forty metres tall. This is totally unknown to most people, including Japanese, and even less so among the Chinese. I feel that in spite of anti-Japan sentiment, friendship can be built up between the two countries. Friendship, not just on the intellectual level but at the heart level, is essential. Japanese who are familiar with China say that despite all the difficulties there are some Chinese who are really men of sincerity. It is possible for a few sincere people to work together and make progress. This again could be a possible breakthrough in the present situation.

The Japanese film star, Takakura Ken, is such a person. He had an impact on people through his commitment to love and justice. Chinese who worked with him were affected and inspired by his example. One was a lawyer. After retirement he was invited by big companies to work for them, but he refused. "No", he said, "I want to help people who are helpless." Why? Because he had been inspired by Takakura Ken and by seeing his films. Another Chinese is now managing an airline company. He has kept the doors open for flights to Japan, whatever the situation. So now through his efforts many Chinese are travelling to Japan. The numbers are relatively small but his commitment is firm. Another, who is a very famous film director, had his eyes opened when he was young by seeing the example of Takakura Ken. He felt he had always been inspired by Ken and said, "I'm so fortunate to have met such a person; I feel, instinctively, that I cannot find such a person in China, and I will not see anyone like him again. But the memory of him remains in my heart." Everybody who participated in making Takakura Ken's last film had such affection and respect for him. He, in turn, appreciated and respected them. Others felt that just by his being there, not saying anything, or doing anything, but just by being there, he inspired them.

Basil: Can I ask you about the present situation? Has Prime Minister Abe been able to change the Japanese constitution, or is he still trying to change the peace constitution?

Minoru: No. He is trying to change it; that is right. But right now it is impossible, though the government is moving towards effecting a change. And America is urging the government to make this change. Although America created the peace constitution after the war, they very soon encouraged Japan to take up arms.

Basil: In 1950 during the Korean War America pressed Japan to form an army and defend herself. In doing so they undermined the peace constitution and Article 9 in particular.

Minoru: Fortunately, at that time, even politicians continued to resist American pressure, but they were forced to compromise and have defence forces. But now America is again pressing Japan to build up its military forces and not to think they can continue to have a free ride, simply relying on the US to protect them. China has become so powerful in military terms that a change is necessary. At the popular level in Japan people feel that China's use of military threats is inexcusable. So affection for China is disappearing in Japan. In the past some ordinary Japanese felt the need to show their penitence for China's sufferings during the war by doing what they could in their personal capacity. They felt it was wrong to depend only on the government to give aid, so they did things like planting trees in China. True friendship between the two countries is essential to counteract the anti-Japan propaganda in China, which is such a harmful policy.

Basil: So is Japan allowed to defend itself, according to the peace constitution?

Minoru: The original spirit of the constitution was that if you attack me, I would just say this is not right. But the actual situation is that if we are attacked, we will do our best to defend ourselves. But we would not give up the ideal of the ninth article of the constitution. That is our lifeline.

Basil: The present situation is that Japan does have an army, navy and air-force for self-defence. But what Prime Minister Abe is trying to do is to extend this right, so that Japan can use their forces to help other countries.

Minoru: Yes, and the government tries to justify its position, but in doing so they are exposed to self-contradiction. However in the Japanese parliament they have the majority.

Basil: According to popular opinion, you say the majority of people in Japan, or more than fifty per cent, are still against any change to the peace constitution and want to preserve it even now.

Minoru: Fortunately young people are gradually being awakened to the situation. They don't have the experience of war shared by the older generations. The politicians of the previous generation knew what war was like, so they tried to resist American pressure. But Abe does not have any experience of war and is now supported by people who are like him. The older generation are just excluded, more and more.

Basil: "No more war" means also no use of violence.

Minoru: That is basically it.

Basil: Gandhi rejected the use of violence to settle any matter. China and Japan both agreed in their 1973 treaty, not to use violence or the threat of violence to settle any dispute between the two countries. Now however China relies on increasing its military might, because they do not wish to be invaded again. However Desmond Tutu believes this is a misconception, for security cannot be found through violence and reliance on arms and weapons. He said, it is a big mistake to think that true security can grow out of the use of weapons. Of course, that reminds us of Mao Zedong's statement that power grows out of a barrel of a gun. Tutu's point is that we have learnt from history that security does not come from relying on military weapons.

Minoru: Yes. The trouble is that the present state of society in Japan is deteriorating. Each morning when I read the newspapers I feel shocked to read of couples being murdered. Every day there is some such news report. It is the innocent who are being killed, including children. This was quite rare in my young days, in spite of the poverty. In this way, by scientific achievement, we have reached the point of self-destruction.

Basil: Another well-known writer, J.P. Lederach, has pointed out that when nation states rely upon weapons, inevitably they use them at the expense of a defenceless population. It is the defenceless who pay the price for a government that depends upon weapons. But what he also says is that nations rely on military force out of fear. It is because of fear that they entrust their security to weapons. So dealing with that fear becomes the task of the peacemakers.

Minoru: The contemporary situation is becoming more and more inhuman. The most civilised nations have the weapons to destroy the whole world! They want to have them and are using whatever they have achieved on the battle ground.

Basil: That may well be true. I did find a good quotation here, which would support what you have said, from Kenzaburo Oe. In a lecture he said: "After the end of the Second World War it was a categorical imperative for Japan to declare that we renounce war for ever as a central part of the new constitution. The Japanese chose the principle of eternal peace as the basis of morality for our rebirth after the World War."

Minoru: Very interesting. He was saying that the Japanese sensitive spirit which has been associated with Dogen and others is gone. Nothing remains. What could take its place? He could find no answer, but he kept on trying to find an answer. One of the key people who opened his eyes was Shigeto Fumio, the doctor who treated many in Hiroshima. He was also impressed by the Okinawan people. They have a unique memorial naming all those who died in the invasion of Okinawa, of all nationalities, both Japanese and American. All of these people believed passionately that there should be "no more war".

Basil: You might agree with the preamble of the constitution of UNESCO, which was written in 1945. "Since wars begin in the minds of men, it is in the minds of men that the defence of peace must be constructed." The conviction is that wars begin in the minds of men, so it is in the minds of men that there must be a change. This is very much what you are saying, because unless our thinking changes, the world will continue to revert back to war.

Minoru: At the same time I feel nervous, because wars often start accidentally. When this happens it is difficult to stop them, and that is fatal. The history of war indicates this tendency. Sometimes war is beyond human control. That is the difficulty. That is why the longing for "no more war" is my prayer.

Basil: Yes. It has to be a prayer for peace.

Minoru: I hope that China and Japan will be fully awakened. Then their existence can be for the enrichment of the entire world and for peace. China's huge military expenditure will then be unnecessary and they can use the savings for the welfare of the people, not only in China but outside China as well. Japan is just a small country, but we are still ready to move together with China. That would then be a worthy response in keeping with our ancient heritage as civilised peoples.

Basil: I don't think that many people in China appreciate the fact that Japan is the only large country in the world, which has a pacifist constitution. Your constitution was adopted, as you have explained, not because of imposition by America, but because of the will of the people and the desire of everyone after the war. To maintain this peace position, this pacifist position for the last seventy years, has not been easy.

Minoru: You know, the pressure for change from America has been just enormous.

Basil: I know. But nevertheless Japan has maintained its pacifist constitution for seventy years. Surely, that should tell China that they don't need to fear Japan, because Japan is deeply committed to peace and has maintained this commitment ever since the War. This commitment is deeply rooted in the nation's experience and it is the present opinion of the majority of people in Japan that the constitution must be kept unchanged.

Minoru: Thank you for your encouragement.

# Nuclear Weapons

*Nuclear weapons remain the most serious threat to world peace. Can there be reconciliation between China and Japan without dealing with the nuclear threat?*

Minoru: This is a fundamental question for me, because I am personally drawn to listen to the witness of the victims of the atomic bomb. My attention is focused on listening to what they are saying. One phrase symbolises the focus of my search: "the cries and silent prayers of the victims of the atomic bomb in Hiroshima ... the place consumed, heaven burnt red and bodies melted."

Shigeto Fumio, the medical doctor responsible for the specialised hospital for the victims of the atom bomb in Hiroshima, was working there for more than thirty years. Daily he was confronted by the sufferings of the victims in an intensive relationship. In this intensive relationship he found these people to be the least and lowest in the contemporary world. So my question, naturally, is this: How does Christ minister to the problems of these who suffer in agony, the weak and the helpless? In this plight both doctors and victims share the same destiny.

Shigeto Fumio strongly felt that nuclear weapons went beyond the limit and that the use of such weapons is clearly a crime against humanity. Shigeto Fumio goes on to say, we are really in the midst of the darkness. We are not aware what we are doing; we are really destroying ourselves, and not only ourselves but nature as well. This is because we remain silent. All kinds of justification are put forward for this silence, but it is still accepted as a way out. The reality is that we are in the dark. But our destiny is to witness to the fact that we are in the darkness, and our task in this situation is to pray.

Basil: How does this relate to the relationship between Japan and China?

Minoru: Can there be reconciliation between China and Japan without dealing with the nuclear threat? I think this is impossible. China's understanding of the threat posed by nuclear weapons is unknown, so far. In view of this, reconciliation is a long way off, quite apart from the many other questions that need to be addressed. If you go this way, relying on nuclear weapons, there is no way out. I don't think they are willing to admit that nuclear weapons have such serious implications, in other words that they threaten to destroy humanity and lead to self-destruction.

Alexei Arbatov, a Russian nuclear expert was recently interviewed by a Japanese journalist. He is a very influential person in Russia, advising on policy matters. He was asked: "Can we destroy nuclear weapons?" He replied: "Sometime in the future mankind will surely destroy nuclear weapons. I believe that. The reason is this: we have nuclear power to destroy the whole world within a few hours. Having such a weapon, how can we ever be secure?" Reasoning quietly, this Russian specialist says: "The civilisation of which we are so proud is not worthy to be called civilisation if we rely on such weapons." He went on to say, we have to abolish nuclear weapons, but this will need enormous patience. These weapons cannot be abolished by slogans. In order to achieve progress we have to have a reasonable degree of unanimity on the necessity for destroying nuclear weapons. To accept this position is enormously difficult. Once arranged, then negotiation with patience is needed, because it will decide the fate of civilisation. For this really strong political leadership is necessary.

Basil: That is good. Are you saying that you feel that in China this is not understood? But China does understand the danger of North Korea achieving their full nuclear capacity.

Minoru: China has such a strong influence over North Korea. They could be a very important ally.

Basil: Even China is finding it difficult to restrain North Korea, and has condemned the recent claim by North Korea to have tested a hydrogen bomb

Minoru: China has had a lot of chances to restrain North Korea. It may be too late now.

Basil: Do you think that China has any intention of using nuclear weapons, or are they simply for defence?

Minoru: A country says it is simply for defence, but that defence is a threat to other countries.

Basil: So can you talk about the Mayors for Peace programme, which began from Hiroshima? Is there any result from this movement?

Minoru: The movement is spreading. The organisers feel that the nuclear threat can be overcome by people's power. There is no real sense of that yet. But the movement is spreading gradually. It takes enormous time to have an effect. Mayors for Peace began in 1982 and grew slowly until it really took off in 2005 with 600 cities joining as members.

Basil: Have any Chinese cities joined the Mayors for Peace programme?

Minoru: Yes, 7 Chinese cities joined the movement in the 1980s, but none since then, which probably indicates the decline in the popularity of Japan in China since the 1990s.

Basil: There are now 6,893 member cities in all continents (as of 2015). The vision is to eliminate nuclear weapons by 2020. The membership is unevenly distributed around the world with Japan far outnumbering any other country, having 1,597 member cities. This reflects the fact that the aim is to convey the message of survivors of the atomic bombs in Hiroshima and Nagasaki. Surprisingly the country with the next largest number of city members is Iran with 770, whereas South Korea has none and Indonesia despite its size has only 3 member cities, and India, the second most populous country in the world only has 19 member cities. So China is not the only one with a small membership.

You have not mentioned so far that your wife, Yoshiko, was living just outside Hiroshima when the bomb was dropped, so you have a personal connection with this tragedy as well.

Minoru: Yoshiko was seven years old at the time. Since then some of her relatives have passed away, because of the effect of nuclear radiation, including her elder sister. She herself remembers the black rain falling on her white school dress, so she has to be ready at any time to face the same destiny. But she does not say much about this. For her, personally, it is just simply a disaster. So very naturally she wants to see no more disasters like this.

## Two Pilgrims Meet

Basil: You go on a peace pilgrimage, together? You have been doing that for many years.

Minoru: From Takamori Soan, yes. I have tried, previously, to describe to you in depth that I think we are in the midst of the darkness. First, we have to be awakened to this, because nuclear weapons show that in destroying man and nature we are at a crucial point in world history. The victims feel Christ is with them, in their cries and prayers.

Basil: Do you also want to say anything about the use of nuclear power reactors in the light of Fukushima and the present situation? Are you against the use of nuclear power, because of the assault on nature?

Minoru: That's right, we are destroying nature. That disaster is just enormous. For example, one village refused to have a nuclear power station, because they did not need that power. The village was beautiful and in harmony with nature and with their community. This is unusual, because nowadays it is very difficult to preserve village life in competition with economic commercialisation. Many Japanese people were attracted to the village and came to find out how they managed to have such an ecological balance. Visitors came to that village to learn from them. It was located far from the power station that exploded, but because of the direction of the wind the whole village was destroyed and they had to be evacuated from the area. For forty years they had really struggled, working hard together. It is a poor area, but they prospered and the village people were satisfied and thankful. Those who came to see this village wondered how such a miracle was possible in such a poor area. By cooperating with each other and also with nature they were able to manage without using chemical fertilisers. But then due to this nuclear disaster everything was destroyed and they had to leave.

Basil: I think, as you say, people are aware of the threat of nuclear power to nature and to the environment, but not so much aware that nuclear bombs are a threat to humanity. During the Cold War period between America and Russia, up to the end of the 1980s, people were terrified about what could happen. After that period, the danger seemed to pass, but the present is even more dangerous for humanity.

Minoru: Yes, but it is amazing that Angela Merkel, the German prime minister, after reflecting on the Fukushima disaster has decided that Germany should not rely on nuclear power any more. She said that when she came to Japan and learnt about the consequences of the Fukushima power station disaster, she decided that Germany would not invest any more in nuclear power.

Basil: That's interesting.

Minoru: Another leader who has changed his opinion on the use of nuclear power is our former Prime Minister, Koizumi. He had been determined to expand the peaceful use of nuclear power and therefore supported the building of nuclear power stations. But, just like Angela Merkel, when he saw the consequences of the Fukushima disaster, he said, "I have been wrong. I accept responsibility for my mistaken policy and now I stand against the use of nuclear power reactors."

*Two Pilgrims Meet*

Basil: I think your quotation from the Russian, Alexei Arbatov, was very significant and important. He seems to understand that nuclear power and nuclear bombs are a threat to the existence of humanity, because the whole world could be destroyed within a few hours. I think that most people don't understand that, even now.

Minoru: To rely on such weapons for our security is not worthy of civilisation.

Basil: That of course is a very powerful point. To be in favour of the use of nuclear weapons is to depart from civilisation. Civilisation is not a fit word to use for the society in which we are now living.

Minoru: Alexei Arbatov is talking about nuclear weapons.

Basil: Yes. But he is right, and you are right, that we are living in darkness and are largely unaware of the dangers. This affects Japan and China as well – not just Japan.

# Ma Licheng's View of Reconciliation between China and Japan

*Chinese writer, Ma Licheng, outlined his view of China-Japan relations in an article in the Japanese journal, Churokouron, in August 2015. Minoru summarises his position here.*

Ma Licheng's basic position is that the process of reconciliation between China and Japan, though not clearly recognised, has always been going on in spite of ups and downs. History shows this has been proceeding from at least 1950 onwards. In China, particularly recently, Japan has been presented as the enemy, with whom there can be no possibility of reconciliation. That is the general contemporary trend in China. But from his point of view the desire for reconciliation and mutual coexistence between the two countries has been repeatedly confirmed. He is convinced that progress towards reconciliation is both necessary and ongoing.

Ma Licheng refers to the views of a Chinese writer, Litong Chou, who believes that the divisions between China and Japan will never be solved, and that Japan is China's main enemy. Ma Licheng rejects this view. He bases his argument on two levels of history. On one level is the history of the war against Japan. On another level is the history of reconciliation and cooperation between the two countries.

On the first level concerning wartime history, he stresses the painful fact of Japan's invasion of China. We cannot forget this disaster, and we should not forget it.

But it is not enough just to remember the war. Regarding the history of Japan's invasion, we know this caused enormous suffering for the Chinese people. It wounded China in heart and mind. The pain cannot be expressed or put into words. But, at the same time, that war inflicted enormous pain and suffering on the Japanese people. After the war, Japanese society and the Japanese government became deeply aware of what they had done to China. Out of that realisation came the desire for reconciliation and the pursuit of peace.

Regarding this history of reconciliation between China and Japan, four important documents have been exchanged, particularly between 1972 and 2008. The first of these was the Joint Statement in 1972 that normalised relations between China and Japan for the first time after the end of the war. Both sides committed themselves to maintain peaceful relations. The second one was on 15th August 1995, when Tomiichi Murayama, the Prime Minister of Japan apologised officially for the harm done to Japan's neighbours during the war period. The Murayama apology clearly established the government's position concerning Japan's responsibility and awareness of the past. It stated that in the past Japan invaded neighbouring countries, which included China, and had inflicted damage and suffering. This statement was welcomed by China and by Japan's other neighbours in East Asia.

Ma Licheng says that he has checked through Chinese records and found that from 1972 to 2008 the Japanese government apologised officially twenty-five times. Japan has repeatedly reaffirmed Prime Minister Murayama's statement.

In April 2007, the Chinese Prime Minister, Wen Jiabao, visited Japan and addressed the Diet. In his official speech, representing China, he delineated China's position in regard to his country's relation with Japan, particularly with regard to the history question. He said, since the establishment of normal diplomatic relations in 1972 between China and Japan, the Japanese government has continued to admit that Japan did invade China. The Japanese leaders are deeply aware of how this invasion caused much pain and suffering to the Chinese people. So, out of this awareness and through reflection on the past they have expressed their regret. The Chinese government and people take this very seriously and accept that statement as the basis for moving forward. In Ma Licheng's understanding this means a kind of reconciliation between both countries and a reason for China to look forward to a creative relationship with Japan.

The fourth important landmark took place in the following year, on 7th May 2008, when President Hu Jintao and Japanese premier, Yasuo Fukuda, signed a Joint Statement to promote a mutually beneficial relationship between their countries. The Chinese side expressed their appreciation for Japan's record as a peaceful nation for more than sixty years, as well as its contribution to the peace and stability of the world. Both governments mutually agreed that all problems would be solved by peaceful means through consultation and negotiation without the use or threat of force. In this way it was similar to the 1972 joint statement, establishing normal diplomatic relations. From Ma Licheng's point of view, these four documents deal with the past problems caused by the Japanese invasion of China and recognise that Japan has taken this very seriously and is determined not to repeat the past.

Ma Licheng now turns to his second level of history concerning the history of reconciliation between China and Japan. This process has been going on ever since the end of the war, with one side repenting for the past and the other accepting this regret as genuine, and both moving forward together. This mutual interaction is reflected in the language of the joint statements.

The Communist Party maintained a positive attitude to Japan from the beginning. Chou Enlai's contribution, in particular, was immensely important. In his view China and Japan had always enjoyed a close relationship throughout their long history, apart from the previous sixty years. It was Chou Enlai, who invited three members of the Japanese Diet to Beijing in 1952. The Japanese delegation led by a lady, Kora Tomi, had no official standing, as formal, diplomatic relations had not then been established between the two governments. However Chou Enlai wanted to start something at an interpersonal level, so an informal agreement was made to improve trade links with Japan.

In 1956 there was an exhibition of Japanese goods based upon the 1952 informal people's treaty. It was opened on 6th October in Beijing in the presence of Mao Zedong. On the opening day Mao met the Japanese representative, Shozo Marata, who was in charge of the special exhibition of Japanese products. After viewing the exhibition Mao said: "Japanese are great people. They are courageous, hard-working and wise. I want to establish good relations with Japan." He then turned to Shozo Marata and asked him to present his best wishes to the Emperor! It was clear from Mao's remarks that he liked Japanese people, particularly their three virtues of courage, hard work and wisdom. He then wrote in the visitor's book, "This is a very encouraging exhibition, and I hope the Japanese people will be successful." So Ma Licheng wants to show that from the beginning the Communist Party wanted to establish a positive relationship with Japan. Eventually this led in 1972 to the establishing of formal diplomatic relations with Japan.

Ma Licheng then enumerates the help that Japan has given to China, beginning with the investment made by private companies as well as by government agencies. Between 1952 and 2014 Japanese companies have invested billions of yen in China. As many as 23,000 Japanese companies are listed as operating in China, employing at least ten million Chinese workers. Japanese government aid, known as ODA, started in 1979 and has continued since then. In 1979 China found it extremely difficult to obtain foreign funding. Ma Licheng likens Japanese aid to a Chinese proverb about the warmth of glowing embers in a snow covered land. We were covered by snow, he says, and Japan sent us fuel to give us warmth. This was an expression of Japanese sincerity in desiring to help modernise China. It was not simply the money that was important, but Japan's action, which showed their sincerity and repentance for what they had done to China. The generosity of the aid can be seen not only in its quantity but by the terms on which it was given. Japan gave something like forty per cent of all foreign aid received by China in this period. Japanese aid was given at an interest rate of 3.5%, whereas the World Bank's interest rate was 6.3% and Chinese banks charged 7%. The World Bank requires repayment of loans within sixteen years, but Japanese aid only has to be repaid within either thirty or forty years.

Ma Licheng notes that Japanese aid was used for 160 infrastructure projects all over China. These included such prestige works as the extension of Beijing airport, the new Shanghai Pudong airport and the building of major bridges. President Hu Jintao acknowledged China's debt to Japanese aid in his speech at Waseda University on 8 May 2008. He said that through these major infrastructure projects Japan had helped to modernise China, in doing so the Japanese people had given sacrificially out of heartfelt generosity. The Chinese people will never forget this generous aid.

Ma Licheng concludes that despite the current wave of anti-Japanese feeling in China, Chinese people have to recognise the importance of Japanese aid. This was given at a time when China was going through a difficult time. Aid was also given officially by the Japanese government to the Chinese government. Ma Licheng considers this to be a sort of reconciliation process, because the help given by Japan shows serious repentance for Japan's invasion of China. We also have a glimpse here of the Japanese appealing for an intimate relationship with China, as the country most close to them. Unfortunately appreciation for China is at an all time low now in Japan.

Ma Licheng then moves from dealing with the economic relations between China and Japan to consider other aspects of their relationship. In 1978 when Deng Xiaoping assumed power one of his early actions was to import Japanese films. Until then China had been closed to anything coming in from the outside. When Japanese films were imported they became very popular and made a great impact in China. This was a big surprise to Japanese film star, Takakura Ken, who became very popular in China. Young people were fascinated by his movies. When Takakura Ken died in 2014 the Chinese Minister of Foreign Affairs said that he had been the bridge between China and Japan. Chinese newspapers described him as an ambassador for Japan in China.

Then in 1984 Zhao Ziyang invited three thousand Japanese young people to come to Beijing in September and October. Their visit culminated in a grand reception at a huge hall in Beijing. On this occasion Zhao Ziyang said that if the young people of China and Japan are determined to develop friendly relations between their countries and if their children are educated to pursue this dream, then relations between China and Japan will be significantly deepened. That was what Zhao Ziyang was hoping for. Ma Licheng notes that 2015 marks the centenary of Zhao Ziyang's birth. His contribution to deepening the process of reconciliation between China and Japan was enormous, and for this Ma Licheng has heartfelt gratitude.

In June 1989 Deng Xiaoping's suppression of the Tiananmen Square protestors provoked a political storm. In July 1989 the G7 leaders reacted sharply and decided to enforce economic measures against China. Japan was one of the G7 members, but disassociated itself from this decision. At that time China was very isolated, her economy was weak and she needed aid. In August Japan restored economic relations with China, despite being a member of the G7. Then some members of the Japanese Diet who were sympathetic to China went to Beijing and met Deng Xiaoping. He was very appreciative of their support and told them: "Japan is our true friend. When we were really desperate, we found we could rely on the friendship of Japan." Ma Licheng wants to remind Chinese again and again that Japan has been consistently acting in this way. So he is pained by the mass media in China stirring up hatred for Japan and threatening to destroy Japan with nuclear weapons. He notes that Deng Xiaoping was then invited to Japan, which was an extraordinary step at that time. Deng immediately accepted the invitation, because China had been pushed into a corner and desperately needed aid.

But from 2010 China-Japan relations were badly affected by the Senkaku/Diaoyu Islands dispute. On an official level, relations between the governments suffered. But in spite of that at the popular level the flow of visitors between the two countries is increasing. The Chinese people coming to Japan are like a swarm. Ma Licheng comments that among the Chinese who visit Japan there is a saying: 'If you go to Japan, your view of Japan will be changed.' The reason is that in their eyes Japan is very prosperous and clean, very polite and civilised, orderly and sensitive. The Chinese are most impressed by this. If the Chinese are interviewed, they say that governments do not meet face to face, as they have done with Japanese people. Ma Licheng expects people to change the negative relationship at the government level. However the majority of people are swayed in mainland China by the mass media's hostile attitude to Japan.

On 13th December 2014, there was a special memorial service commemorating the Nanjing massacre. President Xi Jinping said at this memorial in Nanjing that the purpose was to remember the past and to promote the yearning for peace, not to perpetuate hatred. He encouraged Chinese and Japanese to continue their friendly relationship, always learning from history. With humility, we should contribute to peace - that was his official message. Ma Licheng points out that in this way Xi Jinping refers to the two levels of history, which he has described. Yes, the history of the past disasters of the Japanese invasion cannot and should not be forgotten. But if we only remember this and perpetuate hatred, then the future will be bleak, and we may have to face more wars.

Ma Licheng wants to emphasise that all the Chinese leaders he has mentioned have wanted to stress the importance of encouraging coexistence between China and Japan. Ma Licheng repeats again and again, quoting their authority, that we cannot forget the past disasters caused by Japan. But if we just remember these and carry on pursuing hatred, we will not be building a peaceful future. Therefore, the history of reconciliation and coexistence between China and Japan can be seen to exist from the beginning, and certainly from the establishment of Communist Party rule in China. This policy represents the consistent direction of China's relations with Japan and her hope for the future. Therefore the pursuit of reconciliation is of vital importance.

In conclusion, Ma Licheng wants to see the study of East Asian Reconciliation established as an academic discipline under the subtitle of "Peace, Reflection and Tolerance". He seems to be stressing the need for tolerance, that is tolerance by the Chinese people for Japan, and also the need for Japanese to learn the virtue of tolerance. Differences of opinion are inevitable and should be welcomed. But at the same time there must be tolerance. Tolerance will enable reconciliation to become the way out, in spite of talk of "eternal enemies", which leads inevitably to war.

# Responsibility for the Past

*What responsibility does the present generation have for the past? Do both Japan and China have to change their view of their history?*

Basil: We cannot ignore the past, as the Chukiren (Japanese Association of Returnees from China) insisted. Their motto, as we have noted earlier, was: "Forget not the past; make it your teacher for the future." The present reality is that the memory of Japan's invasion of China seventy years ago separates China and Japan and is a major obstacle to friendship between the two countries. We have to clarify this further by noting that it is the politicisation of history by the two governments that exacerbates the division. This has not always been the case, because after the end of the war China, first under the nationalist government and then under the Communist Party, acted benevolently towards the Japanese and only blamed the Japanese military clique for the war-time invasion. However, after 1990 it became increasingly convenient for the Chinese government to blame Japan for the war, in order to gain popular support and appeal to patriotic sentiment. The Japanese government has also found it convenient at times to draw a veil over the war period and not to address Chinese concerns about Japan's past.

How then is the history problem to be addressed? There are various questions, such as, why are China and Japan so divided by their views of the past, and why should the present generation be bothered by events that happened more than seventy years ago? What responsibility does the young generation have for a war that their grandparents fought? Why do Japan and China not forget the past and concentrate on building a peaceful future? How then do we address the history question, or the historical problem, and the history of the war in particular? Merely ignoring it will never remove Chinese fears or satisfy Japanese integrity.

There are a variety of possible approaches. The first one we have noted comes from the Chinese writer, Ma Licheng. Ma Licheng's approach is that China should give up its attitude of hatred and bitterness for the war. There is no future in persisting in perpetuating hatred for a war that happened seventy years ago, especially, as Japan has done its best to change and has indeed changed dramatically. Japan is not the warring military regime that it once was. Instead it is the only major pacifist country in the world! It has benefited China in so many ways and has given her so much aid and has helped China for a long time. So there is no reason for China not to respond positively, but rather to say to Japan, let us move forward and abandon feelings of hatred and bitterness, which will not be beneficial for either of us in the future.

Another approach comes from the historians Fumitaka Kurosawa and Ian Nish. You will remember that in 2013 you showed me their book published in Japanese, which has a title meaning in English, *A History of Reconciliation*. Prof. Kurosawa argues that the textbook controversy, which first erupted in the 1980s, led to the politicisation of history which became an obstacle to reconciliation between China and Japan. The misuse of history, which this is, should be overcome by a retelling of the past, free from distortion. Their book attempts to approach a history of reconciliation by establishing the facts, looking through a historian's eyes. They make the point that since the memory of the war is the root cause of Chinese distrust of Japan, the key to reconciliation lies in the history itself. For reconciliation to take place, both sides must share historical facts and support them and sincerely face up to their past history. Reconciliation has to be evidence-based; this means history-based. On that theme we are able to say that historians, both Japanese and Chinese, have been working together. For example, we have noted the book, *Toward a History Beyond Borders,* published in 2011. It is a compilation of articles by Japanese and Chinese historians working together, dealing with the contentious issues of Sino-Japanese relations during the past century.

Minoru: This must be very significant.

Basil: This book is a very good example, because these historians are coming together and trying to look at history beyond national borders. Of course they don't agree on everything, but they do come close together.

Minoru: Meetings among specialists, who know the facts so well, enable common problems to be shared and reconciliation to be pursued. This is very interesting.

Basil: The fact of meeting and discussing contentious issues, and also listening first to one side and then to the other is itself an important step forward.

Minoru: In that context, did they discuss the kind of patriotism in China which is identified with hating Japan?

Basil: Maybe, somewhere. Their conclusion was that just allowing the historical issues to be used by politicians is disastrous.

Minoru: Being historians, they recognise that this use of history for propaganda purposes is a manipulation of history at the lowest level men and nations are capable of. I am convinced from my experience that this is the lowest use of history we can stoop to. Nothing good can happen from this misuse. We have to face the reality that such propaganda is common in China.

Basil: That is why these historians are meeting together: to bridge this divide, so that this does not continue, because it is destructive.

Minoru: In Japan in the past we did experience this sort of history propaganda and suffered from it, due to fanatical nationalism. If that attitude really is prevalent in China, I think the poison of hatred for other countries will spread, not only within China, but elsewhere too.

Basil: We all tend to remember the good things we have done and the good our countries have done, just as we remember the bad things done to us – everything else is ignored! The bad things we have done we forget, and the good things others have done we also ignore. We only remember what we have achieved and what we have suffered. The British, for example, remember the Blitz inflicted by German bombers on London, and then afterwards the V1 and V2 missiles fired from Germany. We remember those bad things. We also remember the good things that we achieved, such as the successful D-Day landings. The good things Germany did, or the bad things we did to them, we do not think about. Later on we may open our minds and realise that their side of the story is also important and that we should listen to their point of view as well.

Another approach to history was expressed by an editor-in-chief of the *Asahi Shimbun*, Funabashi Yoichi. He said something very important. "It is deepened historical consciousness that is necessary for reconciliation. More apologies will make the current generation resistant and obstinate. What is important is not an apology but historical consciousness of why we had to apologise." He suggests that demanding apologies is not helpful, but understanding why they are demanded is important. We will come back to this point in a different connection later on, when we think about the younger generation.

A fourth way of looking at the history question comes from a Chinese political scientist, Yinan He, who has written a book on the search for reconciliation. This was published in Cambridge in 2009. Her book compares Sino-Japanese relations with German-Polish relations after the Second World War. She has some interesting things to say. She writes: "For countries that have experienced dramatic conflict, harmonious popular ties are not attainable until historically-rooted animosity has been eliminated. This does not mean that the memory of the conflict will utterly disappear, but if this happens people will be able to research and talk about their history without it being a source of resentment. When new bilateral disputes arise, the tendency is to hold history against the former enemy. To put it simply, popular reconciliation means that peoples of former enemy states need to put their traumatic history behind them. When this has happened the atmosphere between the two peoples will be dominated by mutual trust and a sense of affinity for both sides." She is clear that governments are usually to blame, because they want to continue to use past events for their own purposes and to gain popular support. She argues, and this is the thesis of her book, that we have to deal with the traumatic conflict that has happened in the past, and unless we deal with that we will not root out the animosity. It will not disappear. This is the situation in East Asia, where the animosity between China and Japan has not disappeared, although seventy years have gone by. The animosity does not disappear, if we do not deal with it. It does need to be dealt with somehow.

Another way of looking at the history question is provided by Professor Liu Cheng from Nanjing University, where he is a professor in the history department. He has two different things to say. You will be glad to know that his main advice is as follows: "Generally speaking, aim to improve friendship between China and Japan. Do not focus on the past, but extinguish hatred and extend forgiveness to the enemy." He quotes the famous writer, Hannah Arendt: "Forgiving serves to undo the deeds of the past, whose sins otherwise hang like the sword of Damocles over every new generation." But he has also expressed this point in a different way as well. He says that, "Most Chinese cannot separate the memory of the bitter past actions of militarist Japan from the present problems with democratic Japan. Chinese think of Japan as an invading enemy. This provokes hostile reactions. This attitude then provokes hostile reactions from Japan." He is aware that on China's side there is this critical feeling, but then for Chinese to express that feeling only promotes hostile reactions from Japan. This then becomes a two-way problem, not a one-way problem. How is this situation to be dealt with? Liu Cheng says, we have to extinguish hatred and extend forgiveness. That is not easy.

Another point of view is what we might call a commonsense viewpoint. When we go to neighbouring countries and we hear the other side's views, including their viewpoint on the past and on the wartime past, we find that they are human too. They want peace, and they are not to blame for what their predecessors did. They may not talk about the war at all, but we find that they want peace. We cannot blame them for what was done in the past. So we can work together to build a better future and overcome the legacy of emotional antagonism, as people realise that there is a degree of emotional antagonism to be overcome. But this antagonism can be dissipated, as we have already noted in discussing the importance of youth exchange visits, by the meeting of Chinese and Japanese citizens in China or Japan or anywhere in the world. This process goes on at all levels and is really going to be the best contribution to peace.

An interesting way of looking at history says: "The past is alive, and we move toward the past, not away from it." Now, I think when I read these words, I have to say that this is happening to me. For nearly fifty years I forgot my Chinese past, but in the last fifteen years my Chinese past has revived. I grew up in China, and every day I am thinking more and more about that past, as if I am moving backwards towards it! Not feeling this to be a backward movement, because the past for me in China is where I learned so much. That is part of my identity. It is so valuable and I don't want to move away from it; I want to understand it and build on it. This viewpoint says, the past is part of our identity. When we realise that, we realise that we have to think about it.

A new narrative of the past, a new way of seeing and telling the story is very important, because there are things in the past which need to be healed. That is something that Nelson Mandela touched on when the Truth and Reconciliation Commission was started in South Africa. He said when the Truth and Reconciliation Commission was launched: "The choice we have is not whether we should disclose the past, but how it will be done. It must be done in such a way that reconciliation and peace are promoted." He went on to say that everyone was a victim in the past; everybody suffered. In South Africa, the whole nation suffered, so the process of healing is necessary for everybody. That will be true elsewhere in the world and it will be true now wherever nations have fought each other. It is definitely true for China and Japan. There is a process of healing, which needs to continue and we can continue this process, if we view the past in a positive way.

In China as in all countries the past is always alive. If there is anywhere in the world that values its past, it is China. If anyone in the Communist era wanted to communicate anything, they had to refer to the past. They could not say anything directly about the present, but they could recall the past, such as an incident which might have happened two thousand years ago, because the past for every nation is a treasure store. For every individual it is a treasure store of lessons for their understanding. If we can grasp that, we will see that Japan and China can approach the past in a new light, in a positive light. In this way, both sides can find a way of seeing their history, which allows both to be healed and to be a healing influence in East Asia and the world. Even the period 1939-1945 can be accepted as a time when China learned invaluable lessons and overcame the greatest crisis it has ever faced. So, China and Japan can move forward to the future, not holding back and not being held back by past arguments, but being free to discuss and share together, free to move forward together, free to construct a new future.

The last question I want to discuss is about the responsibility of the young generation. Why should they have any responsibility for what their predecessors did seventy years ago? This is very important and for this I want to turn to the former German President, Richard von Weizsäcker, and to what he said. On 8$^{th}$ May 1985, the fortieth anniversary of the end of the Second World War, he addressed the German Parliament in Berlin. "The vast majority of today's population in today's Germany cannot profess guilt for crimes they did not commit. No discerning person expects them to wear a penitential robe, simply because they are Germans. But their forefathers left them a grave legacy. All of us, whether guilty or not, whether old or young, must accept the past. Anyone who closes his eyes to the past is blind to the present. Anyone who refuses to remember inhumanity is prone to new risks of infection. There can be no reconciliation without remembrance."

The most important word in that statement is the word "inhumanity". We can read that word and not realise what he was saying. What he was saying to his fellow Germans, even to young Germans, was you have to remember the inhumanity to the Jewish people that our nation was guilty of in the Holocaust at Auschwitz and other extermination camps.

It is that inhumanity, or those moments of inhumanity, that are so painful, and they are painful in Japan. It is the inhumanity of dropping an atomic bomb on human beings and seeing them just burned to death and tormented and dying in horrible ways with their flesh being torn off them – this is utterly inhuman. Similarly, in Nanjing we see the inhumanity that happened there; the inhumanity of the dismembering of bodies, the destruction, the burying of thousands upon thousands of soldiers and civilians and the throwing of their remains in bits into the rivers. It is all there in photographs. We have to remember the inhumanity. That is what should never happen again.

I should stop here and let you respond, as there may be many other things to note as well.

Minoru: This is a very complex problem which you have presented. The past is always alive in the present and particularly the heritage of the past in terms of the search for truth. What has been found in the past is inherited by succeeding generations. The truth unites us with each other, in spite of and beyond our differences. This is a most important point. Otherwise, we may just discuss recent history in isolation from this past heritage. We may also fail to question our understanding of our nation's identity. Without being aware of this fundamental question, the discipline of history may focus only on facts. Facts are most important, but it is also important to interpret the facts in relation to our heritage. The question of history demands that a country's spiritual heritage should cease to be a side issue. It is fundamental. In China and Japan the spiritual heritage inherited from the past is more important than the issues which currently divide the two countries. That is my first point.

Secondly, the search for reconciliation challenges a nation's understanding of itself in the light of its actions. What Japan has done to her surrounding countries does not conform to Japan's own self-understanding. By the invasion of other countries Japan destroyed the connection with its own heritage. The result was clearly revealed without any ambiguity, most symbolically and painfully in Hiroshima and Nagasaki and in all our other main cities. Out of this experience Japanese have been awakened to their unforgiveable way of acting in the past. So because of this they seriously examined themselves and asked, 'who am I?', and then, 'what is Japan?'

In my limited experience, because my experience was so overwhelming, I questioned why Japan should exist with such a past? From my self-reflection, I concluded that if there is any purpose in Japan existing, it must be to become a witness for real peace. This then turned into a prayer and became a life-line. Therefore the peace constitution was accepted, formally from the outside. But internally, it was something given from Heaven. That is the core of Japan's position in relation to its recent past.

From my point of view, and I think I share these feelings with the Japanese who were totally crushed, nothing remained. Out of this came repentance for our relationship with others, and that we should never repeat this past history, in which we have caused so much pain and suffering for others. Nevertheless, despite repentance, we were fully aware that the normal reaction from other nations would be hatred and revenge. However neighbouring countries, such as the Philippines, have been so generous. When I first went to Manila in 1960 I did not dare to go out on the streets, but in 1972 I was welcomed by people. It was a great change. It took time, but right now there is no obvious hatred and bitterness against Japan. The difficulties remain: the natural reactions of hatred and revenge are to be expected, if people are not enlightened. Somewhat fortunately, Japan's neighbours have been generous, except in China and Korea. These tolerant neighbours are cooperating together and we benefit mutually, as people are liberated from the natural reactions of revenge.

Basil:  This difference may be partly due to the length of time, in which Japan occupied different countries. Japan ruled Korea from 1910 to 1945, a huge length of time, and occupied China from 1937 to 1945, whereas in the Philippines, it was a more intense, two or three-year period. The difference may be something to do with that. But it is good that in the Philippines they are putting the past behind them and you are welcome there.

Minoru: That is a definite factor. Also in the colonial period much depended on their reaction to their former rulers. In the case of India, I think at least from the beginning of the twentieth century the Independence movement was freed from hatred for the rulers. In this way, I think, bitterness and hatred, amazingly, do not exist in the case of India. Other countries are different.

As far as China and Japan are concerned much depends on the leaders. The old generation of Japanese leaders after the War had experienced real suffering and were depressed by Japan's situation. So because of that they approached other countries with real humility and out of repentance. It was a very humble approach. But then at a later stage things probably changed, because of the prosperity of the Japanese economy. In the first stage, however, Japan had to build herself up from nothing.

Basil: History is a matter of selection. Similarly, countries' views of other countries are a matter of selection. The important thing that I am realising now is that after the War finished in 1945, the Chinese government wanted to make sure that Chinese did not indulge in acts of revenge. Instead all Japanese soldiers and civilians were treated with care and were helped to return to their own country.

Minoru: But not those under Russian control.

Basil: True. But after the War did the Chinese government put you in a camp, did they restrict you? No! This is amazing to me! It may not be to anyone else, but it is to me. No restrictions at all, and also no revenge.

Minoru: Chiang Kai-shek is a strange person, I must say. In 1943 Chiang Kai-shek was invited to the Cairo

Conference, where he met with Roosevelt and Churchill. Roosevelt was determined to demand that Japan should surrender unconditionally and that the Allies would decide the fate of the Emperor. Roosevelt thought that the position of the Emperor should be abolished. Immediately Chiang Kai-Shek said, No. That should not be done, because the role of the Emperor is a lifeline for the Japanese. This was a very tolerant and generous attitude, not motivated at all by revenge.

Basil: That's interesting, because I remember how important the Emperor's broadcast to the Japanese people was, when he told the army to surrender and lay down their weapons. That broadcast may have saved my life and certainly saved the lives of hundreds of thousands of soldiers and civilians on both sides. Also on the other side, Chiang Kai-shek saved many lives by his broadcast, when he told the Chinese people there was to be no revenge.

Minoru: There are many background stories from the period after the end of the war. After the war Chiang Kai-shek was driven out of mainland China by the Communist army. Chiang Kai-shek consulted the former supreme commander of the Japanese army and asked for his help. He immediately responded and asked some Japanese to assist the general in charge of Chiang's forces in the defence of a small island off the coast of the mainland. This Chinese general had distinguished himself by his impressive leadership in command of the Chinese forces who took charge of Shanghai at the time of Japan's surrender. He strictly enforced Chiang Kai-shek's order that there be no revenge against Japanese in the city. The victorious Communist Party army thought they could conquer the island very easily, but they failed. In this way the Japanese commander returned his thanks for Chiang Kai-shek's generosity.

Basil: That helps us to understand why after the War and during the Cold War period Japan appreciated China's tolerance. So when China was completely cut off from the West, Japan was helpful.

Minoru: I remember even when I was still a child growing up in Japan, feeling that we were once again related to China and we were being asking to help them – and why not? We were willing to do so.

Basil: So there was a time even after the war when relations between Japan and China were good. That is something that needs to be remembered now. On that hopeful note we will end this session.

# Student and Youth Exchange Programmes

*Why do we believe that this subject is so important?*

Basil: For both of us this is a crucial subject, since visits to other countries have played a formative part in shaping our outlook on life and our attitudes to other nations. I went to Germany for a month when I was at high school. After school I worked in Malaysia, and later my two years in an Indian university, where I met you, was a life-changing experience. You have described how you were transformed by your years as a student in America and in India. As a result, we long to see students from China and Japan meeting each other and being transformed by these encounters.

Students are the treasure of both nations. Rebuilding relationships between countries that have been separated by conflict is central to restoring true peace and to pursuing reconciliation. There can be no reconciliation without meeting. This meeting is of limited benefit if it takes place in "no man's land". We need to go over to the other side, to see things from the point of view of a neighbouring country. This is even more essential when it comes to those who have been enemies in the past. For example, it was of fundamental importance to me to go to Hiroshima. How would I be able to understand at a deeper level how Yoshiko and Minoru feel about the dropping of the atom bomb, if I never went there? We have to share the pains of others, if we expect them to understand our own.

The importance of youth exchange programmes, whether of students or of teenagers, can be seen from the example of Germany and France after the Second World War. How is it that these two nations not only made peace with each other, but built up the European Union and even today form the two pillars which hold the Union together? Nothing major is decided in the European Union without the agreement of France and Germany. That is amazing when you consider how fiercely they fought in the twentieth century, but also in previous centuries. Many in Europe do not know that both countries encouraged youth exchange visits between their countries. These were encouraged so strongly by their governments and were so successful, that it is estimated that as many as seven million in the sixteen to twenty-five age group took part in these exchanges in the period 1953-1973. Every year, on average approximately four hundred thousand young people went from Germany to France, or from France to Germany. No wonder this created mutual trust between these two nations at the popular level, to counteract the legacy of two deadly wars. In this way, young people from both sides learnt that the other side has its own perspective on the past and were willing to make friends. A change from enmity to amity between neighbouring countries requires this kind of change at the people level. What happens to a nation's students will determine the direction that the country takes in the future.

What about China and Japan? What has happened in the past few decades? Very few people in either county know that in 1984 the Chinese Premier, Zhao Ziyang, invited three thousand Japanese young people to come to Beijing in the months of September and October. That timing was important, because as we know now the first week in October in China is a holiday week. That invitation was a very positive move in the years when China was just beginning to open up to the world. Unfortunately it appears to be an isolated example, but nevertheless an encouraging one.

Since the 1980s there have been a variety of youth exchange programmes. One of the most prestigious was between students of Beijing University and Tokyo University. The Japanese government supported this financially for many years, but that does not appear to be the case now. Similarly China and Japan did have an exchange programme for school students from provincial towns, but China withdrew support for this programme. In 2006 President Hu Jintao and Prime Minister Abe called for the promotion of personal exchanges between the two countries. In addition, students from both countries have been studying at Japanese and Chinese universities.

There have also been non-governmental programmes designed to promote exchange visits between China and Japan. One example of this is the Sasakawa Japan-China Friendship Fund, which was established in 1989 with the aim of promoting peace and mutual understanding between China and Japan. From its beginning the Fund began personnel exchanges with China through its Chinese partner, The China Association for International Friendly Contact. Noted individuals and media representatives from China were invited to Japan, and Japanese language teachers and students were invited to China. In the first decade of the 21st century the Fund adopted two novel programmes: one to promote personnel exchanges in the security field, and the second, to ease tensions over historical issues. By 2007, 5,677 Japanese citizens and 17,270 Chinese citizens had participated in the Fund's projects. The Fund believes: "People are the pivotal factor in maintaining and promoting bilateral cooperation."

## Reflections on Key Issues

What is happening now? I recall what I have discovered on visits to China. Visiting Nanjing on various occasions, I found that the Amity Foundation has promoted exchange visits between Nanjing and International Christian University, Tokyo, in connection with John Rabe House. John Rabe was the German who rescued many Chinese civilians during the Nanjing massacre and his house is now used as a centre for peace studies. A few students from Japan come there, and some have gone from Nanjing to Tokyo. Also in Nanjing I have met several times with Professor Liu Cheng, professor of history at Nanjing University. He has told me that from time to time Japanese students come to his university and he meets with them. They have also had an exchange with ICU. For example, on an exchange programme, four students went from Nanjing University and four from the Nanjing Normal University, which specialises in education and teachers' training. They have arranged for the students to go to Japan for three weeks, including a visit to Hiroshima.

To begin with the Chinese students, before they left, were anti-Japanese in their feeling and sentiment, but when they came back Professor Liu Cheng asked them, "If war between Japan and China happened again, which side would you be on?" They said, "Why, Professor? How could there be a war between Japan and China? The Japanese are very kind and polite. The streets are clean and the food is delicious, so why would China want to fight Japan?" In other words, their attitude had completely changed because of their visit, when compared with their anti-Japanese feelings before they went. As far as the Japanese coming to Nanjing are concerned, the Chinese were concerned to show them both old China and new China. Nanjing, with its famous wall and old buildings, is a wonderful place to visit and see something of old China.

Minoru: Does old Nanjing still remain after the bitter battle with Japan? Is there anything left of the old wall?

Basil: At least two thirds of the old wall still stands. There are about twenty-two kilometres of the old wall still remaining. The wall encircled the old city, thirty-three kilometres in length. A lot of the gates were broken down, but the entire wall was too broad to destroy. It is so broad that you can drive two double-decker buses along the top, side by side. There is also an old Confucian centre, where the ancient Confucian examination hall still exists, and most of it is still preserved. But the students also wanted to show their Japanese visitors new China. In Nanjing one of the big attractions is the bridge crossing the Yangtze from Nanjing to the other side. It was built in the 1960s and is an immense bridge, four and a half kilometres long, and an impressive engineering feat. The river at that point is like an estuary, not just an ordinary river, but several kilometres wide. The railway line goes underneath the road as well. They also wanted to show their Japanese friends the power stations and the new university. This was a very positive exchange.

Minoru: What change was there in the Japanese students' attitude?

Basil: I don't know!

Minoru: I want to know that!

Basil: Prof. Liu could not tell me that. He knew from the Chinese students how they had changed after seeing

Japan, but he could not report on how the Japanese students had changed. However you will remember meeting two of my Chinese friends in Shanghai. One is a palaeontologist and the other is a biochemist. Both of them, as you know, did their training in Japan. Both of them received their Ph.D. in Kyoto.

Minoru: How many years did they stay?

Basil: One was there for at least seven years, because he did his undergraduate study, as well as his doctoral studies in Japan. His wife only completed her postgraduate and Ph.D. studies there. They finished their studies in Kyoto, and they learned Japanese so well, that they were able to translate for you from Chinese into fluent Japanese, when you met them in Shanghai. They love Japan very much indeed. Anybody that I have met who is Chinese and who has gone and stayed in Japan, and studied there like these two, is always enthusiastic about Japan. Now Chinese students are the largest contingent of foreign students in Japan.

Recently, I was talking to a Chinese Ph.D. student who is here in Cambridge from Fudan University in Shanghai. He said that the largest group of foreign students in his university is from Japan, even more than those from Korea. But, he said, the great majority of these come to his university to learn Chinese. They come for maybe six months to a year to learn Chinese. He has learned some Japanese, and he would like to meet you and talk in Japanese with you, because he is frustrated that when he talks to the Japanese students in Japanese they only reply to him in Chinese. They will not talk to him in Japanese. I think this is understandable, because they have come to China to learn Chinese, so they only want to talk in Chinese, but it is frustrating for this Chinese student, because he wants to improve his Japanese. There are also other Chinese trying to learn Japanese from these Japanese students.

Another person I talked to was a Chinese from northern China, she said: "We don't have Japanese students, but we do have Japanese teachers who come to teach Japanese at my university. I am sure that it is also true in many parts of China, that the university arranges courses for anyone who wants to learn Japanese and Japanese teachers are invited." My Chinese friend from Fudan University also said that there are other universities in Shanghai where Japanese students study and they too have programmes for teaching Chinese to Japanese students. However, this is all due to local effort; that is to say, it happens because of the individual initiative of students or through universities arranging such courses, not through government action. He said universities do this to earn money, because universities are trying to attract foreign students. Foreign students are a very important source of revenue in modern university education, everywhere in the world. That is perfectly understandable. It is not a government initiative, either from Japan or from China.

We need more mechanisms to improve the flow of exchange, especially when it comes to high school students. As we noted in the case of France and Germany after the war, they did encourage that at a crucial time, and it was because of government initiatives that the youth exchange was not only so successful, but also involved so many hundreds of thousands of young people. The report prepared for Shinzo Abe by Japanese experts in August 2015 prior to his statement on the 70th Anniversary of the end of the war makes the same point. It goes on to say: "Going forward, it will become necessary to undertake work to move toward reconciliation with China by making exchanges at all levels much more active than before, on the basis of remorse over the past..." (Report of the Advisory Panel on the History of the 20$^{th}$ Century and on Japan's Role and the World Order in the 21$^{st}$ Century).

We could mention another type of exchange, and that is tourism. In the first three months of 2015 one and a quarter million Chinese tourists went to Japan. This was a huge increase on the previous year. Among the tourists are children and young people, maybe students as well, although we have to ask, is this a one-way street? Is there an equivalent flow of Japanese young people, high school children and students, going from Japan to China? It seems that there are not many. This is where I need to ask you: what is your experience in Tokyo, in your university, ICU? I do know, from what I have seen, that you do have a few Chinese students, maybe three, four or five or a few more, who have come from China to Japan, and we know that you have some exchange programmes with Nanjing involving two, three or four students from ICU going there. But these are very small numbers. Are you aware of anything else your university has done, or of what is happening in other universities?

Minoru: I am not related to this area of youth exchange, so I do not have the knowledge to respond to this question.

Basil: I know from other sources that Tokyo's Waseda University used to have a programme for inviting people from China and these may have included students and academics, as well.

Minoru: Unfortunately I am ignorant about this exchange programme.

Basil: Youth exchange is a big concern for us, because dialogue is a constant necessity between people and nations. It requires mechanisms that make such interaction possible at all levels of society, crucially at teenage and student level, for the future. Meeting is not just of importance for leaders, but needs to be facilitated between Japanese and Chinese on a broad scale, and on multiple levels, so that there is genuine human interaction. We know for a fact that when Chinese students meet Japanese, they are impressed. They like them. Their previous opinions are then changed.

As I was talking to the Chinese PhD student from Fudan recently, I asked him, are you influenced by the anti-Japanese media in China? He said, 'No, I am not against Japan at all. I am, as you can see, trying to learn Japanese, and I like the Japanese I meet here.' When people meet it changes their viewpoint. This will help to achieve the harmonious society that China believes in. It will be particularly beneficial to link people in China and Japan who are not like-minded – this is a crucial point – not just bringing people who like Japan already, but as Liu Cheng did with students in Nanjing, sending those who are hostile, to Japan, where their whole attitude can be completely changed. The impossible then becomes possible, as they return home saying, 'Why would we ever think of fighting Japan?' Therefore, we should bring people together, who are not like-minded and have opposing viewpoints, so that from the resulting exchanges, creative new partnerships can emerge, with new understanding, fresh harmony and real peace.

*Reflections on Key Issues*

# United as Brothers and Sisters in the Human Family

*Is reconciliation possible without the realisation that we are all one family, one humanity, and one world?*

Basil: This topic - united as brothers and sisters in the human family – sounds good, but what does it mean, and why is it important? You and I talk about the importance of realising that we are one great family, all part of the human race, and therefore that our old enemies are in fact our brothers and sisters. This sounds noble, but how can it be translated into reality, so that it changes the relations between different countries like China and Japan?

I am reminded of the vision of Martin Luther King, who said in his famous, "I have a dream" speech in Washington in 1962, his vision was that the sons of former slaves and the sons of former slave owners would be able to sit down together at the table of brotherhood. Desmond Tutu also spoke of something similar. He said that in South Africa they realised something of this vision, when they had the election which elected Mandela and were all allowed, for the first time, to go and vote. South Africans made an earth-shattering discovery: 'We are all fellow South Africans, part of God's rainbow people!'

This is a vision few have grasped. Most people in the world do not share this vision. People are more concerned for our group, our vision, our race. This is as true in China and Japan as anywhere else. We are divided in our loyalties. We look down on people who do not belong to our group. We indulge in labelling people according to their race, their gender, their religion, their wealth and many other labels, and so we lose our vision of the one humanity.

There are many things like this that divide and dehumanise us, but most of all war dehumanises. This is something of which Zhou Enlai was fully aware. When one thousand Japanese war criminals were handed over to China by Russia in 1950 he determined to reverse this dehumanisation. He said that the Communist Party believes that even enemies are human; all are human. He sought to understand this in dealing with these one thousand Japanese prisoners. He saw that they had been dehumanised by treating others, especially Chinese, as less than human. He sought to restore their humanity. He did that by treating them so well that in the end they were willing to confess what they had done. In the process the Japanese soldiers themselves realised how inhuman they had been to others. Through this good treatment they recovered their own human dignity and realised that by treating Chinese inhumanely they had lost their own humanity. Zhou Enlai did a great service to Japan, because he wanted the Japanese who went back to Japan not to make the same mistakes again, but to share with their own people what had gone wrong.

In one of your articles about the victims of Hiroshima, you quoted Kenzaburo Oe as saying that humanity is a healing family. It can become a healing family; and it is especially the survivors of violence who are able to teach us a new way forward, and indeed to heal us. This healing takes place in different ways. You gave me an interesting article about the Chinese author, Sun Ge, who wrote about the settlers who emigrated from Japan to North-East China after 1931. They were impoverished Japanese farmers but they enjoyed affluent lives by taking land from local Chinese farmers, whom they employed. But they also experienced great hardship when Japan was defeated, and at the end of the War many committed suicide and those who remained were driven to abject poverty. But some Chinese farmers helped the Japanese who survived. They took pains to adopt Japanese orphans and bring them up. As human beings they generously represent magnificent humanity. So the Japanese settlers who had originally had a sense of superiority came to realise through their own hardships that the Chinese were no different from them as human beings. In that process, they themselves were healed.

The Chinese Nobel Peace Prize winner, Liu Xiaobo, has written about the importance of understanding our shared humanity. He says, as we understand our shared humanity we will find an answer to the hatred and bitterness between nations, when we realise that those we treat as enemies are not faceless objects but people just like us. This has been the discovery of many in different countries, such as Palestine and Israel, as well as in South Africa and in America.

Liu Xiaobo and Desmond Tutu say that when we discover our common humanity, we then discover some important truths. The first thing, I think we discover, is an inclusive principle. Desmond Tutu forcefully emphasises this point. In South Africa, he says, we discovered that we are all God's people. He writes: "In God's family, there are no outsiders. All are insiders. Black and white, rich and poor, Jew and Arab, Palestinian and Israeli, Serb and Albanian, Muslim and Christian, Buddhist and Hindu ... all belong" (*God Has A Dream, p.20*) – and we could also add, Chinese and Japanese, all belong. All are God's creatures. It is radical and it is shocking to some. It is radical because it includes everybody, and it is also a relational principle because it causes us to relate together, for we are not separate, we all depend on God and on one another. It is only through our dependence on each other, or our interdependence, that we find our future and our real humanity.

What has all this got to do with reconciliation? In 2009 the United Nations declared an international year of reconciliation and said that its aim was to restore humanity's lost unity. Clearly without unity there cannot be reconciliation. We see that the discovery of our common humanity is happening in China and Japan. When Chinese come to Japan they discover not just other people but brothers – and friends! They find in Japan so much to admire, so much to appreciate - politeness, order, civility, and the sensitivity of the Japanese. Through the discovery of our family likeness, we experience a healing and a unity which has been lost. When nationalism is downplayed and the common humanity of both Chinese and Japanese is recognised and encouraged at the government and popular and media levels, then we can make progress. This will go hand-in-hand with an understanding of our identity as mutually related people, whatever our country. This will also set us free – free to be the people God has made us to be, free to be able to see others as they really are.

Liu Xiaobo was right when he wrote that he is free, now, to see Japanese as fellow human beings and to reject the false patriotism and propaganda of anti-Japanese war rhetoric, free also to admit past wrongs and to agree that China is not always right, free to abandon China's "we are the centre of the universe" mentality and the desire to dominate. When this happens we become free to wait for God's gifts of peace and reconciliation, free because we recognise each other as related and part of what God is doing and has done in this world. When we are awakened to the reality of God's presence we begin to share God's vision. Not just Martin Luther King's vision or Gandhi's vision or Desmond Tutu's vision or anybody else's vision, but God's vision, here and now, of a new humanity, truly human, truly free.

I will stop here, because I think you have a lot more to say on the healing family and maybe other things as well. In the paper you have written on humanity as a healing family, you talked about Kenzaburo Oe and his discovery of the healing power of the human family through the survivors of the atomic bomb at Hiroshima. He wrote some very moving things, which you have quoted. He said that victims and survivors of the atomic bomb have a power to heal all of us who live in this nuclear age. This thought seems self-evident if you have seen the survivors of Hiroshima or Nagasaki, now frail and elderly, speaking up and taking an active part in the movement to abolish all nuclear weapons – and, we might add, to save humanity. The healing power of suffering restores authentic and humane order within family and in society, and that is self-evident when we see the witness of some who have suffered. That is true in many parts of the world, and it is certainly true in South Africa, as Desmond Tutu acknowledges. He is keen to add that we find, through survivors, the real dignity of the human family, we see human beings as they were meant to be. Perhaps you would like to add more to that.

Minoru: This presentation makes me wonder whether such suffering is normal or abnormal, or, in harsher words, sane or insane. If that question is raised, many people will interpret it very nicely according to their position, according to their self-understanding. In order to get to grips with the difficulties of this question, we recognise that our response will be closely related to where we stand.

For example, taking the example of sea pollution off the coast of Kyushu highlighted by Ishimure Michiko, it made the sufferers exposed to a reality which is unintelligible to outsiders, because they are far removed from that situation. Ishimure Michiko drew attention to the mercury poisoning that caused what came to be known as the Minamata disease. In the case of this sea poisoning, no fish could survive. By this pollution people were affected in a very violent way, dying like mad cats, jumping up and falling down, and passing away in tremendous agony. Ishimure Michiko, who is now over eighty, had little education apart from attending a local vocational primary training school. But she had such sensitivity to the actual condition of the people who were exposed to this disaster and were overwhelmed by despair. The children saw their parents die in misery and were left helpless on their own. Gradually they too were affected by this pollution and died. The sea was totally polluted. Despair prevailed everywhere. When the sea suffers, man suffers –then where is the way out? There is only total darkness. This is how people react who are actually suffering. Meanwhile outsiders cause the pollution through gigantic modern industries and production systems. Somewhere in the midst of the suffering two ways seem to open up. One is suffering together. People are poisoned, the sea is poisoned; they seem to be suffering together. That is a kind of a way out; a very irrational way, but this suffering together gives the courage to endure to the poisoned human beings.

The other way in this situation is that the victims discover that the basic feature of so-called modernisation is that man is dehumanised and nature is destroyed. So one way out for victims is to share their suffering together, and the other way out is to find through this suffering a path to return to the source of life. In the case of the Japanese fishermen, being Buddhist, this means a return to Buddha. Now, how will the outsiders face the same situation? Ishimure Michiko observes that they will look at the situation from their point of view. Some may see in the midst of the disaster a mother holding a child in her arms, suffering together. Seeing this situation, the attitude or sensitivity of the observer is exposed. Ishimure says, that the observer may meet God, for Christians Christ, for the Buddhist Buddha. There is then an encounter between man and God or Buddha. This is a really sacred place. But in most cases observers just don't feel any relationship between the sufferers and themselves. Ishimure believes that this is the contemporary situation. It depends on a person's real state of mind, how they see the modern situation.

Basil: I think we would agree here that sensitivity is a key issue; those who are sensitive see what is really there, and to be human is to be sensitive. When we are desensitised we have lost our humanity. We have noticed in many cases that those who are sensitive show their real humanity. It is surprising that even people who you think are blind suddenly show a spark of humanity and really are sensitive. A case in point occurred recently in the refugee crisis that we are now facing in Europe with refugees pouring in from the Middle East and Africa. One picture of a three year-old boy, swept up dead on the shore, had more impact than all the statistics of desperate refugees risking their lives to reach Europe. All these numbers didn't have the impact that that one photo of an unfortunate three year-old boy swept up dead on the shore had on media viewers. Amazingly, even hardened media people were so sensitive that they dropped everything else to raise money and to draw attention to the plight of desperate refugees. They used all their ingenuity to make people think: what are we doing, how can we allow this to go on? I take it that even hardened people can show a spark of humanity, and the spark of humanity is sensitivity!

Minoru: Yes, that is crucial. Again, it reminds me of our joint project. For example, you raised questions concerning the victims of the atomic bombs dropped on Hiroshima and Nagasaki. How are their cries received today by their contemporaries? You were asking how many cities are participating in the Mayors for Peace programme in response to the appeal from Hiroshima. I found out today that 6,893 cities in 161 countries have responded and have become members. In this way, they are trying to share the Hiroshima and Nagasaki victims' prayers. Their prayer is clearly for the abolition of nuclear weapons.

People should go beyond racial and national boundaries, as you were suggesting, and discover their common humanity, appreciating each other and living harmoniously together. By doing this we would change the world, not simply abolish nuclear weapons and war, and through this effort we might recognise the divine reality behind the flow of current events. Although there are people who respond in this way, nevertheless nuclear weapons are still spreading and becoming more sophisticated. The situation is not easy. The victims feel the urgency of the present situation. For them discussion and yearning for peace is not enough. So they may be encouraged that the non-violent movement is taking more direct action through cities who have agreed on the goal of removing nuclear weapons from the world. For this to be successful constant and continuous effort is needed. On 27 May 2016 President Obama visited Hiroshima and called for the destruction of nuclear stockpiles. He went on to say: "We must re-imagine our connection to one another as members of one human race... We can choose, a future in which Hiroshima and Nagasaki are known not as the dawn of atomic warfare but as the start of our own moral awakening."

Basil: I was going to ask you, whether you think that Desmond Tutu's description of all the races in the new South Africa as "God's rainbow people" would also be a good description for all the races of the world?

Minoru: As you say, the case of South Africa shows the crucial importance of being awakened to the reality that we are all related as human beings. What is needed is to live in harmony and creative coexistence with all humanity, led and inspired by God. This vision affects our understanding of the relationship between China and Japan. First the relationship between the two countries must improve, then only can reconciliation move to a deeper level.

Basil: Of course, reconciliation is a journey, not a point in time or an end result. We can never say reconciliation is complete. Even in South Africa this journey continues, sometimes going down and sometimes rising again.

Minoru: In that situation there is still the necessity to live creatively together.

# Looking Forward Together to a United Future

*How can China and Japan be united by a common vision for the future?*

**Basil:** Despite the present tensions between China and Japan, the overall pattern of history suggests that China and Japan have such close links that both countries will find ways in the future to develop a positive and peaceful partnership. However, both countries need visionaries like Mandela and Martin Luther King in government and society, if a fruitful partnership is to blossom. Respect, trust and friendship, and new initiatives, are needed if reconciliation is to become the goal of both nations. For this, China and Japan need a shared vision for the future of their countries, in which East Asia takes the lead in promoting peace and harmonious coexistence in the global family of nations.

There is reason for some hope for the future when we look at the policy of the Chinese government towards Japan in the last sixty years. From 1972 China has pursued a policy of peace and cooperation, accepting that Japan has apologised for the military regime which led them into war. So for example, the Chinese Prime Minister, Wen Jiabao, said in a famous speech to the Japanese Diet in 2007: "Since the normalisation of diplomatic ties between China and Japan in 1972, the Japanese government and leaders have on many occasions stated their position on the historical issue. They have admitted that Japan committed aggression but has expressed deep remorse and apologised to the victimised countries. The Chinese government and people appreciate the position they have taken."

Wen Jiabao went on to say, looking back at past history: "Beginning with the Qin and Han dynasties, Chinese technologies of rice cultivation, silkworm growing, textile making and smelting were introduced to Japan. So too was Chinese culture, including Chinese characters, Confucianism, Buddhism and Chinese decrees, institutions and art. Japan sent envoys to China on over ten occasions during the Tang Dynasty. The Chinese monk, Jianzhen, tried five times to sail to Japan but failed. He went blind as a result. But Jianzhen did not give up and his sixth journey was a success. That was when he was sixty-six years old. It took him twelve years to realise his life-long dream. When Jianzhen got to Japan, he shared Buddhist teachings that he believed would save the world and the people. He dedicated himself to fostering the Chinese people's friendship with the Japanese people."

Wen Jiabao was determined to make the point that so much of history shows Japan and China to be very closely linked together. He said: "The growth of China and Japan's friendly relations brought great benefits to our peoples. China has received support and assistance from the Japanese Government and people in its reform, opening-up and modernization drive. This is something the Chinese people will never forget. With this in mind, we the leaders of the two countries have reached agreement on building a strategic relationship of mutual benefit. Our goal is to follow the trend of the times and popular aspirations, and lift China-Japan relations to a new historical stage, so that China and Japan will live together in peace, enjoy lasting friendship and carry out cooperation of mutual benefit for common development."

To achieve this goal, Wen Jiabao mentioned several principles; two of them I note here. Firstly, we should "seek common ground, while shelving differences and uphold the larger interests of the two countries. It should be recognized that China and Japan do have differences over some specific interests and some issues. But these differences are of secondary importance compared with our common interests. .....With regard to the issue of the East China Sea, our two countries should follow the principle of shelving differences and seek joint development, and conduct active consultation so as to make substantive progress towards peaceful settlement of the differences and make the East China Sea a sea of peace, friendship and cooperation." Secondly: "China and Japan are both important countries in Asia and the world, and their relations have great impact on Asia and the world. With this in mind, we should maintain close coordination and cooperation, make joint effort to uphold peace and stability in Northeast Asia and promote East Asia regional cooperation, thus contributing to the invigoration of Asia. Also with this in mind, we should jointly address global issues ranging from energy security, environmental protection, climate change, prevention and control of diseases to counter-terrorism, combating transnational crimes and the prevention of proliferation of weapons of massive destruction."

Wen Jiabao concluded by saying: "Despite the twists and turns and setbacks in Chinese and Japanese relations, the foundation of friendship between the Chinese and Japanese people remains as unshakeable as Mount Tai and Mount Fuji. Let us join hands and work together for the everlasting China-Japan's friendship, for a new strategic relationship of mutual benefit between our countries, and for peace and development in Asia and the world."

We should also note the very important speech by China's President, Hu Jintao, on the 8th May 2008, at Waseda University. He said: "China and Japan are close neighbours, facing each other across a narrow strip of water. Our bilateral relations, which are now at a new historical starting point, have new opportunities to grow further. I have come to Japan with the warm feelings of the Chinese people for the Japanese people and the sincere aspiration of the Chinese people to deepen China-Japan relations. The government and people of China sincerely wish to work with the government and people of Japan, to increase mutual trust, to enhance friendship, to deepen cooperation, to plan for the future and to take the all-round growth of the strategic relationship between China and Japan to a new level." That kind of language is impressive and strong.

Hu Jintao added, that with this in mind we need first to increase strategic mutual trust. People become friends when they trust each other. Countries enjoy stable relations when they trust each other. China and Japan should appreciate and see each other's development in an objective and sensible way and regard each other as partners of win-win cooperation, not as competitors. We should support each other's peaceful development. Secondly, we should deepen mutually beneficial cooperation. Thirdly, we must promote people-to-people and cultural exchange, because people-to-people exchange serves as a bridge between the two peoples to deepen mutual understanding and enhance friendship. Fourthly, we must promote Asian rejuvenation, and fifthly, work together to meet global challenges, including climate change and the proliferation of weapons of mass destruction. "We do appreciate that we are different; the people of Japan are hard-working and talented, good at learning and making innovations. The people of Japan have made remarkable achievements and now lead the world in so many fields. This is a source of pride to the Japanese people, and is also worth learning from by the Chinese people."

These are very positive remarks, and should not be taken lightly, because they were given on very important occasions when Chinese leaders came to Japan. We note that they are also making serious suggestions about how to improve relations between the countries. China's basic policy towards Japan has not changed since then, despite the Islands dispute.

To show that China's basic policy toward Japan has not fundamentally changed I quote from a speech by the present leader of China, Xi Jinping, which he gave in Nanjing on December 13th, 2014 at the memorial for the massacre of Chinese in Nanjing in 1937. He said, on that emotional day that he wished the Chinese people would stick to the path of peaceful development and remember history, to cherish peace and create a better future. Chinese and Japanese people should keep their friendship and maintain this from generation to generation, learning from history and looking forward to a future where they can both contribute to the peace of all mankind. He went on to say: "Peace is the most enduring human aspiration; like the sun it warms, and like rain it gives moisture. With sun and rain everything in nature thrives; with peace and stability human beings are able to achieve their dreams. Only when everyone cherishes peace will peace be kept. We hold a memorial ceremony today for the victims of the Nanjing massacre, not to evoke and perpetuate hatred. Sino-Japanese friendship, which has lasted for generations between the two peoples, should continue, learning from history and facing the future jointly, to contribute to the peace of mankind." On that significant occasion President Xi was able to say, that the point of the Nanjing memorial was not to perpetuate hatred, but to underline the importance of Sino-Japanese friendship in the present.

China's basic policy toward Japan has not changed since 2008, despite the various disputes, especially the Islands dispute. These speeches indicate a shared vision, and also a realisation of what Japan and China have in common. The relationship between the two is the key to the future, as is the need to strengthen cooperation beyond trade. This is a point that Professor Liu Cheng of Nanjing University emphasises. He says that China should strengthen cooperation with Japan not only in their economic partnership, but in also other matters as well, such as cultural concerns, matters concerning history, the environment, ecology and so forth. He emphasises the importance of solving issues, like the Islands dispute, together, and finding a joint target for Japan and China which will be beneficial to both sides, whilst always remembering that underlying all this is the need to respect each other's identity, history and achievements, and each other's interests. These are diverse and different, but nevertheless linked together.

Despite the hopeful speeches of Wen Jiabao and Hu Jintao in Japan in 2007 and 2008, we have to say that there has been very little progress in moving both countries toward a heartfelt reconciliation that overcomes the wounds of the past century. Trust, respect and friendship are not the principle characteristics of present relationships between Japan and China. At the governmental level there has been no realistic determination to take advantage of the times when both sides moved closer together, for example in 1989-1990 when Japan was the only major power to support China after the Tiananmen Square massacre, or again in 2007-2008 when Wen Jiabao and Hu Jintao made their friendly visits to Tokyo. As a result no movement has been generated that would move both countries forward toward reconciling their painful differences over the past or the present, that is over China's humiliation in the war period and over Japan's fear of current Chinese expansion in the East China Sea. For true reconciliation we need leaders in both countries, like Nelson Mandela and Martin Luther King, who have undergone a profound transformation enabling them to view their former enemies as friends, because they no longer view anyone with hatred.

Partnership and the future are not simply for governments to determine. It is for the Chinese and Japanese people to work towards. The vision of Chinese and Japanese people will determine the future. Governments come and go, but what the people desire and work towards will endure. Their relationships, their friendships, their cooperation are what are most important.

I think we can see from the point of view of history that the overall trend of China-Japan relations has positive elements, even though the present is a difficult time. This ends my presentation. I now ask you about what can be said from the Japanese side. It is vital that the relationship between Japan and China grows and flourishes.

**Minoru:** Responding to your presentation, as a Japanese, I represent this common programme of looking forward together with China to a united future. First of all, I agree that the historical perspective is very important, and this has been emphasised again and again. In the past we have learnt so much from China on many different levels of life. But most of all we have learnt from the Chinese understanding of the truth, which is at the heart of my understanding of the historical perspective. From ancient times we have been deeply united in search of the truth, mutually appreciating and respecting each other. This is at the core of our mutual learning, since the quest for the truth has been particularly cultivated in Japanese history.

I have personally been involved for forty-five years in a dialogue fellowship between Zen Buddhism and Christianity in Japan. This been a dialogue fellowship between Zen Buddhists and Christians, but it is open to all Japanese religious traditions in search for the truth, particularly from the Buddhist side. Dogen, the founder of the Soto Zen school, went to China in the thirteenth century and stayed there for three years. In the final stage of his stay his master called Dogen to him and said, 'I recognise you are really living in the truth.' Returning to Japan, he shared his understanding of the truth which he had learnt in China, and starting with Dogen this spread from generation to generation until today. From my association with this dialogue fellowship, I have learnt not only through their teaching but also from their way of life. There I could see their deep appreciation of each other, cultivated by the truth, and a mutual relationship, expressing the reality of truth. In their own understanding, it is living together, related to each other as brothers and sisters, and sharing an intimate relationship with respect, love and appreciation, which is the reality of the truth. Through this understanding there comes a deep relationship with each other. Then naturally they find who they are and they realise more and more that their existence is full of meaning, here and now, and that they must live with thankfulness.

Truth is not simply a doctrine, but living fully here and now. From the Christian side, I appreciate their sharing of the reality of the truth, which Buddhists have learned from China. The religions are different, but my heart appreciates their understanding of truth. Here and now we live as human beings, sincerely and thankfully trying to find a more human way of life. In that sense there is no blueprint; each one is responding to their own situation, and together we discover a way out of our predicament, which is full of meaning for us. From a Christian point of view, I learnt about this living reality when I heard Martin Luther King speak in America, while I was a student there at Princeton University. He urged us to live as brothers and sisters, as members of God's blessed family. This vital truth was something that our ancestors inherited from what they learnt in China.

So, in the relationship between China and Japan, I want to stress that what we have learnt from China is immense. We really appreciate China on this level. The relationship between China and Japan has been deep and vast. When I look at the contemporary situation from this point of view, I believe that our mutual appreciation and understanding of our identity should not be ignored and is absolutely fundamental. From this point of view, we do feel the more we go into the truth the more we will be deeply united. Being encouraged by this relationship here and now, we can thankfully and joyfully meet each other. What we learn from the past is an understanding of the relationship between China and Japan at the truth level. I find from my Christian point of view that this is the real core for interpreting the modern situation.

Coming to the second point, in the contemporary situation, it is very painful, but from my point of view in spite of this painful situation, it is important to appreciate the learning which we have inherited from China. Put simply, Japanese have learnt from China the reality of mutual appreciation, mutual respect, appreciation of each other and participation in the blessed reality of being brothers and sisters in the same family. When I say this is

*Reflections on Key Issues*

painful, I am referring to Japan's invasion of China and the suffering and pain caused to our Chinese brothers and sisters. I feel that what we have done in China cannot be erased and cannot be forgiven. The truth is that we have brought disaster on our Chinese brothers and sisters. What kind of relationship can we then hope to establish with China?

In response to this critical question, I believe there are many ways out of this painful situation. I find the example of the European Union, particularly the relationship between France and Germany, to be a very precious witness to the way of going beyond the painful situation which Europe experienced during the past century, particularly in World Wars One and Two. After such wars feelings of hatred and revenge occur naturally. But after World War Two, De Gaulle and Adenauer, the two great leaders of France and Germany, were united by a yearning for peace, believing that peace is the only meaningful hope for the future of Europe. From the beginning they were convinced that reconciliation is absolutely necessary. I was so inspired by the way they cooperated to work for reconciliation. Since then they have been the central core of the European Union, and amazingly in spite of their past history they have overcome the mentality of hatred and revenge. How could this reconciliation take place between these two countries? I have been wondering how their vision for the future gave birth to such fruitful reconciliation.

Then recently, this year, the German Prime Minister, Angela Merkel, came to Japan. She shared in public how Germany had been enabled to respond to the yearning for peace and the longing for no more war. France and Germany respected their differences, but were deeply united in their search for the truth, through consultation and debate. The German Prime Minister said that progress came from seeing history as it is and from the conviction that reconciliation is absolutely necessary. She went on to say that without the tolerance and forgiveness shown by the French, Germany would have found reconciliation very difficult, despite knowing that it was the only way to achieve a successful European Union. Just listening to this, I was astonished. This is a miracle! It is a blessing for the rest of the world.

Personally I feel that exactly what happened in Europe is the only way for the future of China and Japan. The relationship between China and Japan in the past century has been very painful, as I have already explained. But now, somehow, my heart is full of hope. The process of reconciliation has already started. It began in 1952 and was confirmed in 1972, when both countries officially recognised each other and established diplomatic relations. From my point of view China has shown tolerance and forgiveness for what happened during the war and Japan has gratefully accepted this. In our own way the process of reconciliation and cooperation has already begun, and should continue.

In my own experience I saw the despair in Japan after the war. Out of despair came reflection. Japanese reflected on the past, seeing the wrong way they had taken, which had caused great suffering for others in China and the whole of South-East Asia. The peace constitution was then deeply accepted by the Japanese people as their commitment to "no more war" and as a witness that peace is the only way for Japan in the future. This remains the lifeline of the Japanese people, in my observation.

For the present, each person has the opportunity to be aware of their own responsibility for the future and their own God given identity. From my point of view the only hope is for a breakthrough at the person to person level.

If we act together with respect and appreciation for each other we can create a new story. The story of the Chinese women who came to work in Japanese companies and were caught up in the Fukushima tsunami disaster is a significant example. Twenty Chinese girls were taken on as apprentices. When the tsunami struck, their company manager immediately took them to higher ground. He then went back to rescue his family. To the girls' horror their manager and his family were all drowned. They returned to China and shared their experience with neighbours who had previously only been taught to hate Japan by the media. These acts of heroism and loss have united very different people in Japan and China across national boundaries. They have been inspired through love and justice to act together. Such examples, though often not appreciated, can be multiplied many times over.

I hope this history of reconciliation and creative cooperation will spread and be deepened, and in that way the relationship between China and Japan can in future become a light in the darkness. There are many difficulties, but from my personal point of view these have to be overcome, and will be overcome! Through understanding of the truth, and by fully appreciating each other and respecting each other, we will be closely related in the reality of forgiveness.

This is my response to my friend's careful analysis of the relationship between China and Japan in the modern context.

# Postscript

We have a dream of the world awakening to the joy of being God's rainbow family on earth, where although all are different yet all are accepted as brothers and sisters, and where the world is no longer divided into enemies and friends.

In the fullness of time this will happen. In the meanwhile individuals may discover this liberating experience for themselves. If they do it will come to them as a pure gift, in an unexpected moment, and not as something they have achieved.

What makes reconciliation possible in its deepest sense? Minoru witnesses to the revolutionary effect of awakening to God's presence, here and now. This transforms our relationships with everyone, when we come to realise with Martin Luther King that we are all brothers and sisters, whatever our race or religion, or nationality or social status. It is easy to write this down, but this is not a proposition to be agreed with or rejected. We naturally believe that right and truth are on our side; to discover that God also loves our enemies can be very shocking. This only makes sense when we encounter the reality of God's presence. It does not matter how this happens, what matters is that we are awakened and liberated from enmity and division.

Although we write as Christians, the awakening to the reality of God's presence can be experienced by anyone, whether they are from China or Japan or any other country, and whether they have a religion or none.

How does this relate to reconciliation between China and Japan? Whatever governments may do, individuals can change. When anyone is awakened and liberated to see that all human beings are one family, then reconciliation becomes possible. When we first met in India, despite our different nationalities, we met as friends. We found that our wartime past was not a barrier between us. Later we were able to look at the past through each other's eyes and to learn from the past and from one another. Reconciliation has this amazing power to liberate us from all that has divided us in the past. So in the relations between China and Japan, if we begin with the painful past it will be hard to make any progress toward reconciliation. But wherever there is an awakening that enables Japanese and Chinese to view each other as brothers and sisters, there reconciliation will flourish. It will then be possible to learn from the past and not to see it as an insuperable barrier and a cause of undying enmity.

Some say all would be well on earth if there was no suffering. But our experience is that in our suffering we cried for a way out. Because of the desolation in Japan after the war Minoru searched desperately and found hope in Christ. Later in America he was appalled by the strife between black and white Christians and then found liberation in the message of Martin Luther King. Again and again we find that it is the crushed, who cry out in despair and are sustained by the light they see shining in the darkness. When all hope had gone in South Africa and the country was doomed to explode in bloodshed, Nelson Mandela came out of prison to forgive the Africaner whites and usher in a new dawn.

On the other hand the rich and powerful find it almost impossible to awaken to the blessed reality of God's plans and of being liberated as part of God's rainbow people. But as Jesus pointed out the impossible is possible with God. God's plan is not for some people, but for everyone to search and hopefully to find his new order.

Reconciliation is his gift and comes when least expected. This is our experience and gives us hope.

Reconciliation is an ongoing journey. As you can see from the record of our pilgrimage from Shanghai to India and later back to Japan and China, we continue to learn new lessons and to be challenged by new dilemmas. We can never say we have arrived and that our unity is perfect. This is also true of countries. In South Africa Desmond Tutu is fully aware that the reconciliation road can go backwards if leaders are complacent. The road goes on, because even when reconciliation has taken root it can be undone, and much remains to be restored and perfected by truth and justice.

Our prayer is that you will find something that will be of help to you from this sharing of our pilgrimage.

*Postscript*

*Two Pilgrims Meet*